PERSPECTIVES IN
PSYCHICAL RESEARCH

This is a volume in the Arno Press collection

PERSPECTIVES IN PSYCHICAL RESEARCH

Advisory Editor

Robert L. Morris

*See last pages of this volume
for a complete list of titles.*

Elijah Farrington

REVELATIONS OF A SPIRIT MEDIUM

BY
HARRY PRICE

AND
ERIC J. DINGWALL

ARNO PRESS
A New York Times Company
New York – 1975

Editorial Supervision: EVE NELSON

Reprint Edition 1975 by Arno Press Inc.

Reprinted from a copy in
 The New York Public Library

PERSPECTIVES IN PSYCHICAL RESEARCH
ISBN for complete set: 0-405-07020-9
See last pages of this volume for titles.

Manufactured in the United States of America

Library of Congress Cataloging in Publication Data
[Farrington, Elijah]
    Revelations of a spirit medium.

    (Perspectives in psychical research)
    Written by E. Farrington and C. F. Pidgeon.
    Reprint of the 1922 ed. published by K. Paul,
Trench, Trubner, London, and E. P. Dutton, New York.
    Bibliography: p.
    1. Spiritualism--Controversial literature.
I. Price, Harry, 1881-1948. II. Dingwall, Eric
John. III. Pidgeon, Charles F., joint author.
IV. Title. V. Series.
BF1042.F3 1975   133.9   75-7395
ISBN 0-405-07044-6

Revelations of a Spirit Medium

REVELATIONS OF A SPIRIT MEDIUM

FACSIMILE EDITION,
WITH NOTES, BIBLIOGRAPHY, GLOSSARY
AND INDEX

BY

HARRY PRICE, F.R.N.S.

(Member of the Society for Psychical Research; Hon. Librarian, Magicians' Club, London; Member of the Society of American Magicians, etc.)

AND

ERIC J. DINGWALL, M.A.

(Member of the Society for Psychical Research; Member of the Inner Magic Circle, London, etc.)

LONDON:
KEGAN PAUL, TRENCH, TRUBNER & Co., Ltd.
NEW YORK: E. P. DUTTON & CO.
1922

CONTENTS

	PAGE
COMPILERS' PREFACE	vii
BIBLIOGRAPHICAL NOTE . . .	xii
NOTES ON THE TEXT	xvii
BIBLIOGRAPHY	xxix
GLOSSARY	lx
*AUTHOR'S PREFACE . . .	1
*SPIRITUAL MYSTERIES EXPOSED . .	7
INDEX	325

*Reproduced in *facsimile* by photography.

PREFACE

THE stir in the spiritualistic world which accompanied the publication of this book will be easily understood when its contents have been analysed and adequately digested. In 1891 when it was first published, fraudulent mediumship had attained a vogue which it would be difficult to over-estimate. The class of so-called physical phenomena of which the book treats has always been more popular amongst public mediums in the United States than in this country, and has at all times been regarded with suspicion by serious students of the subject. The reason for this is not far to seek. If genuine physical phenomena exist (and we believe such phenomena to be excessively rare), it is scarcely conceivable that such manifestations could take place at the will of any medium on whom a sitter happens to call. Public mediums therefore are to be especially guarded against, and any apparently successful results obtained with them should be scrutinised with the greatest care. The present great increase of interest in psychic phenomena will probably result in the production of spurious physical phenomena by the less honest mediums, and it is with this thought that we have decided to reprint the *Revelations of a Spirit Medium.* The inquirer will find much food for thought in the ingenious devices and methods herein exposed, and the magician cannot fail to profit by a careful perusal of its pages. The literary quality of the work is certainly not of a high order, but we have preferred to reprint it as a whole, thereby retaining the somewhat quaint flavour of the original work.

In conclusion we would remind the reader that no mere knowledge of magical secrets will ever guarantee him from being deceived by fraudulent mediums. Actual acquaintance with practical methods and long experience of the conduct of séances is necessary before he will be able to distinguish the genuine from the fraudulent, and when he finds himself able to discern faintly the line which divides the two he will be in a position to understand more fully the enormous difficulties which confront

Preface

the investigators of psychical phenomena. It is hoped that the reappearance of this mediumistic classic will whet the reader's appetite and make him eager for still further information. The field of inquiry is well nigh inexhaustible and competent researchers are but few. If this book helps to produce even one student who is really capable of distinguishing truth from error the editors will feel themselves amply rewarded.

H.P.
E.J.D.

BIBLIOGRAPHICAL NOTE

The Revelations of a Spirit Medium is a book with a history—of which, unfortunately, we know very little. It was published in 1891 by Farrington & Co., 37, East Tenth St., St. Paul, Minn., U.S.A. The same year it was " entered according to Act of Congress in the Office of the Librarian of Congress at Washington " (corresponding to our Stationers' Hall), by the same firm, under the name of Charles F. Pidgeon, and there our positive information comes to a full stop.

The *real* authorship of the book has long been a subject for discussion and surmise. In an article on Lily Dale, published in the *Proceedings* of the American Society for Psychical Research, 1908, Vol. II., p. 116, Mr. Carrington says : " A number of us have, for some years, been endeavouring to find, with certainty, the author of this book. I tried, and came to the conclusion that it was a medium named Mansfield, because a well-known medium of that name published, some years ago, a little pamphlet entitled *Spiritualistic Phenomena*, explaining a number of slate tricks, materialisation frauds, etc., and in it gives one to understand that he is the author of the larger work, from which he freely quotes. He is careful not to assert that such *is* the case, however. Dr. Hodgson tried, and probably came nearer the truth than anyone else has. In the course of some correspondence I had with Miss Edmunds, after Dr. Hodgson's death, this question of the authorship of the book came up, and Miss Edmunds referred me to a gentleman, living in the West, who had in his possession a copy of this book, on the fly-leaf of which were the following words:

(At top of page.) 'Is the author Donovan or Pidgeon?'

(At bottom of page.) 'Miss H—— writes on December 8th, 1903, that she is sure the authorship of this book is Donovan. Mr. Bundy had told her, but that Donovan had slipped her memory, but was recalled by my note.—R.H.'"

The above explanation sounds highly probable, for we have evidence in the book itself that the author was well acquainted with Mr. J. C. Bundy, editor and owner of the Chicago *Religio-Philosophical Journal.*

But in a note on p. 663 of the same volume of the *Proceedings,* we have the following " correction " : " In Mr. Carrington's *Report* on Lily Dale, he attributed the authorship of *The Revelations of a Spirit Medium* to a Mr. Donovan, on the authority of Dr. Richard Hodgson. Since the publication of that *Report,* information has come from Dr. George B. Warne, President of the National Spiritualists' Association, pointing out a probable error in that statement. We publish extracts from two of his letters which show what information had come to him in regard to that authorship."

The letters in question state that the writer was told by Moses Hull that the book in question was written by Chas. F. Pidgeon, with the assistance of the notorious " spirit photographer," Frank N. Foster. Mr. Harrison D. Barrett, Dr. Warne's predecessor, reports similar testimony, and adds that he is certain the book was written by Pidgeon, though the sources of his information are not given.

Notwithstanding these amended particulars, if Mr. Bundy *really* told Dr. Hodgson that the book was written by Donovan, the Editors of the present edition favour this opinion as being correct, as undoubtedly the author was well acquainted with Mr. Bundy.

The book was such a crushing *exposé* of the methods of the bogus mediums that it created somewhat of a *furore* when it first saw the light. The mediums themselves bought every copy of the work they could find. Many copies were destroyed on the assumption that " dead men tell no tales," and the book soon became *rarissime*. Henry Ridgely Evans, writing in 1909, says (*Old and New Magic*, 2nd Ed., p. 377) : " The *Revelations of a Spirit Medium* is a very rare book," proving that thirteen years ago the work was difficult to obtain. Very few copies found their way to this country. No second edition can be traced, and the publishers went out of business soon after publication.

The remainder of the edition was apparently acquired by Leo L. Williams & Co., of Syracuse, Ind., and a reprint of certain passages in the book was published in Vol. XXXIII. of the *Open Court*, in 1909.

Many alleged *exposés* of mediumistic tricks have been published, but none with the " inside knowledge " contained in this remarkable book, which has the ring of truth in every line.

After a perusal of this most readable volume, truly can we say with Goethe that " it does not follow that what is mysterious must necessarily be miraculous."

NOTES ON THE TEXT

P. 11, line 23.—Deceive. This view is still very commonly held even to-day. As a matter of fact apparatus is by no means always necessary to the magician, some of the very best magical effects being obtained with the audience all round the performer.

P. 14, line 19.—Chirography. This marvel is being constantly related of modern mediums. For an example of how scripts are manufactured and detected see the *Proceedings* of the (English) Society for Psychical Research, 1892, vol. VIII., p.271 and of the American Society for March, 1920, pp. 529-588.

P. 17, line 18.—Preparation. It is generally assumed that magicians are capable of detecting fraudulent mediums. This is not always the case, and it is obvious that the investigating magician ought to be fully acquainted with fraudulent methods. A knowledge of how to manipulate cards and billiard balls will not make a competent investigator, and it will be remembered that both Kellar and Bellachini showed themselves incapable of detecting the ingenious methods employed by Eglinton and Slade. See *Proc. (Eng.) S.P.R.*, 1887, pp. 411*seq.* and *cf. Light*, Oct. 11, 1919, p. 324.

P. 20, line 18.—Proceeding. The same misstatements concerning the influx of spiritualists into asylums is still being repeated. The author sees clearly that such arguments have little substance and rightly condemns them.

P. 22, line 7.—Chase. Dealers in magical apparatus.

P. 26, line 17.—Ears. Searching the mouth and ears was evidently considered an extraordinary precaution in 1887. Such a control would not be thought nearly strict enough to-day.

P. 28, line 26.—It. Similar explanations offered by self constituted investigating committees are often heard even in these days and must afford the mediums the same amusement.

P. 45, line 27.—Maggie. An excellent example of the method employed for guessing names which may be verified by anybody who chooses to attend a séance for clairvoyant descriptions.

P. 54, line 8.—End. A slightly exaggerated description of an Indian " control." One of the editors was once present at a séance in which the medium was alleged to be controlled by a spirit called Whitey, who addressed the sitters in almost the exact way mentioned by the author.

P. 54, line 26.—Spiritualism. This is perfectly true. Once converted, a spiritualist seems able to believe any nonsense. For an amusing example see *Proc. Amer. S.P.R.*, 1908, II., 102--104.

P. 73, line 15.—Match heads. The easiest and commonest method for producing spirit lights. When bottled as described on p. 83, the effect is excellent. The properties of calcium sulphide and similar substances can be turned to good account when lights are to be produced. See Sir E. Thorpe's *Dictionary of Applied Chemistry*, 1912, I., p. 609.

P. 86, line 21.—Slack. The whole secret of successful work with unprepared ropes is to secure slack. There are many ingenious methods for doing this, some of which are here explained by the author.

P. 98, line 7.—Together. Liquid styrax or storax is a balsam obtained from the trunk of Liquidambar Orientalis. It is heavier than water, being about the consistency of honey, and grey or brownish yellow in colour. Alum is also extensively used in experiments of this kind, and magicians have found the same substance useful in the burnt and restored tape illusion.

P. 103, line 21.—Lead. Another contrivance consists of a dummy hand fitted with a spring clasp and rubber fingers which grip the arm of the sitter, making the hold even more deceptive. There is another device for the same purpose the secret of which we are unable to divulge.

P. 108, line 20.—Note books. These note books, " generals," or " pony " books, as they are sometimes called, have been used by American mediums for years for the purpose of gaining information about their sitters. It has often been thought that a great directory commonly called the Blue Book is in existence, and there is a certain amount of evidence which supports such a notion. The truth probably is that in every centre where there are many people interested in spiritualism, and where travelling mediums are constantly calling, the resident medium or some intermediate agent has a few note books or card index containing particulars of prominent spiritualists in the neighbourhood. This information would be supplied to the visiting medium for a consideration, or perhaps exchanged for similar information about another locality. A universal directory of American spiritualists would obviously be far too bulky to escape detection, and would rapidly go out of date, being too costly to keep up for long. Probably some of the larger centres entailed books of somewhat bulky proportions, and this may account for the rumours of the Blue Book which are often heard. That fraudulent mediums make use of information supplied by their colleagues in the same trade is certain, but the assertion that all the information received was filed together in an immense directory is, to say the least, extremely doubtful.

P. 116, line 25.—For it. Such a guitar would be useless under modern test conditions where the investigators invariably supply all the apparatus used.

P. 117, line 5.—Heel. The same device has been used in connexion with handcuff work.

P. 120, line 26.—Muriatic. *i.e.*, hydrochloric acid.

P. 131, line 16. This ingenious slate would be very useful in ordinary work, where no test conditions were demanded. In these days no investigating committee of any importance would consent to the medium working with his own slates.

P. 140, line 18.—Slates. A good example of the limits of deception when confederates have to be employed.

P. 147, line 3.—Slate. As in psychic photography the mind's eye is responsible for more than half the recognitions.

P. 152, line 23. The writer is evidently fully acquainted with the total unreliability of the average observer. With his opinion before us the exceedingly valuable test séances given by

Mr. S. J. Davey should be examined and the results compared. The accounts of Mr. Davey's sittings are published in the *Proceedings* of the Society for Psychical Research. (See *Bibliography*.)

P. 157, line 14.—Abbott. For some account of the exploits of these ladies, see *Jour. S.P.R.*, V., 168; *Proc. S.P.R.*, XI., 219, 223, 224, and No. 1 of the Lulu Hurst series (Rome, Ga., 1897), which deals with Lulu Hurst, the Georgia Wonder.

P. 164, line 27.—Or "magnetic" power, etc. See *The Magnetic Lady*, by J. N. Maskelyne, 16 pp., 8vo., published as an appendix to *The Supernatural?* Contains many diagrams and scientific explanations of the tricks and "experiments" worked by Lulu Hurst and Mrs. Abbott. See also Lulu Hurst's *Autobiography*.

P. 165, line 17.—It in this way: See *Secrets of Stage Hypnotism; Stage Electricity; and Bloodless Surgery*, by "Karlyn" (J. F. Burrows), for a very complete and concise *exposé* of fake electro-medical "cures" and methods, as used on the vaudeville stage. The spectacular experiments founded upon static electricity fully explained.

P. 167, line 20.—Essential oil of mustard. Essential oils of mustard or cayenne, if suitably " broken down " with alcohol or olive-oil, have a truly magical effect on the nervous system, when applied outwardly. In cases of neuralgia or sciatica, the relief is almost instantaneous.

P. 169, line 19.—" Table-tipping." See *Table Turning and Table Talking*, with Professor Faraday's experiments and explanation.

P. 170, line 18.—Fox girls. See the *Deathblow to Spiritualism*, by R. B. Davenport, which gives a full account of the confessions of the Fox sisters. It is only fair to add that they afterwards disavowed their " confessons."

P. 172, line 16.—Of use to you. For varieties of this trick, see *Behind the Scenes with the Mediums*, by David P. Abbott; also consult *Bibliography*.

P. 178, line 12.—In connection with " slate writing." " Dr." Henry Slade, the famous medium, was the High Priest of slate-writing, and its ablest exponent. For classical examples of his work, see *Trancendental Physics* (Zöllner, translated by Massey). Whether Slade was a fraud, or Zöllner a madman, is still hotly debated. See also, the *Report of the Seybert Commission on Spiritualism.*

P. 179, line 27.—Saturated with alcohol. Must be *absolute* alcohol. The slightest trace of water in the spirit causes a conspicuous patch to form on the envelope where the paper has dried unevenly. This trick is much used in pseudo-spiritualistic entertainments.

P. 181, line 7.—Sheets of the paper. This method is now obsolete. Annie Eva Fay used pads interleaved with waxed sheets of paper. Writing upon the top sheet would leave an invisible impression in wax upon one, two, or three sheets lower down the pad. These impressions were then taken behind the scenes and " developed " by having powdered plumbago dusted over them—causing the writing to appear in black characters. There are still more subtle and up-to-date methods of arriving at the same result.

P. 186, line 8.—Announcing a name. See *History of a Strange Case*, by David P. Abbott, for a remarkable exposition of " trumpet voices," and a suggested explanation. The cases of Mrs. Harris and Mrs. Wreidt, other well-known " trumpet mediums," are likewise worthy of study.

P. 195, line 5.—Filled with flour. A favourite " test " with the Davenport Brothers.

P. 220, line 2.—Connected with wires. These so-called mind-reading and thought-transference acts have been very much elaborated since the first edition of this book was published in 1891. Many other systems are employed, but they are all based on clever code work.

P. 225, line 7.—Although he may be mistaken. Washington Irving Bishop was one of the greatest " fakers," and published a little book (written actually by Frederick Wicks) called *Houdin and Heller's Second Sight Explained*, in which are exposed several codes for " second-sight " effects. J. N. Maskelyne, in *The Supernatural?* p. 189, makes a slashing attack on Bishop as a rank impostor.

P. 226, line 12.—Wonderful now, is it ? This " experiment " is well-known to conjurers as the Dictionary Trick.

P. 241, line 5.—Leverage. A *very little* vaseline is also smeared on the jointed rod or bolt, making it absolutely impossible to get a grip on the object—should the experiment be tried.

P. 247, line 4.—He would "grab" the "spirits." See *Spookland*, by T. Shekleton Henry, for a vivid account of the " grabbing " of Mrs. Mellon, the notorious medium.

P. 254, line 10.—Like an ordinary mortal. Compare this description of a "materialization" with Sir William Crookes' experiments with Katie King, the spirit " control " of Florence Cook. (*Phenomena of Spiritualism*, by Sir William Crookes, F.R.S., 1874.)

P. 259, line 18.—Foolish actions receive. David Dunglas Home, the famous medium, was, on May 22nd, 1868, ordered by the Court of Chancery to disgorge some £30,000 which he had received from a Mrs. Jane Lyon, who had been induced to part with this sum by means of alleged " spirit messages " from her dead husband.

P. 268, line 8.—John King. " John King" and his family are very famous " controls " or " guides," and have been used by thousands of mediums. King, *père*, was known as " Sir Henry Morgan," when on earth, and is supposed to have been a pirate. His daughter, "Katie," has been immortalized—if one can apply this term to a "spirit"—through her connection with Sir William Crookes, F.R.S. See his *Phenomena of Spiritualism*. A very detailed description of "John" can be found in *The Medium and Daybreak* for August 8th, 1873.

P. 321, line 16.—Language of a coal-heaver. One cannot help recalling that amusing joke which appeared in a humorous weekly a short time ago:

> Investigator: "Is that the spirit of William Ewart Gladstone speaking?"
>
> Shade of the "G.O.M.": "Yus, I'm 'im!"

BIBLIOGRAPHY

THE following bibliography is intended to offer a representative selection of books and articles which throw some light upon the fraudulent aspect of psychic phenomena. In making our selection we have been guided rather by a desire to help the student than to compile a catalogue which would be of interest to bibliographers. In some cases we have included works, which, although not dealing directly with fraudulent methods, present detailed descriptions of alleged physical phenomena which can hardly fail to be of interest, whilst in others we have inserted books containing some account of the lives of celebrated impostors of past epochs. As we have not attempted to give any detailed list of periodical literature, further information should be sought in the *Journals* and *Proceedings* of the English and American Societies for Psychical Research, in spiritualist papers such as *Light,* or the *Annales des Sciences Psychiques,* or in magical journals such as the *Sphinx.*

In conclusion we must say that the reason why many of the entries are incomplete is that being of an ephemeral nature, these publications unfortunately escape the notice of contemporary bibliographers.

BIBLIOGRAPHY

ABBOT, David P. "Some Mediumistic Phenomena." Article in the *Open Court* Magazine, Chicago, Aug., 1905.
—— "Mediumistic Reading of Sealed Writings." Article in the *Open Court* Magazine, April, 1906.
—— "Half-Hours with the Mediums." Article in the *Open Court* Magazine, Feb., 1907, Chicago.
—— Behind the Scenes with the Mediums. 8vo.; pp. 328. *Chicago*, 1907.
Later editions are published.
—— History of a Strange Case. 8vo.; pp. 60. *Chicago*, 1908.
An account of Mrs. Blake, the trumpet medium. *cf.* also Proc. Amer. S.P.R., 1913, VII., pp. 570-788.
—— Independent Voices. pp. 15. *Chicago*, 1911.
—— Spirit Portrait Mystery. 8vo., pp. 33. *Chicago*, 1913.
See also his *Behind the Scenes with the Mediums.*
—— Spiritualistic Materialization and other Mediumistic Phenomena. *Open Court*, 1919, XXXIII., 257-276.
ABBOTT, Orrin. The Davenport Brothers. 8vo., pp. 48. *New York*, 1864.
ADAMS, M. P. The Rich Uncle from Fiji; a Collection of Swindles. 8vo., pp. 110. *Melbourne*, 1911.
ADAMS, W. H. Davenport. Dwellers on the Threshold, or Magic and Magicians. With some illustrations of human error and imposture. 2 vols., 8vo., pp. 308. *London*, 1864.
ADARE, Viscount. Experiences in Spiritualism with Mr. D. D. Home. With introductory remarks by the Earl of Dunraven. Pp. XXXII., 179. *London, n.d.*
Gives an account of the famous levitation phenomena.
ADY, Thomas. A Candle in the Dark; or, Advice to Judges, Grand-Jury-men, etc. . . What to do before they passe sentence on such as are arraigned for their Lives as Witches. 8vo., pp. 164. *London*, 1656.
An able refutation and exposure of the arguments of witchmongers and witch-finders.
AIDE, H. "Spiritualism." Article in the *Nineteenth Century Magazine*, London, April, 1896.
ALBERTUS (*pseud.*). Conjuring, Hypnotism, Muscle and Mind-Reading. 8vo., pp. 118. *Pentre, Glamorgan* [18—].
ALEXANDER, C. The Life and Mysteries of the Celebrated Dr. "Q," *Los Angeles*, 1921, 8vo., 123 pp. An epitome of the tricks of fraudulent mediums.
D'ALMERAS, Henri. Cagliostro, et la franc-maçonnerie et l'occultisme au XVIIIe Siècle; pp. 386. *Paris*, 1904.

ALRUTZ, Sydney. Zur Psychologie der Taschenspielerkunst, Zeit. f. allg. Psychol., Leipzig, 1914, VIII., 181–192.

AN OPTICAL ILLUSION ; one of the tricks performed by the Fakirs of India. Article in the *Weekly Times*, St. Thomas, Ontario, Aug. 1st, 1901.

ANDERSON, Prof. J. H. The fashionable science of parlour magic . . . . to which is added for the first time the magic of spirit rapping, writing mediums and table turning. . . ; 8vo., pp. 60. *London* [c. 1855].

Mentions a mechanical rapping table.

—— Anderson's Exposé of spirit rappings, being a series of letters to the editors of the *Baltimore Sun*, together with a writing medium's reply. 12mo., Baltimore, 1853.

ANIMAL MAGNETISM : An exposure and explanation. In nos. 1 and 2 of *The Oracle of Health*, London, Oct. 22, 29, 1834.

An amusing plate of Mesmer magnetising ten persons is contained in No. 1.

ANON. " The Boy's Own Book of Indoor Sports ; . . . . Conjuring and stage magic fully explained." *New York* (187?), 4 pts. in one vol. Spiritualistic tests with some curious cuts are to be found in part two. pp. 37-70.

ANON. " A History of the Ridiculous Extravagancies of Monsieur Oufle ; occasioned by his reading Books treating of Magick, the Black Art, Dæmoniacks, Conjurers," etc. *London*, 1711., 303 pp., 8vo. Trans. from the French of the Abbot B. . . . Exposes the tricks of fortune-tellers, astrologers, magicians, etc.

ANON. A Fearless Investigator. *Chicago*, 1896, 8vo., 353 pp. Anti-spiritualistic.

ANON. Art of Spirit Rapping and Table Turning. 8vo., pp. 76. *Colchester* [c. 1884.]

ANON. Confessions of a Medium. 8vo., pp. XVI., 232. *London*, 1882.

A highly-coloured narrative, supposed to have been written by a medium named Thompson (or Thomson).

ANON. A Full Exposure of Ann Moore, the Pretended Fasting Woman of Tutbury. London, 1813. 30 pp., 8vo.

ANON. Caraboo. A Narrative of a Singular Imposition practised upon the Benevolence of a Lady residing in the vicinity of Bristol, by a Young Woman of the name of Mary Willcocks, *alias* Caraboo, Princess of Javasu. *Bristol and London*, 1817. 8vo., pp. 68 Complete history of an extraordinary impostor and charlatan.

ANON. Spirit Rapping in England and America. *London*, 1853. 120 pp., 8vo. Exposes Mrs. Hayden and other American mediums, etc.

ANON. Theosophy : What is it ? *Madras*, 1894. 16 pp., 8vo. " Exposure " of Madame Blavatsky and Mrs. Besant, and their work in India.

ANON. Madame Blavatsky : Her Tricks and her Dupes. *Madras*, 1894. 44 pp., 8vo.

ANON. Who is Mrs. Besant ? And why has she come to India ? *Madras*, 1894. 44 pp., 8vo. Exposure of the Theosophists and Mrs. Blavatsky.

BIBLIOGRAPHY

ANON. Theosophy Exposed : or, Mrs. Besant and her Guru. An Appeal to educated Hindus. *Madras*, 1893. 113 pp., 8vo.

ANON. Maud Blount, Medium. A Story of Modern Spiritualism. *London*, 1876. 339 pp., 8vo. Anti-spiritualistic, and exposes some of the tricks of the mediums. (Written by the Rev. C. Maurice Davies, D.D.)

ANON. Conjuring and Stage Magic. Wonders of Spiritualism ; Table-Turning ; tricks of the Davenport Bros., etc. *New York*, 1881. 94 pp., 8vo.

ANON. Curiosities of Modern Travel. *London*, 1846. 8vo., 310 pp. The exposure of Abd-el Kader, the " Magician of Cairo," pp. 1-30.

ANON. Das Gedankenspiel oder die Kunst der Menschen Gedanken zu erforschen. 8vo. *Halle*, 1782.

ANON. Das Neue Universum. *Stuttgart*, c. 1899. 396 pp., 8vo. Spiritualistic tricks, illusions, spirit photography, etc. *Cf.* Hopkins' "*Magic.*"

ANON. Mrs. Etta Roberts, the so-called Cage Medium ; her Strange Career of Deceit, with variations. 3 pp., 8vo. (*U.S.A.*), c. 1890.
—— The Spirits Exposed. *New York*, n.d. ; 8vo., 58 pp.
—— The Art of Stage Mind Reading or Second Sight. *New York*, n.d. ; 8vo., 55 p.p.
—— The Book of Hindoo Mysteries and Spiritualistic Work Revealed. *New York*, 1908 ; 16mo., 59 pp.
—— Magic Explained ; Magic Pretended ; Miracles and Remarkable Natural Phenomena. *Philadelphia*, n.d. ; 8vo., 192 pp.; a reprint of a R.T.S. publication.

ANON. Der Spiritische Schwindel Enthuellungen von einem Eingeweihten. 2e. Aufl. 8vo. pp. 96. Leipzig, 1885.

ANON. Discours contre le spiritisme, par un médium incrédule. *Paris*, 1860.
By Camille Debans.

ANON. Fraud masquerading in Saintly Robes : how thousands were mystified by cheap jugglery. pp. 8. *New York* (18—).

ANON. Ghosts at Holly Court ; by a genuine Medium. Articles in the *Boys' Own Paper*, London, 1879, Vol. 2 ; pp. 158-165 and 188-205 ; exposes several tricks of the bogus mediums.

ANON. How to do Second Sight. *New York*, 1900 ; 8vo. pamph.

ANON. Mind Reading. pp. 32. *London*, 1901.

ANON. Modern Miracles in Magic, ventriloquism and spirit mysteries.
Pagination wrongly printed throughout and no place or date ; American ; about 1880 ? Probably made up copy. Ellison Coll.

ANON. Mr. Stuart Cumberland. Der antispiritische Taschenspieler und sein Gedankenlesen. 8vo., pp. 32. *Leipzig*, 1884.

ANON. Secrets of Clairvoyance : How to Become an Operator. *New York*, 1884 ; 8vo., 95 pp.

ANON. Sketches of Imposture, Deception and Credulity. *London*, 1837 ; 8vo., 368 pp.

ANON. Spirit Mysteries Exposed ; being a full and plain explanation of the wonderful feats of the Davenport brothers and other " mediums." pp. 58 ; *New York* (188–?).

ANON. Spiritualism Exposed. pp. 16. *Philadelphia*, (18—).
ANON. Spiritualism Exposed, or Lighting up a Dark Séance. 8vo., pp. 16. *Birmingham* [c. 1875 ?]
Amusing account of the aerial transit of Mrs. Guppy.
ANON. Table Turning and Table Talking. 8vo., pp. 191. *London*, [1853.]
Two editions were published. The second contains Faraday's experiments and explanation.
ANON. The Art of Mind-reading. pp. 40 ; *New York* (1880).
A. J. Brown's methods are herein described.
ANON. The Book of Hindoo mysteries and Spiritualist work revealed. pp. 59. *Providence*, 1908.
ANON. The Rappers, or the mysteries, fallacies, and absurdities of spirit rapping . . . by a Searcher after Truth. pp. 282. *New York*, 1854.
ANON. The Wizard's Manual of Mind-reading, Magic, Spiritualism, etc. (No. 337, *Leisure Hour Library*) ; 8vo., pp. 122. New York, 1895.
ANON. Trees grown while you wait ; what Indian Magic can do. Article in *Penny Pictorial*, London, Oct. 25th, 1902, Vol. 14, pp. 290-292.
ANTI-CANIDIA ; or, Superstition Detected and Exposed. In a Confutation of the Vulgar Opinion concerning Witches, Spirits, Demons, Magick, Divination, Omens, Prognostications, Dreams, Augurys, Astrology, etc. *London*, 64 pp., 8vo., n.d.
ASTOR, PHILIP. A Séance with the Lights Up ; Some Spirit Mysteries Exposed. Article in the *London Magazine*, Sept., 1902 ; pp. 220-224.
ATKINSON, W. W. Secrets of Mental Magic ; obl. 8vo., pp. 380. *London*, 1917.
BAGGALLY, W. W. Telepathy, Genuine and Fraudulent. 8vo., pp. 94. *London*, 1917.
Has a preface by Sir Oliver Lodge, and Part III. is devoted to the Zancigs' thought-reading entertainment.
BAILEY, F. H. Hindu Jugglery. *Journal of Education* (Boston) ; Vol. xliv., p. 378.
BALDWIN, Prof. S. Secrets of Mahatma Land Explained. 2nd ed., 4to., pp. 120. *Brooklyn*, 1895.
Originally published in Australia. For a account of the Baldwins' entertainment see Proc. S.P.R., xi., 225-228.
BALLARD, Rev. Dr. Frank. Eddyism, miscalled Christian Science ; a Delusion and a Snare. *London* ; 8vo., n.d., 205 pp.
BANCROFT, Frederick. Yogi Magic in India. *Scientific American Supplement ;* Vol. xciii., pp. 1784-5.
BARNUM, P. T. The Humbugs of the World. 8vo., pp. 424. *New York*, 1866.
Mentions the Davenport brothers and " fake " Spiritualism.
BARTHEZ, Dr. E. Empress Eugenie and Her Circle. *London*, 1912. Account of the " exposure " of D. D. Home, the medium. 8vo., pp. 139-166.
BARTLETT, Geo. C. An Episode in the Life of a Medium. Article in the *Open Court Magazine*, Feb., 1909. An " editorial comment" gives explanations of the effects described in the article.

BARTLETT, J. Second Sight. *Scientific American Supplement*, vol. xlii., pp. 1777-8.

BAYLEY, R. Child. Faked Spirit Photographs. Article in the *London Magazine*, Jan., 1910.

BEADNELL, C. M. The Reality or Unreality of Spiritualistic Phenomena ; being a criticism of Dr. W. J. Crawford's investigations into levitations and raps. pp. 23. London, 1920.
Of little value to the magician.

BEARD, George M., M.D. The Study of Trance, Muscle-Reading, etc. New York, 1882 ; 8vo , 40 pp Explanations of the tricks of the " mind-readers."

—— Current Delusions Relating to Hypnotism (artificial trance). *St. Louis*, 1882 ; 8vo., 9 pp. Reprint from *The Alienist and Neurologist*.

BELLACHINI, *the younger*. Wie es gemacht wird ! Vorführung von Zauber-Kunststücken, magnet und spiritist Experimenten, sowie Hellseherkünsten. 8vo., pp 26. Berlin, 1894.

BENJAMIN, M. Modern Magic and its Explanation. *The Chautauquan*, Vol. xi., p. 731.

BENSON, E. F. Queen Lucia. London (1920) ; 8vo., 304 pp.
A good-natured satire on the various modern crazes which attract the idle rich, who in this story are exploited by a cunning Indian Guru, or teacher.

BERTRAM, C. A Magician in Many Lands. 8vo., pp. 315. London, 1911.
The feats of Eastern jugglers are dealt with.

—— Are Indian Jugglers Humbugs ? Article in *Strand Magazine*, London, Dec., 1899.

BESANT, W. Herr. Paulus ; his rise ; his greatness ; his fall. New York ; 8vo., 342 pp., n.d. ; anti-spiritualistic.

BIBLIOGRAPHIE DES OUVRAGES relatifs aux Pélerinages, aux Miracles, au Spiritisme et à la Prestidigitation . . . 8vo., pp. 70. Turin, 1876.

BIEN BOA. The Hypothesis of the Artist, G. von Max, concerning the Clothing of " Bien Boa," and the Replies of Mm. Barmann, Peter, Richet, and Dienhard. *Ann. of Psych. Sci.*, 1906, iv., 38-54.
Important for the Villa Carmen controversy

BISHOP, Washington Irving. Houdin and Heller's second sight explained. 8vo., pp. 78. Edinburgh and London, 1880.
Actually written by Fred. Wicks. Codes for thought transmission are given.

BISSON, J. A. Les phénomènes dits de Matérialisation. pp. xx., 311. Paris, 1914.
Discusses fraud in the case of the Medium " Eva C."

BISONETTE OF SICOTTE AND HIS MANY DUPES. Article in *New York Sun*, Oct. 27th, 1901.

BLACKBURN, Douglas. Thought Reading ; or, Modern Mysteries Explained. Being chapters on Thought-reading, Occultism, Mesmerism, etc. ; forming a key to the Psychological Puzzles of the Day. 12mo., pp. 101. London, (1884).

BLAKEMAN, Rufus. A Philosophical Essay on Credulity and Superstition. *New York,* 1849 ; 12mo.

BLACKWELL, H. Spirit Photographs. Article in the *London Magazine,* Jan., 1910.

BLITZ, Signor. Fifty Years in the Magic Circle. 8vo., pp. 432. *Hartford, Conn.,* 1871.

An interesting account of the early spiritualists and their tricks.

BLUNT, Chiistiana. A Midnight Dialogue between Joanna Southcott and Satan ; translated from a Luciferian Manuscript. 2nd Ed., 12 pp. *London,* 1814. Exposure of this celebrated charlatan.

BODIE'S STAGE CURES AND TRICKS EXPLAINED. See London Press for period, Nov. 1st—14th, 1909.

BOHN, E. Der Fall Rothe. Eine criminal-psychologische Untersuchung. 8vo., pp. xii., 157. *Breslau,* 1901.

BREITHAUPT, C. Disquisitio historica, critica, curiosa de variis modis occulte scribendi. 4to., pp. 65. *Helmstadii,* 1727.

BREWSTER, Sir D. Letters on natural Magic. 16mo., pp. xi., 351. *London,* 1832.

Other editions, including a French translation by A. D. Vergnaud, were published.

BRIGNOGNAN, *pseud.* La sorcellerie amusante. 8vo., pp. 188. *Paris,* [1897].

BROWN, J. H. Spectroscopia. Spectral illusions showing ghosts everywhere and of any colour. 4to., pp. 44. *London,* 1864.

Coloured plates. Part I. only was published, and a portion called *Ghosts* was reproduced as No. 2 of Vol. I. of *Magic,* Kansas City, 1910.

BROWNSON, O. A. The Spirit Rapper. 8vo., pp. xii., 402. *Boston,* 1854.

An early and amusing exposé. The author was editor of Brownson's *Quarterly Review* and the book is in the form of an autobiography.

BURKE, Walter. The Fire-Walkers of Fiji. Article in Frank Leslie's *Popular Monthly,* New York, April, 1903.

BURLINGHAME, H. J. Around the World with a Magician and a Juggler. 8vo., pp. 172. *Chicago,* 1891.

Written in 1872. Contains explanation of Eastern tricks.

—— How to Read People's Minds. 8vo., pp. 48. *Chicago,* 1905.

A useful little book on mind and muscle-reading.

See also *Twenty Years of Spoof and Bluff,* by Carlton, for explanations of some wonderful mind-reading tests.

—— Leaves from Conjurers' Scrapbooks. 8vo., pp. 274. *Chicago,* 1891.

Deals with fake hypnotism, mind-reading, second sight, instantaneous memorization, etc.

BURMESE MAGIC, M.S. Sixty beautifully-inscribed palm-leaves, with three covering leaves lacquered in gold and red. Describes the Indian fakir tricks. Executed by a scribe at an Indian Court. from particulars supplied by itinerant conjurers. *In the Harry Price Collection.*

BUSH, EDWARD. Spiritualism Explained and Exposed. *Wakefield* (1920) ; 8vo., pp. XI. 83.

BUSH, EDWARD. Spirit photography exposed. pp. 40, 8vo. *Southport*, 1920. An attempted exposure of the Crewe Circle.
CADET, Max. Les Trucs de la Mémoire. pp. 28. *Rennes*, 1911. [publd. by the Author].
CAPPER, Alfred. A Rambler's Recollections and Reflexions, with portrait. 8vo., pp. 330. *London*, 1915.
—— Confessions of a Thought-Reader. Article in the *Universal Magazine*, Xmas No., 1901 ; pp. 105-111.
CAPRON, E. W. Modern Spiritualism, Facts, Fanaticisms, Consistencies, and Contradictions. 8vo., pp. 438. *Boston, U.S.A.*, 1855.
CARLTON (pseud., i.e., Arthur Philps). Twenty years of spoof and bluff. 8vo., pp. 299. *London*, 1920
Describes muscle-reading entertainments, telephone " telepathic " acts, etc.
CARLYLE, Thomas. Count Cagliostro (in his Miscellaneous Essays). A brilliant sketch of this famous charlatan and pretended wonder-worker. See, also, the French translation of the original Italian Inquisition Biography: *La Vie de Joseph Balsamo, connu sous le nom de Comte Cagliostro. Paris*, 1791.
CARPENTER, W. B. Mesmerism, Spiritualism, etc,, Historically and Scientifically Considered. 8vo., pp. 158. *London*, 1877.
—— Epidemic Delusions. 8vo., pp. 27. *Manchester*, 1871.
Report of a lecture delivered in Hulme Town Hall, Manchester, Dec. 8, 1871.
CARPENTER, William H. At an Algerian Aissaoua. *Current Literature*, Vol. XIX., pp. 409-11.
Describes the " supernatural " tricks of the Algerian wonder-workers.
CARUS, Dr. Paul. An article on David P. Abbott's New Illusions of the Spirit World. In *The Open Court* for February, 1912. Chicago. Exposes the spirit paintings, " talking kettle," etc.
—— Revelations of an Ex-Medium. Series of articles in the *Open Court Magazine*, Chicago, commencing Feb., 1909. In the same issue : Healing by Conjuration.
CARRINGTON, Hereward. Eusapia Palladino and her Phenomena. 8vo., pp. XIV., 353. *London* [1910.]
An account of many sittings with this famous medium. Both fraudulent and genuine phenomena described. For the full report of the Naples Sittings see Proc. S.P.R., Vol. 23, pp. 309-569.
—— Hindu Magic. 8vo., pp 52. *London*, 1909.
An edition was also published in Kansas City in 1913.
—— My Experiences with Present Day Mediums. Article in the *Bohemian Magazine*, Oct., 1909.
—— Personal experiences in Spiritualism. 8vo., pp. XVI., 274, *London* [1913].
—— Report of a two weeks' investigation into . . . Lily Dale. Proc. Amer. S.P.R., 1908, II., 1-117.
Materialising and slate-writing mediums are exposed.
—— The Physical Phenomena of Spiritualism. 8vo., pp. 426, *London*, 1907-8 ; 2nd Ed., *London*, 1920.

CASTON, A. de. Les marchands de miracles. 8vo., pp. 338. *Paris*, 1864.
—— Tartuffe Spirite. 8vo., pp. 316. *Paris*, 1866.
CAUZONS, T. de. La Magie et la Sorcellerie en France. 4 vols. *Paris*, [1910-11].
" CAVENDISH " (*pseud.*) Second Sight for Amateurs. pp. 100 ; edition of 25 copies only. *London*, 1888.
CHARLATANS (Les) Célèbres. 2nd Ed. [by J. B. Gouriet], 2 vols., 8vo., pp. 782. *Paris*, 1819.
CHAUTARD, E. Les Révélations d'un Magnétiseur. 8vo., pp. 69. *Monceau-les-Mines*, 1904.
CHINESE MAGIC MIRRORS. Article in *Open Court Magazine*, Chicago, April, 1901.
CLAIRVOYANCE, HYPNOTISM, AND THOUGHT READING EXPLAINED. Article in the *Ludgate Weekly*, London, Vol. I., Mar. 5th, and 12th, 1892.
CLARKE, E H. Visions : A Study of False Sight (*pseudopia*). 8vo., pp. XXII., 6-315. *Boston*, 1878.
CLEMENT, H. Le Spiritisme. Ses pseudo-manifestations. pp. 35. *Lyons*, 1914.
CLODD, Edward. Is Sir Oliver Lodge Right ? In the *Strand Magazine*, London, July, 1917. A criticism of *Raymond*.
—— The Question : If a Man Die, Shall He Live Again ? *London*, 1917 ; 8vo., pp. 314.
COATES, J. Photographing the invisible. 8vo. pp. XII., 399. *London* 1911.
Gives a good idea of psychic photography.
COLLINS, A. F. The Book of Magic. 8vo., pp. 177. *New York*, 1915.
Describes a wireless rapping table.
COLLYER, R. H. Automatic Writing : the Slade Prosecution. 8vo., pp. 23. *London*, 1876.
CONFESSIONS OF A BOGUS MEDIUM : How I made £1,000 a Year by Faked Séances. A series of articles in the *World's Pictorial News* (Eng.), commencing Feb. 20th, 1920.
CONJURERS AND SPIRITUALISTS. Article in *Chamber's Journal*, Oct. 14th, 1876, London.
CONRADI, F. W. Telepathische Unterrichtsbriefe. pp. 48. *Berlin*, 1918.
CONWAY, Moncure Daniel. Autobiography. *London*, 1904, two Vols., 8vo., 404 and 428 pp.
Account of sitting with, and exposure of Mrs. Guppy, the medium, etc.
COOK, Walter. Reflections on Raymond. *London*, 1917 ; 8vo., 94 pp. A Criticism of Sir Oliver Lodge's book.
COOVER, J. E. Experiments in Psychical Research at Leland Stanford Junior University. pp. XXIV., 641. *Palo Alto*, 1917.
CORELLI, Marie. Spiritualism : An Exposure of Automatic Writing, etc., in the *Daily Telegraph*, Feb. 10th, 1920.
CRAFT, Amos. Epidemic Delusions, with especial reference to Modern Spiritualism. 8vo. pp. 341. *Cincinnati*, 1881,

BIBLIOGRAPHY   xxxix

CRAMER, W. Ik Kan Goochelen ; Vermakelijke Proeven Op, Natuurkundig Gebied Voor Jong En Oud. *Leiden*, n.d. (c. 1914). 8vo., 349 pp.
Chapters on optical " ghosts," " spirit " photography, etc.

CRAWFORD, W. J. The Reality of Psychic Phenomena. pp. VII., 246. *London*, 1916.

—— Experiments in Psychical Science. pp. VII., 191. *London*, 1919.
Deals with levitation phenomena and the direct voice.

CRICHTON-BROWNE, Sir James. Account of Failure of Experiments in Thought Transference with Blackburn and Smith. In the *Westminster Gazette*, Jan. 29th, 1901.

CROOKES, Sir W. Researches in the phenomena of Spiritualism. *London*, 1874. pp. 112, 8vo.

The classic investigations into Home's phenomena which have never been satisfactorily explained. Sir William's investigations of the medium, Florence Cook, were described in brief letters in *The Spiritualist*, in 1874. These, together with the *Researches*, were reprinted by the *Two Worlds* Publ. Co. in 1903.

CRUIKSHANK, G. A Discovery Concerning Ghosts, with a Rap at the Spirit Rappers. 8vo., pp. 48. *London*, 1863. 2nd Ed. 1864.
A Skit on contemporary table turning.

CUMBERLAND, A. W. Der Experimental Spiritist als Orakel, Hellscher, blinder Rechner und Gedächtnisskünstler. 8vo., pp. III., 132. *Stuttgart*, 1895.

CUMBERLAND, Stuart. Illusionary and Fraudulent Aspects of Spiritualism. *J. of Mental Sci.*, Lond., 1881-2, n.s. XXVII., 280 ; 628.

—— People I have read. 8vo., pp. 192. *London*, 1905.

—— Spiritualism : The Inside Truth. 8vo., pp. 157. *London*, 1919.

—— A Thought Reader's Thoughts. 8vo., pp. 326. *London*, 1888.

—— That Other World ; Personal Experiences of Mystics and their Mysticism. *London*, 1918 ; 8vo., 253 pp.
Contains exposures of the mediums Bastian, Home, Philippe, Rasputin, Slade, etc., etc.

—— Cumberland's Mind-Reading ; An Explanation of the Tricks by which Some Mediums Impress their Dupes. Interview with Stuart Cumberland in the (New York) *Evening Post*, Dec. 8th, 1882.

CUNNINGHAM, P. C. Six Visits to a Clairvoyant : Secrets of a Strange Profession. Series of six articles in the Chicago *Inter-Ocean*, Sunday editions, commencing Feb. 12th, 1905. Very complete exposure.

D., E. J. Fraud. *Freethinker*, March 14th, 1920.; pp. 164-165.
The sixth of a series of articles.

D.M. On the Rev. J. Cumming ; being an Exposure of the Sham Miracle of Table-turning. With a Supplementary Review of Popular Delusions, ancient and modern. *Worcester*, 1854 ; 8vo., pp. 32.

DACK, Prof. Les rappels, les trucs et les fantaisies de la mémoire. 8vo., pp. 41. *Paris*, 1912.

DAILY NEWS, Sept. 1st and 5th 1911. Confession of and explanation by Blackburn, of the code used in the "thought-transference" experiments of Blackburn and Smith at Brighton.

DAVENPORT BROTHERS' ENTERTAINMENT. Report of, in *The Lancet*, October 8th, 1864.

DAVENPORT BROTHERS' ENTERTAINMENT. Report of, in *The Times*, Sept. 30th, 1864.

DAVENPORT, R. B. The Death-blow to Spiritualism. 8vo., pp. 247. *New York*, 1888.

    An account of the confession (afterwards withdrawn) of the Fox sisters.

DAVEY, S. J. Spurious Mediumship. Jour. S. P. R., 1888, III., 199-207. [See also Hodgson, R.]

DAVIES, Rev. C. Maurice. Mystic London, or Phases of Occult Life in the Metropolis. *London*, 1875; 8vo., 406 pp. Account of exposure of Annie Eva Fay and other mediums.

DAVIS, A. J. The Diakka and their Earthly Victims. *New York*, 1873.

DAVIS, P. La fin du monde des esprits. Le spiritisme devant la raison et la science. 8vo., pp. XXIV., 294. *Paris* [1892].

DEBAN, C. See Anon. Discours contre le spiritisme, etc.

DE FONVIELLE, W. Comment se font les miracles en dehors de l'église. pp. XII., 348. *Paris, n.d.*

DELANNE, G. Recherches sur la mediumnité. 8vo., pp. XII., 515, *Paris*, 1902.

—— Les apparitions materialisées des vivants et des morts; 2 vols.; 8vo. *Paris*, 1909-11.

DE LAWRENCE, G. The Mysteries of Crystal Gazing. *Chicago*, 1920; 4to.. ll. 22.

    Complete exposé of vaudeville mind-reading and sealed billet-reading acts.

DEVANT, David. Interview with. Conjuring and Spiritualism. Article in *To-Day*, London, Jan. 28th, 1899; pp. 401-2.

DEVIL'S LEGACY TO EARTH MORTALS, The. Being the keynote to Black Art, Witchcraft, etc. *New York*; 8vo., pp. 96, *n.d.*

DESSOIR, M. The Psychology of Legerdemain. *Open Court*, 1893, VI., pp. 3599-3602; 3608-3611; 3616-3619; 3626-3627; 3633-3634.

DICKSONN, Prof. Trucs et mystères dévoilés. pp. 280. *Paris* [1911].
—— La Vérité sur le spiritisme. pp. 216. *Arnouville*, 1917.

DICTIONNAIRE de trucs, illusions de physique amusante. 2 vols., pp. 878. *Paris*, 1792.

DINGWALL, E. J. Magic and Mediumship. *Psychic Research Quarterly*, Jan., 1920.

DIRCKS, H. The Ghost, as produced in the *Spectre Drama*. 8vo., pp. 102. London, 1863.

    A description of Pepper's Ghost, of which Dircks was really the inventor.

DOBLER, Herr [G. W. Smith]. Exposé of the Davenport Brothers. 8vo., pp. 48. *Belfast*, 1869.

BIBLIOGRAPHY xli

DOUGLAS, E. Jesting with Death. Article in the *Royal Magazine*, April, 1899, London.
Explanations of the optical and other illusions of the Cabaret du Néant, Paris.

DOUGLAS, James. Are the Dead Alive ? A series of articles in the London *Sunday Express*, commencing October 23rd, 1921. Very cautiously written, and valuable as accurately describing the various phases of modern Spiritualism. Spirit photography, the dark séance, trumpet mediums, etc., investigated.

—— Is Spirit Photography Genuine ? Article in the London *Sunday Express*, December 11th, 1921. Tells how a conjurer produced " spirit " photographs before committee of Spiritualists under test conditions identical to those imposed upon Hope, of Crewe.

DOWNEY, June E. Studies from the psychological laboratory of the University of Chicago. Control processes in modified handwriting ; an experimental study. 8vo., pp. VII., 148. *Baltimore*, 1908.

DUCRET, E. Les fourberies des charlatans. 8vo., pp 176. *Paris, n.d.*

—— Le charlatanisme dévoilé. 8vo., pp. 319. *Paris* [1892].

—— Le Spiritisme Dévoilé. *Paris*, n.d. 8vo., pp. 327.

—— Récréations Géométriques, Illusions D'Optique, Fantasmagorie, etc. *Paris*, n.d. 8vo., pp. 180.

DUPREZ, Prof. Drawing Room Magic and Spiritualism. 8vo., pp. 28. *Plymouth, n.d.*

DUTROIT, J. Spiritismus und Gefängnis. 8vo., pp. 80. *Pössneck*, 1903.
On the Anna Rothe case.

EARTHLY MATTER. An article in *Punch*, March 9th, 1921, No. 4157, Vol. CLX., pp. 188-9. Humorous skit on public clairvoyant delineations.

EVANS, Henry Ridgely. Cagliostro ; a Study in Charlatanism. Article in *The Monist*, Vol. XIII., July, 1903, Chicago ; pp. 523-552, with portraits, etc.

—— Hours with the Ghosts. 8vo., pp. 302. *Chicago*, 1897.
Afterwards published in an abridged form as *The Spirit World Unmasked*. A popular exposé.

—— Ingenious Devices of Spirit Mediums ; how to produce spirit hands, rappings, music, and the ghosts themselves. Article in the Chicago *Tribune*, Feb. 3rd, 1901.

—— Madame Blavatsky. An article in the *Cosmopolitan*, New York, December, 1899 ; pp. 241-248.

—— Ghost-making Extraordinary. Article in the *Open Court Magazine*, Chicago, Feb., 1905.

—— The Rationale of Ghosts. Article in the *Cosmopolitan Magazine*, New York, Feb., 1905 ; pp. 427-432.

—— The Old and the New Magic. 2nd Ed. ; 8vo., pp. 517. *Chicago*, 1909.

F., J. [John Falconer]. Cryptomenysis Patefacta, or the Art of Secret Information. 8vo., pp. 180. *London*, 1685.
An early treatise on secret writing, etc.

F., J. S. Demonologia . . . being an exposé of ancient and modern superstitions, credulity, fanaticism, enthusiasm, and imposture. 8vo., pp. 438. *London*, 1827. A second edition was published in 1831.

FARMER, J. S. How to Investigate Spiritualism. *London and Chicago*, 1883; 8vo., 32 pp.

—— 'Twixt Two Worlds: a narrative of the life and work of William Eglinton; 4to., pp. 196. *London*, 1886.

Not an exposure but an excellent account of fraudulently produced phenomena.

FAWKES, F. A. Spiritualism Exposed; 8vo., pp. 143. *Bristol and London*, 1920.

FEARLESS (A.) Investigator. 8vo., pp. 353. *Chicago*, 1896.

An anti-spiritualistic novel.

FELLOWS, G. S. Loisette Exposed; together with Loisette's Complete System of Physiological Memory. *New York*, 1888. 8vo., pp. 224.

FEERHOW, F. Wie es gemacht wird ! Die Technik schwindelhafter Psychophänomene. 8vo., pp. 45. *Berlin*, 1913.

FIEDLER, J. Mnemotechnik. pp. 29. *Wien*, 1911.

FIGUIER, L. Histoire du merveilleux dans les temps modernes. 4 vols. *Paris*, 1860.

Several later editions were published.

FITZGERALD, Frank. Tricks of the Trade Exposed. No date or place of publication (published in Australia); 8vo., pp. 33; explanations of spiritualistic " effects."

FLAMMARION, C. Les forces naturelles inconnues. 8vo., pp. XI., 604. *Paris*, 1907.

FLOURNOY, T. Esprits et médiums. pp. VIII., 561. *Genève et Paris*, 1911.

Abridged Eng. trans. entitled *Spiritism and Psychology* was issued in 1911.

FONTENAY, G. de. La Photographie et l'étude des phénomènes psychiques. pp. XIV., 113. *Paris*, 1912.

Excellent survey of the " spirit " photograph controversy.

FOWLER, Robert, M.D. Complete History of the Case of the Welsh Fasting Girl. *London*, 1871; 8vo., pp. 307. An exposure of a great imposture.

FOX SISTERS. Confession of the, in the *New York Herald*, Sept. 24th, 1888.

F.R.A.S. (Capt. Noble). The Exposure of Anna Rothe, the Medium, in *The English Mechanic*, April 17th, 1903.

FRASER, Dr. James. A New Visual Illusion of Direction. Reprint from the *Journal of Psychology*, vol. ii., part 3, January, 1908.

FROST, H. J. Prof. H. J. Frost's A.B.C. of Parlour Magic and Spiritualism. pp. 8. *S(an) F(rancisco)* (188—?).

GANDON, F. La seconde vue dévoilé. 8vo., pp. 112. *Paris*, 1849.

The foundation of Houdin's second-sight act.

GANTHONY, R. Bunkum Entertainments. 8vo., pp. 188. *London*, 1893.

GARRETT, E. Isis very much unveiled. 8vo., pp. 136. *London*, 1895.
An exposure of Theosophical claims. See W. Q. Judge's reply: *Isis and the Mahatmas*. London, 1895.

GARRETT, Julia E. Mediums Unmasked; an exposé of modern spiritualism, by an ex-medium. *Los Angeles, Cal.*, 1892; 8vo., pp. 56.

GASPARIN, Comte A. E. de. Des tables tournantes. 2 vols. *Paris*, 1854.

—— Science v. Modern Spiritualism. 2 vols. *New York*, 1857.

GATCHEL, C. The Methods of Mind Readers. *Forum*, 1891, XI., 192-204.

GERLING, R. Spiritisten ohne Geist. 8vo., pp. 169. *Berlin*, 1912.

GHOST STORIES, collected with a particular view to counteract the vulgar belief in ghosts . . . 8vo., pp. XX., 292. *London*, 1823.
Most of the " phenomena " are due to trickery.

GHOSTS, THE MANUFACTURE OF. Methods of fraudulent spirit mediums. Article in *Kansas City Star*, Oct. 19th, 1902.

GILBERT, Emile. Autrefois—aujourd'hui. Sorciers et Magiciens. *Moulins*, 1895; 8vo., 263 pp.

GOLDSTON, Will. More Exclusive Magical Secrets. *London*, 1921; 4to., pp. 500.
Contains a section on the latest spiritualistic tricks and subtleties, illustrated. See the same author's *Exclusive Magical Secrets* (1912) for other mediumistic "effects."

—— Fake Mediums and their Tricks. An article in *The Magician Annual*, London, 1910-11; pp. 79-86.

—— Fake Mediums; Some of their Tricks Exposed. An article in the *Daily Express*, Feb. 28th, 1919; p. 4.

—— Latest Magical Secrets. *London*; 8vo. (in preparation).
Deals largely with spiritualistic tricks.

GOODCHILD, Geo. The Barton Mystery. *London, n.d.* (c. 1920); 8vo., pp. 208.
The story centres round a remarkable medium, half fraudulent, half genuine.

GRASSET, J. Le spiritisme devant la science. 8vo., pp. XXIX., 392. *Paris*, 1904.

GREY, Dr. R. Memoria Technica, or Method of Artificial Memory. *Oxford*, 1861; 8vo., pp. XXIII., 215.
Directions for acquiring an abnormal memory as used by charlatans, etc.

HAMILTON, Herbert. The Spectre Scope. Article in *Pearson's Magazine*, London, March, 1900; Vol. 9 pp. 330-331.

HAMILTON, W. H., SMYTH, J. S., and HYSLOP, J. H. A Case of Hysteria. Proc. Amer. S.P.R., 1911, V., 1-660.
A case of physical phenomena of unusual interest. The report should be carefully studied.

HAMMOND, W. The Physics and Physiology of Spiritualism. 8vo. *New York*, 1871.

HARKNESS, A. Ku Hova Medium Trapped by the Police: Confesses Fraud at Last. Article in *Daily News*, Atlanta, Ga., March 13th, 1901.

HART, E. Hypnotism, Mesmerism and the New Witchcraft. new ed.; pp. VIII., 212. *London*, 1896.
  The second edition (Ed. 1, 1893) contains chapters on the confessions of a professional hypnotist.
HARTMANN, C. R. E., von. Der Spiritismus. 12mo., pp. 118. *Leipzig*, 1885.
—— Die Geisterhypothese des Spiritismus und seine Phantome. pp. 126. *Leipzig*, 1891.
  Philosophical treatises.
HATTON, Henry. How Magic is Made; Spirit Cabinets, Second Sight, etc. Articles in *Harper's Round Table*, New York, 1895-6; Nos. 844, 852, 862, 866, 869, 873.
—— Secrets of Conjuring. Article in *Scribner's Magazine*, Vol. 21, pp. 304-310, New York, Dec., 1880.
  Exposes the spiritualistic bench, basket trick, etc.
—— Secrets of Second Sight. Article in *Scribner's Magazine*, Nov. 1880; pp. 65-69.
HAVEN, Dr. Marc. Le Maitre Inconnu Cagliostro; Etude Historique et Critique sur la Haute Magie. *Paris*, 1912; pp. 332, 8vo.
  Contains a comprehensive bibliography of works relating to Cagliostro.
HELM, Harry. How Fraudulent Mediums Work; Schemes and Tricks; Voodooism, etc. (?)
HENDERSON, Alexander, M.D. An Examination of the Imposture of Ann Moore, called the Fasting Woman of Tutbury. *London*, 1813; 8vo., pp. 52.
HENRY, T. S. Spookland. 8vo., pp. 73. *Chicago*, 1902.
  Originally published in Sydney, N.S.W. in 1894. Contains an exposure of Mrs. Mellon; cf. also A Counterblast to Spookland, or Glimpses of the Marvellous, by Psyche.
HERMANN, Alexander. Light on the Black Art; Tricks of East Indian Jugglers; Spiritualism; Spirit Photography. Article in the New York *Cosmopolitan*, Dec., 1892, Vol. 14; pp. 207-214.
—— Necromancy Unveiled; Talking Hand, Second Sight, etc. Article in *Lippincott's Magazine*, Philadelphia, Oct. 1893, Vol. 52; pp. 475-481.
HERMON, H. Hellerism. 16mo., pp. 129. *Boston*, 1884.
  Deals with thought transference.
HERO, of Alexandria. Quatro theoremi aggiunti a gli Artifitiosi Spiriti. *Ferrara*, 1589; sm. 4to.
—— Spiritalia. Giorgi edn. *Urbino*, 1592; 4to., 82 ff. Automata.
  Explanations of automata used in Greek temples to produce "miracles." Other edns., 1575, 1589, 1680, etc. See Woodcroft.
—— Spiritalia (Commandinus edition). *Urbino*, 1575; sm. 4to.; and other editions.
HICHENS, Robert. Mrs. Marden. *London*, 1919; and reprints; 8vo., pp. 247.
  Anti-spiritualistic novel; detailed account of a fake medium's business.
HICKEY, Preston Langley. Exposure of the Magical Crystal-gazing Globe. An article in *Science and Invention* (U.S.A.) for September, 1921.

BIBLIOGRAPHY   xlv

HILLIARD, J. N. Not in League with the Spirits; an exposé of Annie Eva Fay. Article in the *Post Express*, Rochester, N.Y., Jan. 29th, 1904.
HODGSON, R. Account of personal investigations in India, and discussion of the authorship of the " Koot Hoomi" letters. Proc. S.P.R., 1885, III., 207-381.
    Deals with the Theosophical controversy.
HODGSON, R. Indian Magic and the Testimony of Conjurers. Proc. S.P.R., IX., 1893-4, 354-66.
—— Mr. Davey's Imitations by Conjuring of Phenomena, sometimes Attributed to Spirit Agency. Proc. S.P.R., 1892, VIII., 253-310.
    A most important paper on mal-observation in slate-writing séances
—— The Defence of the Theosophists. Proc. S.P.R. IX., 1893, 129-159.
—— and DAVEY, S. J. The Possibilities of Mal-observation and Lapse of Memory from a Practical Point of View. Proc. S.P.R. IV., 1887, 381-405.
    Very valuable from a psychological point of view.
HOFFMANN, Prof. [Angelo Lewis]. How and What to Observe in Relation to Slate-writing Phenomena. Jour. S.P.R. 1886, II., 362-75.
HOLMES, D. A Mind-reading Act. 8vo., pp. 20. *Kansas City*, 1913.
HOME, D. D. Lights and Shadows of Spiritualism. 8vo., pp. 483. *London*, 1877.
—— 2nd ed.; 8vo., pp. XI., 412. *London*, 1878.
    A portion of the book deals with fraudulent mediumship.
HOME, J. Spirit Rapping Exposed. 8vo., pp. 32. *London*, 1860.
    Later eds. were published.
" HOME " THRUSTS; or, Raps at the Rappers. By an Undeveloped Poet. *London*, 1861; 8vo., pp. 64.
HOPPE, J. I. Erklärung der Sinnes-tauschungen (Hallucinationen und Illusionen aller fünf Sinne) bei Gesunden und bei Kranken. 4e Aufl., pp. VIII., 306. *Wurzburg*, 1888.
HOUDINI, Harry. Magical Rope Ties and Escapes. *London*, 1921; 8vo., pp. 96.
    Explanations of many mediumistic ties and releases.
—— Miracle Mongers and Their Methods; a complete exposé of the modus operandi of fire-eaters, heat-resisters, poison-eaters, venomous reptile-defiers, sword-swallowers, human ostriches, etc. *New York*, 1921; 8vo., 420 pp.
—— Spirit Manifestations. An article on fake mediums in the Christmas number of *Variety*, New York, 1920.
HOVEY, W. A. Mind-reading and Beyond. 8vo., pp. 201. *Boston and New York*, 1885.
HUBBELL, G. C. Fact and Fancy in Spiritualism, Theosophy and Psychical Research. *Cincinnati*, 1901.
HULL, Burling. Real Secrets of Stage Second Sight. 8vo., pp. 19. *New York*, 1916.
—— Sealed Message Reading. *New York*, 1911.

HULL, Burling. Sealed Mysteries. 4to., pp. 28. *New York*, 1910.
Excellent exposures of little-known methods.
—— Thirty-three Rope Ties and Chain Releases. 8vo., pp. 118. *New York*.
—— Twelve Sealed Message Reading Methods. *New York*, 1920 ; 4to., pp. 19.
HUNT, Fred. How to do Second Sight. pp. 60. *New York* [c. 1883].
HURST, F. How to do Second Sight. *New York*, c. 1912.
HURST, Lulu (the Georgia Wonder), Autobiography of. 8vo., pp. 267. *Rome, U.S.A.*, 1897.
An account of the feats of this performer. For one exposure. *cf* J. N. Maskelyne's *The Magnetic Lady*.
HYPNOTISM and HUMBUG. Article in the *New York Herald*, Oct. 21st, 1900.
Exposé of the methods of operators who impose on the credulous by imitating the phenomena of hypnotism and anæsthesia.
HYSLOP, J. H. See Hamilton, W. H.
INCOGNITO. Clairvoyance No Mystery, or the Fore-Sighted Lady Unveiled. pp. 26. *London*, 1876.
INDIAN FAKIR'S TRICKS, An. Article in the *New York Sun*, March 3rd, 1901.
Explained by a British officer.
INDIA-RUBBER SPOOKS ; Kings and Clowns on Tap for the Credulous. An article in *John Bull*, Vol. XXX., No. 789, July 16th, 1921.
Exposes contemporary mediums.
IOTA. £1,000 Reward, Maskelyne and Cooke. pp. 20. *London*, 1873.
Deals with the Davenport Brothers and their cabinet.
IRWIN, W. The medium game. Behind the Scenes with Spiritualism, 4 pts. *Collier's Weekly*, New York, 1907, XXXIX ; no. 25, 13-15 ; no. 26, 17-19 ; XL., no. 1, 15-17 ; no. 2, 14-15, 18.
INNES, A. Taylor. The Psychical Society's Ghosts. A challenge renewed. Article in the *Nineteenth Century*, London, Nov., 1891. No. 177 ; pp. 764-776.
JACOBY-HARMS. Eine Geister-Soiree Illustrirtes Prachtwerk. pp. 19. *Leipzig*, 1886.
A poem, illustrated with a number of original spirit photographs.
JACOLLIOT, L. Occult Science in India. pp. 274. *London*, 1884.
A translation from the French.
JANET, Dr. Pierre. Névroses et Idées fixes. 2 pts. *Paris*, 1898·
—— Etat mental des Hystériques ; les Stigmates mentaux. Preface de M. le Prof. Charcot. pp. 233. *Paris*, 1893.
—— Etat Mental des Hystériques ; les Accidents Mentaux. pp. 304. *Paris*, 1894. Eng. trans., 1901.
—— L'Automatisme Psychologique. pp. 496. *Paris*, 1889.
JASTROW, Joseph. Involuntary Movements. *Popular Science Monthly*, Vol. XL., pp. 743-750.

An interesting explanation of the movements in muscle-reading, planchette-writing, the Ouija-board, etc. See also his *Psychology of Deception*, the *Psychology of Spiritualism*, and *Facts and Fables in Psychology* ; pp. XVII., 375. London, 1901.

JEWETT, Pendie L. Spiritualism and Charlatanism ; or Tricks of the media. pp. 83. *New York*, 1873.

JONES, F. E. Mind Readng Secrets and Sealed Billet Reading. 8vo., pp. 31. *N.P.*, 1911.
An interesting little pamphlet containing practical instructions.

JUDGE, William O. Isis and the Mahatmas. 8vo., pp. 32. *London*, 1895.
A reply to *Isis Very Much Unveiled*.

KARLYN, [J. F. BURROWS]. Secrets of Stage Hypnotism, Stage Electricity and Bloodless Surgery. 8vo., pp. 77. *London*, 1912.
An exposure of stage " cures."

KATERFELTO. Spirit-rapping Made Easy ; or, How to Come Out as a Medium. Articles in the London *Once a Week*, 1860 ; Oct. 6th, pp. 403-407 ; Oct. 27th, pp. 489-494 ; Nov. 3rd, pp. 512-519.

KELLAR and TELEPATHY ; Muscle-reading, etc. Article in *Suggestion*, Chicago, Jan. 10th, 1905.

KELLAR, H. Magic Among the Red Men. *North American Review*, CLVIII., 591-600.

—— High Caste Indian Magic. *North American Review*, CLVI., 75-86.

—— A Magician's Tour. 8vo., pp. 214. *Chicago*, 1886.

KEMNITZ, M. von. Moderne Medium forschung. pp. 96. *München*, 1914.
An attempt at exposing the " teleplastic " mediums, " Eva C " and Stanislawa P.

" KHALDAH." Mind Wonders that Make You Gasp ; exposé of magical secrets. Article in the New York *Sunday World*, Oct. 28th, 1906.

KING, G. Experiments with Dr. Slade. Priv. printed. *London*, 1876.

KIRBYE, George W. The Wonderful and Incomprehensible Acoustic Telegraph ; or the Second Sight Mystery Unmasked. Also containing an exposure of many frauds practised by magicians, clairvoyants, etc. ; pp. 36. *Lowell*, 1859.

KLEINPAUL, Rudolf. Modernes Hexenwesen. Spiritistische und anti-spiritistische Plaudereien. *Leipzig*, 1900 ; pp. 238, 8vo.

KOCH, C. Table Moving and Table Talking. pp. 15. *Bath*, c. 1853.

KREBS, Stanley L. The Frauds of Spiritualism. Articles in *Suggestion* Magazine, Chicago, Vol. 7, Nos. 1, 2, 3 ; Vol. 8, No. 1. Many mediums exposed.

KREBS, S. L. Tricks and Methods of Eusapia Palladino. pp. 47. *Philadelphia*, 1910.

LANG, A. Cock Lane and Common Sense. 8vo., pp. XVI., 357. *London*, 1894.

LANG, Andrew. Historical Mysteries, in the *Cornhill Magazine*, April, 1904. Account of the lawsuit of D. D. Home and Mrs. Lyons.

LANCELIN, Charles. La Fraude dans le production des phénomènes médiumniques. pp. 129. *Paris*, 1912.

LANKESTER, Sir Ray. Criticism of Sir Oliver Lodge's Theories on Spiritualism, in *Bedrock*, January, 1913.

LANSLOTS, Ildephonsus. Spiritism Unveiled ; a critical Examination of Some Abnormal Psychic Phenomena. *London, Edinburgh and St. Louis*, 1913 ; 8vo., pp. XII., 216.
    Account of exposure of Harry Bastian, the medium, etc.

LAURENCE, John. Everyday Swindles and How to Avoid Them. *London*, 1921 ; 8vo., pp. 125.

LAWRENCE, Edward. Spiritualism Among Civilised and Savage Races. *London*, 1921 ; 8vo., pp. 112.
    The author attempts to show that no essential difference exists between the conceptions of the most degraded races and those advocated by leading Spiritualists.

LAY, Wilfred. Man's Unconscious Spirit. The Psychoanalysis of Spiritism. *London*, 1921 ; 8vo., pp. 335.
    A Psycho-analytical inquiry into Spiritism, raising the question whether we are entitled to say that certain phenomena have actually happened, when we really, as yet, know so little about the part played in all these phenomena by the unconscious wishes of the medium and the observers.

LEBLANC DE PREBOIS, F. Budget du Spiritisme, ou exploitation de la crédulité humaine. *Paris*, 1863.

LEHMANN, A. Aberglaube und Zauberei von den ältesten Zeiten an bis in die Gegenwart. pp. XII., 665. *Stuttgart*, 1908.
    Criticizes Crooke's experiments.

LENTON, ——. Art and Mystery of Second Sight. pp. 24.; *n.p., n.d.*

LEVITATION (the " Aga " Illusion). Articles in the *New York Telegraph*, July 19th, 1903, and in the *New York World*, July 24th, 1903.

LEWES, G. H. Exposure of Mrs. Hayden, the Medium, in *The Leader*, March 12th, 1853.

LEWIS, Carvill. Accounts of some so-called " spiritualistic " séances. Proc. S.P.R., 1887, pt. XI., 338-381.
    An account of a séance with Eglinton where every move was detected.

LIFE. Special Psychic No., Vol. 75, no. 1956. *New York*, April 29, 1920.
    A skit upon contemporary psychic activities.

LOISETTE, Prof. A. [M. D. Larrowe]. Physiological Memory or the Instantaneous Art of Never Forgetting. pp. 200. *New York*, c. 1911 ? See Fellows, G.S.

LILLIE, Arthur. Madame Blavatsky and Her " Theosophy " ; a Study. *London*, 1895 ; 8vo., pp. 228.
    Exposure of the Theosophical movement.

LUSTIG, David J. La Vellma's Vaudeville Budget for Mind-Readers, etc. With supplement : Twenty Minutes with the Spirits. *Somerville, Mass.*, 1921. pp. 96.

LUSTIG, D. J., and SHERMAN, K. Vaudeville Hypnotism. *Somerville, Mass.*, 1920.

—— Magic and Mind Reading Tricks. pp. 42. *Somerville, Mass.*, 1920.

LUSTIG, D. J., and SHERMAN. K. Vaudeville Mind Reading and Kindred Phenomena. pp. 63. *Somerville, Mass.*, 1920.
LYNN, J. W. The Famous Box Trick which obtained Five Hundred Pounds Reward from Mr. Maskelyne, now explained for the first time by the inventor. Article in the *Strand Magazine*, London, March, 1907.
—— Secret of the Great Packing Case Trick. Article in the *Strand Magazine*, April, 1907.
M. S. [Simon Miaille]. Exposé . . . des cures opérées en France par le magnétisme animal. *Paris*, 1826.
MCCABE, Joseph. Is Spiritualism Based on Fraud ? 8vo., pp. 160. *London*, 1920.
Anti-Spiritualistic. Some methods of mediumistic tricks are given.
—— Spiritualism ; a Popular History from 1847. 8vo., pp. 243. *London,* 1920.
Anti-Spiritualistic. The author covers familiar ground.
MCIVOR-TYNDALL, Dr. J. Alexander. How to Thought-Read. *Denver, Colorado*, 1909 ; 8vo., pp. 48.
MACAIRE, Sid. Mind Reading or Muscle Reading ? 8vo., pp. 80. *Dublin*, 1889.
MACK'S (Wm.) Strange Power Baffles Strong Men. Article in the Des Moines, Iowa, *Daily News*, Feb. 14th, 1901.
Tricks of the Lulu Hurst type.
MACKAY, Charles. Memoirs of Extraordinary Popular Delusions and the Madness of Crowds. 8vo., 3 vols. *London*, 1841. Later editions were published.
Long accounts of the Magnetisers, Fortune-tellers, etc., etc.
MACWALTER, G. J. Modern Mystery, or Table Tapping. 8vo., pp. 175. *London*, 1854.
An historical survey of spirit rapping.
MAGIC, PRETENDED MIRACLES, and remarkable natural phenomena. pp. 192. *London* [1848].
MAGIC and Mind-reading. Article in the *Boston Herald*, Feb. 21st, 1904.
MAHAN, A. Modern Mysteries Explained and Exposed. pp. XV., 466. *Boston*, 1855.
—— The phenomena of Spiritualism Scientifically Explained and Exposed. pp. XIV., 421. *London*, 1875.
MAHATMA (The). A Tale of Modern Theosophy. 8vo., pp. 284. *London*, 1895.
MANETHO, G. Aus Uebersinnlicher Sphäre. Die Wunder der modernen Magie in den Phänomenen des Gedankenlesens, des Hypnotismus, Mesmerismus, der Telepatie und der sogenannten mediumistischen Erscheinungen. *Wien and Leipzig*, 1904 ; 8vo., pp. 184.
MANN, W. Follies and Frauds of Spiritualism. pp. VIII., 191. *London*, 1919.
MANSFIELD, —. Spiritualistic Phenomena. 8vo. *New York*, [c. 1900].
Slate tricks and materialisations are dealt with. The author, according Dr. Carrington, was a medium.

MANVILLE, C. An Exposé of Spiritualistic Phenomena and Mind Reading Tricks. 8vo., pp. 47. *Minneapolis*, 1893.

MARION, F. L'Optique. *Paris*, 1867.

An Eng. trans. was published in 1868 entitled *The Wonders of Optics*.

MARRIOTT, William. On the Edge of the Unknown. A series of articles on the frauds of the mediums, in *Pearson's Magazine*, London, June, etc., 1910.

—— The Realities of the Séance. Article in *Pearson's Magazine*, London, March, 1910.

MASKELYNE, J. N. Explanation of the Annie Eva Fay " Cotton Bandage Test," in the *Pall Mall Gazette*, April 18th, 1885.

—— Modern Spiritualism. 12mo., pp. 182. *London* [1876].

—— Sharps and Flats. 8vo., pp. 335. *London*, 1894.

—— The Art and Craft of Thought Reading ; Secrets of Trick Telepathy. Article in the *Pall Mall Magazine*, London, March, 1907.

—— In the *English Illustrated Magazine*, January, 1895 ; pp. 78, etc.

Account of the revival of the Davenport Brothers' " act," Eglinton's tricks, etc.

—— The Fraud of Modern Theosophy Exposed. 8vo., pp. 95. *London*, 1912.

A second edition was published. Contains Mr. Maskelyne's explanation of the Indian rope trick.

—— The History of a Thousand Pound Challenge. *London*, 1906.

The history of the Maskelyne-Colley controversy.

—— The Magnetic Lady, or a human magnet. 8vo., pp. 16.

Published as an appendix to *The Supernatural* ?

MASSE, Pierre. De l'imposture et tromperie des diables, devins, enchanteurs, sorciers, noveurs désguillettes, cheuilleurs, necromanciens, chiromanciens, et autres qui par telle inuocation diabolique, ars magiques et superstitions abusent le peuple. *Paris*, 1579 ; 8vo., ll. 280.

Cf. R. Scot's *Discoverie of Witchcraft*, London, 1584.

MATHIAS P. The Case of Johanna Southcott, as far as it came under his Professional Observation. *London* (1815) ; 8vo. pp. 22.

Exposure of this religious charlatan.

MATTISON, H. Spirit Rapping Unveiled. 8vo., pp. 192. *New York*, 1853.

MAULE, B. Second Sight Explained. pp. 12 ; *n.p.*, *n.d.*

MAXWELL, J. Metapsychical phenomena. pp. XXIV., 448. *London*, 1905.

Discusses fraudulent methods.

MAYO, Herbert. Religious Delusions ; the Possessed, etc. In *Blackwood's Magazine*, vol. 61 ; pp. 673-681. *Edinburgh*, 1847 ; 8vo.

MELTON, J. Astrologaster, or the Figure-caster. Rather the arraignment of artlesse astrologers, and fortune tellers, that cheat many ignorant people. 4to., pp. 80. *London*, 1620.

MENCKEN, J. B. De Charlataneria Eruditorum Declarationes Duæ. *Lipsiæ*, 1715; 8vo., pp. 154. Another ed. in French: De la Charlatanerie des Savans; par Monsieur Menken. *A la Haye*, 1721, 8vo., pp. 242. Both editions have engraved frontispieces showing mountebanks going through their performances.

MERCIER, C. A. Spiritualism and Sir Oliver Lodge. pp. XI., 132. *London*, 1917.
An attempted exposure of trance-mediumship.

—— Spirit Experiences. pp. 54. *London*, 1919.
An amusing skit.

MEYER, J. E. Protection: the Sealed Book. 8vo., pp. 123 (privately printed). *Milwaukee, Wis.*, 1911.
Swindlers' and gamblers' devices are treated, including many devices of use to mediums.

MIDDLETON, A. E. All about Mnemonics; with a special chapter on Memory Feats for Entertainers. *London*, 1887; 8vo., pp. 100.

MILES, Pliny. American Phreno-Mnemotechny. *New York*, 1846; 12mo., pp. 268.
Chapters on lightning memory feats.
How to become a lightning memoriser.

MIND-READING. A Complete Course in the Art of. *Chicago*, 1900; 8vo., pp. 40. In two parts: tricks and telepathy.

MINNOCK, Thomas J. A Fakir's Exposé of a Fakir's Fakes. Three articles in the *St. Louis Sunday Star*, Aug. 28th, Sept. 4th, Sept. 11th, 1904.

—— Confessions of a Hypnotic Subject. *New York*. Articles in *Varieties*, Sept. and Oct., 1896.

MORROW, A. Thought Reading Exposed. pp. 32 (Daisy Bank Series). *Manchester*, 1914.

MORSELLI, E. Psicologia e spiritismo. 2 vols. *Torino*, 1908.

MORTON, W. Maskelyne and Cooke, Illusionists and Anti-Spiritualists; programme and key to the entertainment. *London*, c. 1873. Pamph. 8vo., pp. 30.

MOSELEY, S. A. An Amazing Séance and An Exposure. pp. 166. *London*, 1919.
A description of the "Medium in a Mask."

MUENSTERBERG, Prof. Hugo. Problems of To-day. *London and Leipsic*, 1910. 8vo., pp. 220.
Criticism of Eusapia Palladino, the medium, etc.

MULLER, E. Das spiritistische Medium Anna Rothe: ein echtes Medium und wissenschaftl. nicht entklärt. 8vo., pp. 16. *Ebd.*, 1902.

MUSICAL Medium, The. Article in the *Royal Magazine*, London, Sept., 1904.

My Friends, the Spiritualists; Eusapia Palladino Exposed. Article in the *Metropolitan Magazine*, New York, Feb., 1910.

MYERS, F. W. H. Resolute Credulity. Proc. S.P.R. XI., 213-34.
A valuable paper.

MYSTERIES of the Séance, and Tricks and Traps of Bogus Mediums. By a life-long Spiritualist. *Boston, Mass*, 1903; 8vo., pp. 64.

MYTHICAL Miracles of Notting Hill; cold light on the so-called "cures" at the Horbury Chapel, Notting Hill (the West London Lourdes). Article in the (London) *Evening News*, Nov. 16th, 1921.

NEWLIN, J. J. Some Secrets of Electrical Stagecraft; "Shadows" from the Underworld. In *Popular Electricity*, part 3 of the series; pp. 14-18; New York (c. 1912).

NICHOLS, T. L. A biography of the Brothers Davenport. 8vo., pp. 368. *London*, 1864.

A French translation by Mme. Bernard was published in 1865.

NIXON, W. J. Spirit Paintings. 8vo., pp. 14; *n.p.* 1916.

NORMAN, Samuel. Authentic Anecdotes of George Lukins, the Yatton Demoniac; with a View of the Controversy, and a full Refutation of the Imposture. *Bristol*, 1788; 8vo., pp. 45.

NOTABLE Charlatans Exposed in the Past: a Weird History that Leaves Spiritualism Undaunted. Article in the *Sunday Union*, Springfield, Mass., Nov. 1st, 1909.

OCHOROWICZ, J. La question de la fraude dans les expériences avec Eusapia Palladino, *Ann. d. sc. psych.*, 1896, VI., 79-123.

O'DONNELL, E. Spiritualism Explained. 8vo., pp. 119. *London*, 1920.

Some explanations of tricks are included.

OLLIER, Charles. Fallacy of Ghosts, Dreams and Omens. *London* 1848; 8vo., pp. 251. Reprinted from the *Ainsworth Magazine*.

ORACLE, (The) of the Arts; or Entertaining Expounder of the Wonders of Science. 12mo., pp. 212. *London*, 1824.

Contains an account of Sementini's experiments into the methods of fire-eaters and fire-walkers.

PAGE, C. G. Psychomancy; Spirit Rappings and Table-tippings Exposed. 12mo. *New York*, 1853.

PARISH, E. Hallucinations and Illusions A Study of the Fallacies of Perception. 8vo., pp. 390. *London*, 1897.

PATRICK, C. Vincent, and W. Whately SMITH. Spirit Photographs. In the *Psychic Research Quarterly*, Vol. I, No. 4; pp. 313-355. *London*, April, 1921.

An exposure of fraudulent methods.

PEARSON'S WEEKLY, January 31st, 1920. Exposure of faked "spirit" photographs, by means of trick apparatus.

PEEBLES, J. M. The contemptible, damaging and ghostly frauds perpetrated under the name of Spiritualism. pp. 40. *Los Angeles* (18— ?).

PENLAKE, R. [P. Salmon]. Trick photography. 8vo., pp. 40. *London*, 1906.

Full directions for the sulphate of quinine invisible photos are given.

PEPPER, Prof. The True History of the Ghost and all about Metempsychosis. 8vo., pp. 46. *London*, 1840.

An account of the optical illusion invented by Dircks.

PEROVSKY-PETROVO-SOLOVOVO, Count. The Hallucination Theory as applied to Certain Cases of Physical Phenomena. Proc. S.P.R., 1909, XXI., 436-482.

PETERSON, A. Spirit Slates (Wellington series of original magical effects). *Glasgow*, 1920.

PILLEY, Charles. Amazing Spirit Camera Frauds. Article in the London *John Bull*, Dec. 17th, 1921, p. 4. Alleged exposure of a "photographic medium."

BIBLIOGRAPHY

PHILADELPHUS, T. Phantasmagorie, oder die Kunst Geister erscheinen zu lassen. *Quedlinburg*, 1833.
PHILPS, A. See Carlton, *pseud.*
PHYSICIAN. Practical Instructions in Table Moving, with Physical Demonstrations. By a physician. 16mo. *London*, 1853.
PINKERTON, A. The Spiritualists and Detectives. pp. 354. *New York* [1877].
PODMORE, F. Modern Spiritualism. 2 vols. *London*, 1902.
    The second volume contains many attempts at explanations.
—— The Newer Spiritualism. 8vo., pp. 320. *London*, 1910.
PORTA, Joan. Baptista. De Furtivis Literarum notis vulgo, de Ziferis Libri IIII. *Neapoli*, 1563; 4to.
    An extremely rare work on secret writings, silent codes, signals, and signs.
PREL, C. du. Ein Problem für Taschenspieler. 8vo., pp. 28. *Breslau*, 1885.
PRICE, Harry. Half-hours with the Mediums; How to Give a Spiritualistic Entertainment (in preparation).
—— Mediums and Magic. *Magazine of Magic*, 1920, VIII., pp. 7 seq.
    Deals with the indebtedness of spirit mediums to magicians and *vice versa*.
—— Psychic Photography; the Hypothesis of Fraud (*in preparation*).
PRINCE, Dr. Walter. In the *Proceedings* of the American Society for Psychical Research, vol. XIII., Part II., March, 1920.
    Complete exposure of the Keeler-Lee-Bocock " spirit " photographs.
QUEUX, William Le. Rasputin, the Rascal Monk. *London, n.d.* (1917); 8vo., pp. 176.
    Complete life and exposure of this notorious Russian medium and mystic.
QUINN, J. P. Fools of Fortune. pp. 640. *Chicago*, 1892.
    An exposure of gamblers' devices.
RADCLIFFE, J. N. Fiends, Ghosts and Sprites. 8vo., pp. 276. *London*, 1854.
    Raps, illusions of hearing and similar subjects are dealt with.
RAMBACHER, A. Das grelle Licht der " Antispiritistin " Dr. med. M. von. Kemnitz. sm. 8vo., pp. 19. *München*, 1915.
RAPPERS (The), or the Mysteries of Spirit Rapping. pp. 288. *New York*, 1854.
RAYNALY, E. La vérité sur la mnémotechnie. pp. 72. *Paris*, 1897.
—— Les Propos D'un Escamoteur : étude Critique et Humoristique. Histoires, Souvenirs, Réflexions, Observations et Confidences sur les Prestidigitateurs, Physiciens, Escamoteurs, Magiciens, Illusionnistes, Thaumaturges, Charlatans, Banquistes, Spirites, Jongleurs, Trucqueurs, Hypnotiseurs et Magnétiseurs. *Paris*, 1894; 8vo., pp. 242.
REDDALLS, G. H. Modern Spiritualism: An Examination and Exposure, by G. H. Reddalls (an " infidel medium "). pp. 38. *Birmingham*, 1875.

REECE, Richard M.D. A Correct Statement of the Circumstances that attended the Last Illness and Death of Mrs. Southcott, with an Account of the Appearances Exhibited on Dissection ; and the Artifices that were Employed to Deceive her Medical Attendants. *London*, 1815 ; 8vo., pp. 107.
Complete exposure of this religious visionary and impostor.

REIMERS, C. The Trapped Medium, or Two Clever Sceptics. pp. 30. *London*, 1877.
An amusing pamphlet, describing the attempts of Prof. Molecule, F.R.S., X.Y.Z., B.I.G.A.S.S., and Dr. Protoplaster to control a physical medium.

REMY, M. Spirites et illusionnistes. pp. 257. *Paris*, 1911.

REPORT on a Series of Sittings with Eva C. In the *Proc*. S.P.R., Jan., 1922, Vol. XXXII. pp. 209-343.
The hypothesis of fraud is discussed.

RICHMOND, A. B. What I Saw at Cassadaga Lake. A review of the Seybert Commissioners' *Report*. 2nd ed. ; pp. 244. *Boston*, 1888.

ROBERTSON, — Handbook of Second Sight, Clairvoyance and Thought Reading, pp. 44. *Birmingham*, 1883.

ROBERTSON, E. G. Mémoires physiques et phantasmagorie. 2 vols. *Paris*, 1840.
Optical effects are described.

ROBERTSON, J. M. A Spiritualistic Farce, in *The National Reformer*, Sept. 20th, 1891.
A criticism of Crookes' experiments with D. D. Home.

ROBIN, D. L'Almanach illustré de Cagliostro, 1865, 2nde année. Histoire des spectres vivants et impalpables. *Paris*, 1864.
Cf. the works of Dircks and Pepper.

ROBINSON, W. E. [Chung Ling Soo]. Spirit Slate Writing and Kindred Phenomena. 8vo., pp. 148. *New York*, 1899.
Much of the information is now obsolete.

ROCHAS, Albert de. La Science des Philosophes et L'Art des Thaumaturges Dans L'Antiquité. *Paris*, 1882, ; pp. 218, 8vo.
Descriptions and explanations of old-time " miracles."

—— Trials by Fire and Fire Jugglers. *Popular Science Monthly*, XXI., 645-650.

ROCHFORT, William Henry. A Treatise upon Arcanography ; or, a New Method of Secret Writing Defying Discovery or Detection. *London*, 1836 ; pp. 19, 4to.

ROMBERCH, Joan. Congestorium Artificiose Memorie. *Venice, M.Sessa*, 1533 ; 104 ff , 8vo.
A rare mnemotechnical treatise, illustrated with a large number of woodcuts of various objects, including bells, household utensils, animals, diagrams, etc., designed to induce an abnormal memory.

ROSS, Alex. M.A., LL.D. Second Sight : A Spiritual Toilet Tale. *London, n.d.* (*c*. 1850) ; 8vo., pp. 29.
Amusing skit upon contemporary mediums and séances ; really an advertisement for toilet preparations.

ROUBAUD, F. La danse des tables, phénomènes physiologiques demontrés. 2nde ed. ; 16mo. *Paris*, 1855.

S., E. C. Thought Reading Investigated. 8vo., pp. 8. *Manchester*, 1883.

BIBLIOGRAPHY

SAINT-GERMAIN, Comte. C. de. [E. de Valcourt-Vermont]. Palmistry for Professional Purposes, with 1,252 illustrations. 4to. *Chicago*, 1897.

SAPTE, W. An Indignation Meeting of the Spirits. (*Printed for Private Circulation*). 8vo., pp. 85. *London*, 1883.
  A facetious story dedicated to the Society for Psychical Research.

SCEPTIC (*pseud.*) An Exposition of Spiritualism. pp. XII., 314. *London*, 1862.
  Deals with Home and the mediums of his period.

SCEPTICISM and Spiritualism. By the Authoress of Aurelia. pp. 190. *London*, 1865.

SCHNAUSS, H. Photographic Pastimes. pp. 204. *London*, 1892.

SCHRECK, Prof. The Mystery Book. *New York*, 1920.
  Contains a few spiritualistic tricks.

SCHRENCK-NOTZING, F. A. P. W., von, *Baron*. Der Kampf um die Materialisations—phänomene. pp. VIII., 147. *München*, 1914.
  Discusses the hypothesis of fraud in the case of the medium, "Eva C."

SCIENCE of Marking Playing-cards. Confessions of a Card Shark. Article in *Kansas City Journal*, May 31st, 1903.

SATTHIANADHAN, S., M.A. Theosophy: An Appeal to my Countrymen. *Madras*, 1893; 8vo., pp. 18.
  Exposure of Madame Blavatsky, etc., written to counteract the effect of Mrs. Besant's visit to India.

SCOT, Reginald. The Discoverie of Witchcraft. sm. 4to., pp. 576. *London*, 1584.
  Deals with every variety of charlatanism, including many magical effects. James I. ordered the book to be burned by the common hangman. A reprint was issued in 1886.

SECOND-SIGHT Tricks: Greatly simplified by the grouping of the so-called cue questions. Article in the *New York Sun*, Feb. 18th, 1901. Copied from the *Times Democrat*, New Orleans.

SECRET (Le) des frères Davenport dévoilé. pp. 15. *Bruxelles*, 1866.

SEXTON, G. Spirit Mediums and Conjurers. *London*, 1873.
  By a firm believer in the reality of psychic phenomena and the inability of magicians to reproduce them.

SEYBERT Commission on Spiritualism. (Report of), pp. 160. *Philadelphia*, 1887; new ed. *London*, 1920.
  Valuable material on the Slade-Zöllner investigation. See Richmond, A.B. and *cf.* F. J. Lippitt's *Physical Proofs of Another Life*. pp. 65. *Washington*, 1888.

SHAW, Bradley. Mediums and Their Dupes. A complete exposure of the chicaneries of professional mediums. pp. 54. *San Francisco*, 1887.

SHAW, W. H. J. Magic and Its Mysteries. pp. 60. *Chicago*, 1893.
  Contains methods for materialization.

—— New Ideas in Magic, Illusions, Spiritualistic Effects. pp. 93. *Blue Island, Illinois* [18—].

SIDGWICK, Mrs. H. On Spirit Photographs. Proc. S.P.R., VII., 1891, 268-89.

Exposé of Mumler, Hudson, Parkes and Buguet. See Miss Houghton's *Chronicles of the Photographs of Spiritual Beings* for specimens of Hudson's work.

SIDGWICK, Mrs. H. Results of a Personal Investigation into the Physical Phenomena of Spiritualism. *Proc.* S.P.R. IV., 1886, 47-74.
Tests with the Misses Wood and Fairlamb (Mrs. Mellon) are described. *cf.* T. S. Henry's *Spookland*.

SKINNER, W. E. Wizard's Manual. *New York, c.* 1912.

SMYTH, J. S. *See* Hamilton, W. H.

SOLOVYOFF, V. S. A Modern Priestess of Isis. pp. 366. *London,* 1895.
An exposure of Mme. Blavatsky.

SOME Account of the Vampires of Onset. *Boston,* 1892.

SPICER, H. Sights and Sounds : A History of American Spirit Manifestations. *London,* 1853.

SPIRIT HEALING FRAUD. THE. An Exposure of " Dr. Beale." Article in London *Truth,* Jan. 18th, 1922. pp. 87-8.

SPIRITUAL Manifestations. 8vo., pp. 15. *London,* 1853.
From *Blackwood's Magazine.* An amusing skit.

STAGE Feats of Strength ; novel tricks of muscular legerdemain. Article in *Sunday Herald,* Boston, Mass, May 1st, 1904. Exposes Annie Abbott's act.

STANYON, E. Silent Thought Transmission. pp. 30. *London,* 1904.

STEELCRAFT, F. Some Peculiar Entertainments. *London,* Articles in the *Strand Magazine,* March and April, 1896.
Accounts of charlatans, fire-resisters, stone-eaters, etc.

STONE, S. How to be Quick at Figures. *London, c.* 1890.

STORY of Indian Magic. Article in the (New York) *Current Literature,* Nov., 1899 ; Vol. 26th, pp. 439.

SUHR, H. E. C. Wunder aus der vierten Dimension oder Jedermann Medium. pp. 164. *Stuttgart,* 1904.

SUTEKEN, Rotoff. I Segreti Della Magia Bianca. *Milano,* 1908. 8vo., pp. 223. Il Magnetismo, lo Spiritismo e l'Ipnotismo, offrono fenomeni molti interessanti da meravigliare e sorprendere persone e specialmente gli studiosi dello Spiritismo.

SUTHERLAND, H. How to Become a Mind-Reader. Article in the New York *Home Magazine,* Nov. 1900 ; pp. 448-457.

T., E. and N., F. Exposition of Washington Irving Bishop's Thought Reading. pp. [London, 1883 ?]

[TAYLOR, J. T.] The Veil Lifted. *London,* 1894.
On spirit photography in Glendinning's work.

THAYER, F. G. The Mysterious Séance. *Los Angeles, n.d.*
A spiritualistic act for magicians.

TELEPATHY, Mental, and How it is Done. Article in the (Baltimore) *Evening Herald,* Feb. 26th, 1906.

THE Falacie of the Great Water-drinker Discovered, fully representing what are the ingredients that provoke him to so wonderful a Vomit, etc. *London,* printed by B. Alsop for T. Dunster, 1650 ; 8vo., 4 leaves.
A rare tract, with large woodcut, relating to Manfré, the water-swallower.

THE TIMES, June 22nd, 1909. Report of *Daily Mail* investigation into the question of Spirit Photography.

   The Committee came to the conclusion that no evidence had been put before them showing that spirit photography was possible.

THISELTON-DYER, T. F. The Ghost World. 8vo. *Philadelphia*, 1893.

THOMAS, Frank W. Confessions of a Mind-reader. Articles in *Magic*, London, 1902, vol. 2, pp. 68, 76, 84, 96.

   Very complete information for a mind-reading act. Copied from the *Saturday Evening Post*, Philadelphia, Nov. 10th, 1900.

THURSTON, Howard. The Truth of Indian Mystery. *Cos Cob, Conn.*, 1911 ; 8vo., pp. 150.

   The secrets of the fakir illusions laid bare.

TODD, T. O. Hydesville : The Story of the Rochester Knockings. 8vo., pp. 62. *Sunderland,* 1905.

TUCKETT, Dr. Ivor. The Evidence for the Supernatural. *London,* 1911 ; 8vo., pp. 399.

   Account of the exposure of Monck, the medium, etc.

TRIPLETT, N. The Psychology of Conjuring Deception. *American Journal of Psychology,* 1900, XI., 439.

TRUCS, (Les) du médium Bénévol. pp. 8. *Paris, n.d.*

TRUESDELL, J. W. The Bottom Facts Concerning the Science of Spiritualism. pp. 331. *New York,* 1883. 2nd ed., 1892.

   Very valuable work. Twelve full-page illustrations were issued after the book was bound up.

TRUMBULL, M. M. Psychological Deceptions. *Open Court,* 1893, VII., 3639-3640.

TRUTH, London, July 13th, 1921. An Exposure of a Fashionable Medium ; again mentioned Sept. 28th, 1921.

TYNDALL, John, F.R.S. Fragments of Science. *London,* 1871.; 8vo., pp. 449. 2nd ed. the same year.

   Contains essay, *Science and Spirits,* an exposure of a spiritualistic séance.

VASSEUR-LOMBARD. Les Manifestations spirites dévoilées, ou les médiums et les spirites devant la raison humaine. *Paris,* 1860.

VERRALL, H. de G. The History of Marthe Béraud. Proc. S.P.R., 1914, XXVII., 333-370.

   Discusses the hypothesis of fraud in the case of " Eva C."

WALKER, J. Spiritualism Exposed. Full report of the Blackburn Séances of the Rev. Dr. Monck. 12mo. *Blackburn, n.d.*

WATKINS, John E. The Manufacture of Ghosts ; on Fake Mediums. Article in the *Kansas City Star,* Oct. 19th, 1902.

WEATHERLEY, L. and MASKELYNE, J. N. The Supernatural ? 8vo., pp. 273. *Bristol and London,* 1891.

   Chapters on Oriental Magic. An appendix was added later. See J. N. Maskelyne's *The Magnetic Lady.*

WARD, James, R.A. Some Account of Mary Thomas of Tanyralt in Merionethshire, and Ann Moore, the Fasting Woman of Tutbury. Accompanied with portraits and illustrative etchings. *London*, 1813, folio, XI. pp. Printed for the Author. *Cf.* Dr. Henderson's *Examination of the Imposture of Ann Moore*, London, 1813.

WEBSTER, John. The Displaying of Supposed Witchcraft. Wherein is affirmed that there are many sorts of Deceivers and Imposters, and divers persons under a passive delusion of Melancholy and Fancy. *London*, 1677; pp. 352, folio.

WELTON, T. Mental Magic : A Rationale of Thought Reading and its Attendant Phenomena. 4to., pp. 178. *London*, 1884.

WERNER, H. Moderne Medium—Forschung und gesunder Volksverstand ; 8vo., pp. 55. *Bamberg*, 1915.

WICKS, F. Thought Reading, Second Sight and Spiritual Manifestations Explained. 8vo., pp. 104. *London*, 1907.

An enlarged edition of Bishop's *Houdin and Heller's Second Sight Explained* (q.v.)

WIESENDANGER, R. Ist Frau Anna Rothe ein Medium ? : ein Mahnwort. 8vo., pp. 52. *Leipzig*, 1902.

WILKINS, Rt. Rev. John. Mercury ; or the Swift and Secret Messenger. Shewing how a man may with privacy and speed communicate his thoughts to a friend at any distance. *London*, 1641 ; pp. 172 ; 2nd ed., 1694.

Early treatise on the art of conveying secret information by means of signs, gestures, codes, etc.

WILSON, Daniel. Satanic Agency not Connected with Tableturning. A reply to two publications on the subject by the Rev. N. S. Godfrey. *London*, 1853 ; 8vo., pp. 16.

WILLIAMS, Sidney. Spooks ; How Ghosts are Manufactured by the Camera. Illustrated with photographs by T. C. Hepworth, in *The Royal Magazine*, vol. 6, 1901 ; pp. 156-9.

WILLMANN, C. Enthüllungen über das Treiben der Spiritisten. 8vo., pp. 133. *Hamburg*, 1885.

—— Moderne Wunder. 8vo., pp. VIII., 240. *Leipzig*, 1886.

—— Modern Wonders. *Chicago*, 1892. Portraits of Slade, Bastian, etc.

WILLMANN, Carl. Die Zauberwelt. Monthly magazine, *Hamburg*, 1895—1904 ; 10 vols.

This magazine specialised in exposing the methods of fraudulent mediums, and very many spiritualistic tricks are explained and illustrated.

—— Taschenspieler contra Gelehrte ; eine Entgegnung auf die Brochüre "Ein Problem für Taschenspieler" pp. 64. *Rostock*, i. M., 1886.

An answer to Carl Du Prel.

WOODCROFT, Bennet. The Pneumatics of Hero of Alexandria ; translated from the original Greek. *London*, 1851 ; 4to., pp. 117. Explanations of automata used in Greek temples, etc., to produce "miracles."

WOODBURY, W. E. Photographic Amusements. *New York*, 1896.

Trick photography is dealt with.

BIBLIOGRAPHY

X., M. Humbug in photography. *Annals Psychical Science*, Lond., 1909, VIII., 459-466. With four plates.

YOUNG, Filson. Hymns and Humbug at a Séance. Sir A. Conan Doyle takes me to hear Spirit Voices, and I discover Self-deception and Humbug. Article in *The Saturday Review*, London, Jan. 21st, 1922. pp. 54-7. Conan Doyle's Answer, and Final Remarks, Jan. 28th.

ZERFFI, G. G. Spiritualism and Animal Magnetism. *London*, 1871.
    Anti-Spiritualistic.

ZOLLNER, J. C. F. Transcendental Physics. Tr. by C. C. Massey pp. 266. *London*, 1882.
    An account of the Slade sittings. *Cf.* the Seybert Commissioners *Report*.

—— Zur Aufklärung des deutschen Volkes über Inhalt und Aufgabe der wissenschaftlichen Abhandlungen. pp. 204. *Leipzig*, 1880.
    Concerning Slade and Hansen.

GLOSSARY

OF WORDS AND PHRASES USED IN THE TEXT.

ASTRAL MAGNETISM. The name of a hypothetical "force," supposed to be derived from the stars. Much used by charlatans.

AURA. An alleged emanation of "force"; a supposed psychic influence said to emanate from persons in the trance or semi-trance state.

BABY ACT, To play the. To behave like a child.

BACKSLIDER SPIRITUALIST. A believer who, having investigated the claims and phenomena of Spiritualism, is disgusted and renounces his faith.

BEST LICKS. Finest efforts.

BROTHERHOOD, The. The fraternity of mediums who help each other with information and data concerning the dupes that attend their séances.

BUCK-EYE STATE. Ohio, where the buck-eye (horse chestnut) flourishes in great profusion.

BUCKET-SHOP. An office where people may gamble in fractional lots of stocks, etc., which are bought or sold on the official Exchanges.

BUG IN HIS EAR, To put a. To warn him.

BUNDYITE SPIRITUALIST. One who believes that all mediums are frauds and all phenomena fraudulent until they have demonstrated it differently to their own satisfaction. From Jno. C. Bundy, late editor of the *Religio-Philosophical Journal*.

CABINET. A permanent or temporary structure or recess, capable of being enclosed on all sides, in which a medium produces his various phenomena.

CABINET SEANCE. A séance in which all or most of the "phenomena" are produced by means of a cabinet, *q.v.*

CIRCLE. An association of persons banded together to witness, investigate or develop occult phenomena in a "medium," *q.v.*

CLAIRAUDIENCE. Ability to perceive sounds not within reach of the ear under normal conditions; alleged especially of persons in the trance or hypnotic state.

CLAIRVOYANCE. Ability to see or discern objects not within reach of the eye under normal conditions; alleged especially of persons in the trance or hypnotic state; second-sight; seer-ship.

CONTROL. See Guide.

COUGH MEDICINE, Mediums' slang term for phosphorised oil. See spirit lights.

DARK SEANCE OR CIRCLE. A séance where all, or most of the "phenomena" take place in the dark.

DEVELOPING CIRCLE, or Séance. Formed for the purpose of developing the "powers" of a budding medium.

GLOSSARY

DOCTOR, TO. To "fake" with evil intent.

DRUMMER-BOY CONTROL. A very fashionable "control" a few years back, and taken, no doubt, from Glanvil's account of the phantom drummer that terrorised the family of Mr. Mompesson in the reign of Charles II.

DUMMIES. Mediums' technical term for extra pieces of paper or "billets" surreptitiously added to a genuine heap. By this means they are enabled to "read" the contents of the real notes.

FAKE. Fraudulent; phenomena produced by fraudulent means.

FEEL HIS OATS. Very pleased with himself.

FEELER. Something put forth indirectly to gain information difficult to obtain by direct means, as the sentiments or designs of others.

FISH STORY, A. A highly-improbable yarn.

FLOOR-WORKERS. Confederates employed by a medium to mingle with the sitters or audience. By their aid he exhibits some "marvellous" "tests," Sometimes called "boosters" or "horses."

FULL-FORM MEDIUM. A medium who specialises in materialising full-length "spirits."

FULL-FORMS. Mediums' technical term for full-length materialised "spirits."

GRAB. To suddenly seize a materialised "spirit." The bug-bear of all bogus mediums.

GRIP. Any kind of small bag or case, capable of being carried by hand.

GUIDE or CONTROL. A particular spirit that "controls" and attaches itself to a medium. Many mediums use the same guide, such as " John King," " Prairie Flower," etc.

HELPING OUT the " Spirits." A polite term for doing the phenomena yourself.

HORN MANIFESTATIONS, or Trumpet Séance. A séance by a medium who specialises in producing "spirit" voices by means of a trumpet or horn.

INDEPENDENT SLATE WRITING. Writing that appears magically upon slates; answers given to questions written upon papers enclosed between closed and sealed slates.

INSPIRATIONAL SPEAKER. A speaker, medium, or lecturer who thinks that his utterances are inspired and Heaven-sent.

KICK. To offer resistance.

KING. The name given to an ardent male Spiritualist who has become enamoured of a female " spook." See Queen.

LOADED. A conjurer's term for filling an article or piece of apparatus for the purpose of deceiving his audience.

MANAGER. The technical term of the mediums for an assistant or confederate, who "helps out" in various ways. See "*Floor-workers*" and "*Pass-in*."

MATERIALISE. To assume a material and bodily form; a "materialisation" is the production of spirits or entities in the form, likeness or appearance of human beings.

MATERIALISING MEDIUM. A medium who specialises in "materialising" spirit forms; generally an "artist" in his particular line. Bastian was a notorious example.

MEDIUM. A person professing to be possessed or controlled by the personality of some person who has died, so as to speak or act from the intelligence of that person ; also, one whose organisation supplies the " force " used by spirits in " materialisation."

MOP-BOARD. A board skirting the lower edge of the wall of a room. ; wash-board ; wainscot.

NAILED TO THE CROSS. A euphemistic term for " swindled " ; " sold " ; " taken in."

NIGGER IN THE FENCE. The " fly in the amber " ; the vulnerable point.

NOTE-BOOKS. The technical name of the lists of information, data, etc., concerning a medium's potential " clients " ; called also Blue-books.

OUT OF SIGHT. Splendid ; " A.1." ; unbeatable.

PARALYZED, To be. To be aghast with astonishment ; to be " staggered."

PASS-IN, To. To convey (by means of the " manager " or other confederate) to the materialising medium, various " properties " for the formation of his spirit " guides " or " controls."

PEACHING. The act of confessing, informing, or betraying an accomplice.

PERSONATING MEDIUM. A medium who specialises, or excels in impersonating the " spirits " of the relatives of his " clients."

PHASE. A particular aspect in the phenomena of Spiritualism.

PHYSICAL MEDIUM. A medium who excels in, or specialises in producing " physical " phenomena, *e.g.*, " slate-writing," " materialising," etc.

PICTURE-MEDIUM. A medium who specialises in the production of " spirit " pictures or paintings.

PLATFORM TESTS. Alleged phenomena that are exhibited from a platform or stage, as in a concert-hall.

PLUCK, Ready to. Time to relieve him of his money ; ready to swindle.

POINTERS, Getting the. Acquiring data from victim or by other means, enabling the medium to give a good " test " or " reading." Useful information or hints.

POP-BOTTLE DIAMOND. Cheapest form of paste.

PRIVATE SEANCE or CIRCLE. A gathering of friends who meet together to witness occult phenomena as opposed to " public " séance, where anyone can attend.

PRODUCE, Sucker will. The fool will pay up.

PROPERTIES. The impedimenta, such as robes, wigs, etc., used by bogus mediums.

PSYCHOMETRIC. From psychometry, an alleged occult power, said to be possessed by persons of divining, by means of physical contact, the properties or character of a thing or things with which it has been associated.

QUEEN. The name given by an enthusiastic, if foolish, male spiritualist to the materialised female " spirit " of his choice. He is then known as her King.

QUEERED. Upset ; spoilt.

RAIL-SPLITTER'S MAUL. A heavy wooden mallet, used with wedges.

GLOSSARY

RAPPINGS. Taps produced upon tables or elsewhere by alleged spirit agency.
RHINESTONES. Cheap paste, backed with vari-coloured tinsel.
ROAR, He will. The victim will be seriously angry and probably will make it very unpleasant for the people who have tricked him.
ROASTS. Severe criticisms; ridicule.
ROBE. The mediums' technical name for a costume or similar make-up used when materialising a " spirit."
RUSTLE, To. To hustle, to exert oneself.
SAILING THE SAME DESCRIPTION OF CRAFT. Doing the very same thing.
SAW WOOD AND SAY NOTHING, To. To mind one's own business; to get on with one's work.
SEANCE. A meeting of persons, interested in Spiritualism, for the purpose of witnessing or inducing psychic phenomena.
SEA-ROOM. Nautical term, denoting plenty of working-space in which to manœuvre.
SEERESS. A female medium.
SHINGLE WILL BE SWUNG TO THE BREEZE. He will hang out his sign-board. The flat slabs of wood used for roofing purposes are called " shingles."
SITTINGS or SEANCES. Public or private meetings or series of meetings for the purpose of studying, or for the production of, psychic phenomena.
SKEPTICS. Specifically, persons attending a séance with *a priori* convictions that the whole affair is a fraud.
SKIP FOR NEW PASTURES. To quickly leave the district for fresh ground.
SKIPPING OUT. Quickly leaving the district.
SLATE-WRITING MEDIUM. A medium who specialises in slate-writing effects. Slade and Eglinton were two notorious slate-writing mediums.
SLOPE. To suddenly disappear; to leave the district.
SNARE-DRUM. A small side-drum, beaten only on one end.
SNEAK. A surreptitious call or visit.
SPIRIT BAND. The collection of " spirits " supposed to be connected with, and at the command of, every individual.
SPIRIT COLLAR. A faked mechanical collar, of metal, used by the medium, and out of which he makes a " miraculous " escape.
SPIRIT-LIGHTS (usually the " outward and visible sign " of phosphorised oil or damp match-heads) are lights seen hovering around during a " dark séance."
SPIRIT PHOTOGRAPHER. A person who works for the mediums by producing photographs of alleged " spirit " forms from data supplied; a medium who specialises in this branch of fraudulent phenomena.
SPIRITS. The unseen operators who produce the phenomena at séances; usually the medium himself or his confederates.
SPIRITUAL ROSTRUM, On the. Touring the cities, etc., giving lectures and discourses on spiritual philosophy, etc.

SPIRITUALIST. One who believes that departed spirits communicate directly with men through the agency of mediums and by various signs; an adherent of the spiritual philosophy.

SPOOKS, Female or male. The mediums' technical term for confederates employed to impersonate the spirits of their "clients'" relatives.

STRANGE MAGNETISMS. Baleful influences that would effect the proper development of the "phenomena."

SUCKER. An enthusiastic novice or beginner; in plain English, a fool.

SUMATRA GEMS. Trade name for a very cheap quality of paste.

TABLE TIPPING. The phenomenon of a table rising or swaying without apparent human aid.

TEST and BUSINESS SITTINGS. Séances for soliciting and giving advice upon business matters, etc.; usually privately.

TEST CONDITIONS. Conditions under which it is apparently impossible for a medium to commit any sort of fraud or trick.

TEST MEDIUM. A medium who specialises in giving "tests" (proofs of psychic phenomena).

TESTS. Specifically, proofs.

TIRED. Bored, wearied.

TOP-HEAVY INVESTIGATORS. Scientific men, "overloaded" with degrees, who fail to detect the simplest tricks of the medium; "high-brows."

TOUCHED. Slang phrase for extorting money from a person.

TRANCE MEDIUM. A medium who specialises in giving supernormal information and divinations, etc., whilst in the hypnotic or "trance" state.

TUMBLES. He realises the fact that he is being swindled.

WAYFARING-MAN. Americanism for "man in the street."

WHITE MEN. Honest mediums.

WORK. To. To exploit—usually for the benefit of the exploiter.

Revelations of a Spirit Medium

or

Spiritualistic Mysteries Exposed

By A. Medium.

REVELATIONS

OF A

SPIRIT MEDIUM;

OR

Spiritualistic Mysteries Exposed.

A Detailed Explanation of the Methods Used

by Fraudulent Mediums.

BY

A. MEDIUM.

ST. PAUL, MINN.
FARRINGTON & Co., PUBLISHERS,
37 East Tenth St.
1891.

Entered according to Act of Congress in the year 1891, by
FARRINGTON & CO.,
In the office of the Librarian of Congress at Washington.
All Rights Reserved.

PREFACE.

The author of this book does not consider it a "literary gem," by any means, but claims that it accomplishes the object for which it was written, viz.: gives the reader an expose of the methods pursued by the "spiritual medium" in the various deceptions they practice in their "circles," "sittings," and "seances," which *does* expose. The author has been a working "medium" for the past twenty years, and is not *guessing* or *theorizing* in what he has written. He will experi nce great pleasure in demonstrating to the *scientific* and *reverend* would-be exposers of spiritual phenomena how infinitely wrong have been the theories advanced by them as an explanation of the wonderful manifestations occurring at the seances of the "medium." He will exult in proving to such persons and their followers and admirers, that however learned they may be, or are supposed to be, they have never yet offered an explanation that would hold water, no matter what their followers may have thought regarding it. It has been a case of the "blind leading the blind." Nothing but facts and actual experiences will be mentioned, and when an explanation of any of the phenomena is given, the reader, by a little experimenting, can easily demonstrate to himself that the writer is not *guessing*. There will also be a grim sort of satisfaction experienced by the author to see the wonder-working shops of various "mediums" throughout the country close their doors who were not content to attend strictly to their own particular "fakes," but spent much of their time and went out of their way to hinder the writer's business prosperity. There is a large number of "mediums" who are "white men," that the writer would be very much pleased to pass, leaving them to continue their tricks undisturbed; but by so doing this book would be of no more value as an expose than any of the abortive efforts of the egotistical preacher or the amusing mistakes of the scientist. The most wonderful of the "medium's" phenomena will be so thoroughly explained and so completely dissected that, after reading this book, you can perform the feats yourself. The work is anonymously written for reasons that the average reader will understand without an explanation being necessary. The author is going to engage in other business: possibly not so profitable, but altogether more pleasant and honorable, and will partially atone for his past career by exposing the methods employed by himself and others while playing the role of "medium." No phase of "mediumship" but will be treated to a general overhauling and ventilating. The reader may rest assured that after a perusal of this book he will search long and diligently for a "medium" he can not show to be a fraud. There has not, at any time in the past, been anything written on the same subject by any one who knew that what they wrote were facts, and when the *theories* offered were put to test they would not stand. It is said, "it takes a thief to catch a thief," and it is the writer's opinion that a "medium" of twenty years' experience in almost every phase, is a very well qualified individual to tell you all about the way it is done. The writer was never one of the jealous, back-biting species of the animal known as the "spiritual medium," and at no time derived any pleasure from gaining business by exposing the tricks of other "mediums." He did not give out the impression that he was the only genuine "medium" now on earth, nor intimate that other "mediums" were afraid to give a "seance" when he was present. But, when he did make up his mind to do any exposing, he determined that *everything* should be given, including his own work. If any "medium" has even a remote idea that the writer has gone out of the business through fear of them, they can dismiss it at once, as, in an experience of twenty years there is not a solitary expose to his credit. However, it is usually the female "medium" who is up to tricks of that kind, and they are generally very poor workers indeed, and have not the ability to do any work that will interest any but the most simple of minds and persons not capable of taking good care of themselves. The average professional female "medium" is a very detestable personage. The author intends to write such a book that no "medium" will feel safe until he or she has read it, and after reading will be under the necessity of getting up something new or of quitting the business.

SPIRITUAL MYSTERIES EXPOSED.

In the year 1871 the writer of the following pages was a young man aged 17 years, working steadily at his chosen occupation in one of the capital cities of the middle States. There was nothing out of the ordinary in his physical, moral or mental organization, which is true of him to-day, with the exception of a portion of the moral attributes. No individual can become a spiritual "medium" and retain *all* his moral qualities. To be sure, there are "mediums" full to overflowing with the milk of human kindness, who will divide his last dollar or dime with a poor, hungry wretch, and whose tears are as ready to spring forth at a tale or sight of misery or suffering as the most humane and kindly-hearted Christian or stainless humanitarian. Yet they are ready, the next quarter-hour to prey upon those same human affections in quest of the almighty dollar.

Nearly all "mediums" are, in reality, Materialists, Atheists or Agnostics. The writer, at the date above given was a Materialist of the most pronounced type. He did not *believe* anything, holding that what was truth, could be demonstrated, beyond cavil, as true, hence there was no excuse to take *anything* on faith, simply because the principle was pleasing or in accordance with his views of what was right, and pleasant to contemplate.

Although he was satisfied that his views and ideas were correct, and that Materialism covered and answered every question in regard to man's immortality, and a life beyond the grave, he, like all humanity, craved something different, better, more in accord with the crudest idea of justice. Still he had unanswerable, logical argument to support his views at command, and with all his yearning and researches for something better to replace his Materialism, did not expect to find it. Later on we will see if anything *has* replaced it.

He had been, up to the date given, a frequent attendant at the churches of various denominations, but could not understand from whence the ministers derived the authority for the statements they were making each Sabbath, and why there should be such a wide difference of opinion between the ministers of the various denominations.

He was quite a Bible student himself, and could not understand why he was not as well qualified as the minister to read and understand plain English. He could not conceive any reason why the preacher should say that in the account of the creation the Bible means to say that the earth was created in six epochs or six ages when it says in plain English "six *days*." Their reasons for interpreting "days" to mean "ages" or unlimited "epochs" he could understand easily enough; but how they were to prove that they were correct, if questioned, he could *not* understand, and cannot yet; for if there is an anthropomorphic Deity who created the earth in six billion years, he believes he could have done it in six days of twenty-four hours each. He may have been wrong, and the preacher have some special pull on divine sources of information not accessible to ordinary mortals who have not passed through a theological college-course.

Such was his religious attitude at the time his attention was drawn to Spiritualism.

His family, with the exception of his father, were converts to Spiritualistic philosophy and phenomena, and were regular attendants at the seances of the three or four local mediums and the meetings held on Sunday by the organized society of Spiritualists of his city. The family, at no time, obtruded their views upon him, nor said anything in opposition to the ideas held by himself. He was as generously thoughtful of their feelings, and no word of cavil or argument was uttered in their presence.

Not being given to airing his opinions in speech at any and all places and times, it came about that the members of his family had been numbered in the fold of the Spiritualistic flock for the period of about four years before his attention was sufficiently attracted to the subject to undertake an investigation of its peculiar claims. Knowing that the members of his family were possessed of ordinary intelligence and exhibited average powers of logical argument on questions other than religious or Spiritualistic he concluded that, either there was some fire beneath the smoke, or there were some very clever artists engaged in the business. From the accounts of the phenomena occurring with and in the presence of their favorite medium, given him by his eldest married sister, a lady with a liberal education, an even, cool, analytical mind, with travel and associations with experiences and cultured people of the world, not given to accepting everything for what it appeared on the surface to be, he was forced to the conclusion that those "kings of magic," Hermann, Heller and Baldwin, still had a few things to learn. He had witnessed the performance of the expert gentlemen named, besides the entertainments of others, in the same line, who had not the reputation, but were equally as skilfull performers and performed as apparently wonderful feats of magic or legerdemain, but, in comparison with the "medium's" achievements, as they were related to him, they were as amateurs. Knowing, as he did, the immense quantities of apparatus carried about by the prestidigitateur, to aid in his deceptions; that at the conclusion of each feat he invariably retires behind the wings to dispose of the apparatus used and supply himself wth a different piece for the next trick, also that the stages are admirably fitted up for his use; and that he holds his audience at a distance of at least twenty feet from the seat of his operations, he knew that it would be a very easy matter to deceive. But, in the case of the "medium" it was entirely different. The "medium" referred to, was a gentleman of perhaps thirty years of age, weighing about one hundred and fifty pounds, something like six feet tall, dressed in an ordinary business costume. His clothing was subjected to a searching inspection for apparatus, and he was placed in a cloth "cabinet" furnished by a stranger to himself. The cabinet was erected in a house and room, never having been previously visited by the "medium."

Under these circumstances, it was said, with the "medium" securely bound, hand and foot, to the chair he sat in, that faces, hands, feet, arms, legs and even the busts of supposed dead persons were protruded through the openings in the curtains. Messages were written to different members of the "circle," giving the full names and relationship of the spirit to the sitter. At intervals of a few minutes the members of the "circle" would make a critical examination of the condition of things in the "cabinet;" but at no time could they detect the slightest evidence that the "medium" had even stirred. Now, here was legerdemain with a vengance. The physical part of the seance might possibly have been perpetrated by the "medium," but where did he get the full names of the sitter's spirit relatives and friends? From whence came those faces that were positively recognized as belonging to the relatives of some of the sitters present? That was the point that puzzled him and he could scarcely credit the recital, although given by his sister who could possibly have no reason to deceive him in the matter. He will tell you where they came from later on. Little did he think while listening to the recital of above facts that at one day in the future he would have the reputation, and deservedly too, of being the best and most satisfactory phenomenal "medium" in the United States. Little did he suspect that he should be able not only to duplicate the above performance, but improve it, and be the means of converting hundreds to a belief in the phenomena of modern Spiritualism. Such, however, are the facts in the case. He has not only converted the lowly and ignorant, but individuals of great learning; people of all classes and conditions; the day laborer, physicians, lawyers, bankers, preachers, college professors and presidents; statesmen and scientists. He has been "tested" by self-constituted committees of learned men and women, who, through the reports of the wonderful nature of the phenomena occurring in his presence, have sought to explain the occurrences, through other than supernatural power. They have invariably given up the task, either convinced that the "medium" had genuine spirit "manifestations" or had been the first to discover some law in nature that gave the key to the entire class of phenomena produced by him, and was making the best possible use, financially, of his discovery. Another scientific error.

Science, many times, in dealing with the question in hand, undertakes too complicated a method in their efforts to discover a natural solution to the mysterious and wonderful works of the, generally, "illiterate ignorant medium." It does not seem to occur to their pregnant minds that ignorance and illiteracy is many times assumed by the "medium" for the very purpose it serves so well on occasions.

"Mediums" have been known who obtained written messages from Spiritland in from six to a dozen different languages, and in as many as twenty totally different styles of chirography It is possible that under the eye of an exper the twenty different specimens of penmanship would be accredited to one and the same hand, but every investigator is not an expert in chirography, hence a "medium" can build up quite a reputation on the ignorance of those who imagine themselves competent judges of the phenomena passing under their observation.

It is a fact, though, that the "medium" would a hundred times over rather be "investigated" by the man reputed by all his friends to be an uncomonly shrewd or "fly" man. The reason is obvious. He has satisfied his friends that he knows a thing or two about legerdermain and has exposed to them a few of the old moss-grown feats that have done duty ever since the prestidigitateur has been in the business, and through his knowledge of the few antediluvian tricks, he is credited with a knowledge of *all* the arts of deceit. This is the foundation for his alleged brilliancy.

When such an one visits a "medium" for the phase of "independent slate-writing," he does so with the system by which the "medium" does his work already exposed in his own mind. This being the case, he is in the best possible condition to be bamboozled by even an ordinarily sharp "medium."

The "medium," sharper and more "fly" than his "fly" sitter, in a few moments knows by the talk and actions of the sitter just what system he is watching and does his own work without his sitter noticing a wrong move, for the reason that he was intently watching for his own ideas to be worked upon him, and goes away without any more knowledge of the *modus operandi*, although he has received writing, than he had before.

In order to watch a "medium" with any show of success, one must not go into his presence with the idea that he knows how the fraud is perpetrated, for by so doing he disarms hunself to a great extent. Go, keep your mouth shut and eyes open. You cannot expose his methods of procedure at home with paper and pen, without having visited him in his lair and, ninety nine times in a hundred, not then exsept you have a hundred times greater knowlege of magicians and magician's tactics than most of those who star the dime museums throughout the country as Wizards of the Wand."

With the aid of apparatus and the facilities afforded by the ordinary theatrical stage, Hermann, Kellar, Heller and a number of others perform some startling deceptions; but in their efforts at exposition of the phenomena of Spiritualism they are at sea. Did they *know* the means by which the "mediums" obtain their results, they would not be slow to use them, for the reason that the act would be enhanced, and bear some resemblance to the "seance" of the "seance-room." As they do it at present, not one man or woman in one million, who had attended even *one* "seance." but would go away disgusted with the miserable attempt to carry out what the program promised. There is absolutely no resemblance of any kind or description, to the "seance" of the "medium," in these alleged exposes of the professional magician. They reflect great discredit on the cunning of the "medium;" for, with their ton or so of tables, chairs, cabinets, wooden skeletons, sheets, poles, and various other properties, absolutely essential to the success of their "manifestations," they do not even approach the "medium" in the variety of phenomena produced, nor the noiseless, beautiful, accurate work of *one* man, against from four to six. Besides, the "medium" has no apparatus, or, if he has, it cannot be found, and he gives his "seances" in strange rooms, with but a few minutes for preparation.

Ordinarily, the "physical medium" is an artist in his line. He must be, else his calling is soon gone, and he must earn his bread in other and perhaps better occupations. If a man become at all clever in giving "physical manifestations," he is assured of plenty of remunerative business, and can travel 'round the world and have his entertainment at the hands of Spiritualists, no matter in what country he may tarry. And just here it may be said that his entertainers, would by no means be the people of the lower classes.

Those whose business it is to attempt an expose of the phenomena of Spiritualism in order to please and gratify the desires of their congregations, or to create a little cheap notoriety for themselves make many gross misstatements regarding the believers and adherents of that religion. They are invariably depicted as "a mob of free-loving, licentious and bestial lunatics and criminals," and it is claimed that "the insane asylums and penitentiaries are overflowing with them." They are said to be "lean lank and lantern-iawed, with clammy hands and long or short hair," as best suits the fancy of the speaker. It is the writer's intention in this work to demonstrate that the ranks of the "medium" is overflowing with tricksters and humbugs of the first water, and their most wonderful phenomena will be described, and so thoroughly dissected and fully explained that the "wayfaring man, though he be a fool" can understand, and can perform the same feats with a very little practice and patience. But, while doing so, it is his intention to confine himself strictly to the truth regarding the believers to the best of his knowledge. He is not writing this book on the strength of some pet *theories* as to the manner in which the phenomena is produced, but as one who has made use of the ideas divulged for a number of years. It is not being written for the purpose of persecuting or maligning any one, but for the purpose of explaining, in as plain language as can be used, what the writer is positively certain of, through his experiences as a "medium" for twenty years, and through his associations with scores of other "mediums" in all branches of the business. This work will not be a compilation of opinions—persecutions of malicious priest or preacher, who speak without knowledge, and trust to the equal ignorance of his congregation to give weight and seeming knowledge to his abusive rantings. Neither will it be long drawn, technically worded, ambiguous *mistakes* of our scientific gentry; nor yet the wild and wide-of-the-mark guesses of the notoriety seeking news reporter.

As to the morality of the Spiritualists, as a class, outside of the fraternity of mediums, it would prove a difficult task to establish their rating one jot below that of the Methodist, Presbyterian, Catholic or any other denomination of Christians. At the same time it is probable that any of the denominations mentioned, outside the fraternity of preachers, are equally as moral as the Spiritualists. But when you get down to the insane statistics of the country, you will find that the orthodox religious lunatics outnumber the Spiritualistic lunatics about one hundred to one. In the penal institutions the odds are very much greater in favor of our friends the Spiritualists. Denunciation of the Spiritualists, as a class, will not answer for arguments agaiust their philosophy, nor disprove one of the miraculous "manifestations" they will tell you they are receiving daily. When one begins the use of abuse and villification of his opponent in debate or out of it, it begins to appear that he knew he was fighting a losing battle or had exhausted his stock of arguments and knowledge on the subject in hand. To abuse anything or anybody is a cowardly proceeding.

The writer, it will be seen, is especially disgusted with the rattletrap explanations offered by the learned gentlemen occupying pulpits in the churches of various denominations. The reason for this will be apparent to any one who has ever listened to one of their spiteful, malicious, and slanderous denunciations against the Spiritualist. It is certainly true that the preachers can not *prove* to you the *truth* of what they are teaching. They may convince you they are right, but they do not offer such proof as you would desire produced against you were you on trial for your life. It is especially distasteful to the author to listen to a man denouncing ANYTHING *that he knows nothing about*. Did they *know*, for a certainty there is nothing in Spiritualism, it would imply that they were familiar with the methods of the "medium" used to produce the phenomena. Oh! did they but *know* those things, Spiritualism would long ago have been an ism of the past. But, *not* knowing what they would have their congregations believe they do, and, of course being unable to demonstrate the methods of the "medium", thus proving to their congregations that they are only *guessing*, and *know* no more than their own ordinary selves, Spiritualism thrives and grows apace. There have been clerical efforts enough made to crush Spiritualism, to move the earth; but they amounted only to a general abuse and slandering of the Spiritualist, and have come to naught. Their explanations did not explain.

In order to successfully contradict and refute the claims of the Spiritualist, you will find it necessary to devote several years to the study of its "mediums" and phenomena, and become something of a chemist. Among the first things you will learn is the fact that the "medium" is not under the necessity, neither does he, buy any apparatus of the magical supply houses throughout the country. It had previously been your opinion that you could have expended a hundred dollars with Martin & Co., J. W. Judd, or C. M. Chase, and duplicate the phenomena of any "medium" on the globe. This was your idea previous to your having witnessed any of the phenomena.

It is only necessary, in order to have the whole phenomena of Spiritualism exploded and explained, to form the acquaintance of a gentleman wearing a seedy silk hat in connection with a "blazer" shirt, pop-bottle diamond and loud pantaloons, who has executed the wonderful (?) rope neck-tie trick at the county fairs, while selling his soap or plating compound; or has fed the monkeys in some fourth-class travelling menagerie. The only other qualification absolutely necessary is that he never saw anything of the phenomena, nor ever read anything of the philosophy; never attended their lectures or circles. This description of man can give you more information to the square inch of his silk tile than it would be possible to obtain from any other source.

It depends in a great measure on the ignorance and intensity of a man or woman's prejudice against the subject, as to just the number of preposterous explanations they will offer. And it depends entirely on the ignorance of their listener, as to the amount of confidence they place in the revelations made.

A sample verdict of a learned and scientific committee will be of interest here, as illustrating the far-fetched and absolutely ridiculous solutions of the "physical phenomena," concocted and offered the hungry skeptic and churchman, by those who, through their intellectual capabilities and scientific attainments are supposed to be eminently fitted for the task they assume.

The writer had been giving "seances" in a western city, for a number of weeks, in 1887. The phenomena produced at these "seances" had created considerable discussion and newspaper comment, besides converting quite a number of well-known, and a portion of them prominent citizens of the town. In a near by city there lived and transacted business a preacher, of the Presbyterian persuasion, and a physician of great prominence and supposed learning in the sciences and wiles by which the ancient Prince of Black Magic, Cagliostro, produced the results that puzzled the wiseacres of his day and generation. These gentlemen concluded to form an "investigating committee" of a dozen persons, from among their large number of friends, choosing none but those gifted beyond the ordinary in intellectual attainments, or versed in some of the sciences that it was supposed would materially aid in disentangling the web of mystery surrounding this young man and his strange phenomena. Accordingly, there finally was associated together the minister, who was noted for his scholarly sermons, disclosing a deep knowledge of many of Nature's laws and the isms and ologies that perplex so many of lesser learning and researches; the physician, who also bore a reputation for a profundity of information on subjects other than physics; a very popular lecturer on occultism, hypnotism and kindred subjects; two wholesale merchants of the city, who were blessed with extraordinary large bumps of self-esteem, with the perceptive faculties largely developed; and a state legistator, who had the points down fine, but withal a well informed individual. Each gentleman was accompanied by his wife, each one of whom was accredited with a large share of brilliancy in an intellectual way. This composed the circle or "committee" of twelve, sharp and keen, who were to wrest from the blonde, hatchet-faced, gentle-eyed "medium," all his secrets, whether he would or no. One of the merchants was deputized to visit the "medium" and bargain with him for his services one evening, to be designated by himself. The visit was duly made, arrangements satisfactorily concluded, and the "medium" was in for it. A few evenings after the merchant's visit, found the "medium" in one of the drawing-rooms of the minister's residence, in the presence of the aforementioned dozen of investigators. The time set for the "seance" to open was eight o'clock. At half past seven the ladies withdrew to another apartment, and the preliminaries began by the minister saying:

"Mr. Smith," I call the "medium" Smith for convenience, "It is my duty to inform you that you were engaged for this evening for the purpose of more fully and carefully "testing" your claims than possibly has ever yet been undertaken. Will you submit to the means proposed to be used by us, in our work?"

"I will submit to anything reasonable, and do all in my power to aid your experiments," replied Mr. Smith, "but as to my claims, I will say that I make none whatever."

"We have understood that you are a Spiritualistic "medium," for materialization and physical phenomena," pursued the minister.

"I believe myself to be the equal of the best of them, and yet do not make any claims for the 'phenomena' produced in my presence. I leave all conclusions and deductions to the investigators, and am satisfied to have them name it what they choose. What I do claim is that the phenomena is very wonderful and given under "test" conditions that make my participation in its occurence, apparently one of the impossibilities. It is your business to discover whether I *do* have a hand in it or not," replied Mr. Smith.

They now searched his clothing thoroughly, and even took the precaution to explore his mouth and ears. After satisfying themselves that he carried nothing contraband, he resumed his clothing, the ladies re-entered the room, and he proceeded to arrange them in a semi-circle, male and female alternating, in front of the cabinet, which was constructed by hanging a pair of heavy portierre curtains across a corner of the room and making a cover to it with a pair of blankets.

The "seance" now began, it will be minutely described later on, and continued about one hour and a half, to a successful termination.

Everythmg, including the "medium," was examined every few minutes, by the learned gentlemen, who felt the pulse, took the temperature, and affixed some kind of apparatus on his limb for recording the muscular activity or contractions, pried into his eyes and mouth, and. conducted themselves very much as learned men are supposed to do in their experiments in quest of more light. At the conclusion of the "seance" the ladies were a unit in declaring it as wonderful as the printed stories of the wonders worked by the fakirs of the Indies. The gentlemen held a conference of their own in one corner of the spacious apartment, in low tones, while the "medium" made mysterious passes about his own anatomy, presumbly to aid in recovering the exhausted vital forces, expended during the "seance." After some thirty minutes had passed, the gentlemen, after making a last examination of the "medium's" condition, confided to him that they were positive that "the manifestations were not caused by the spirit-world, at all." They also stated to him, in reply to an interrogation, that they did not think, in fact were positive, that he did not cause the manifestations, knowingly, but innocently made the entire entertainment. On being asked for an explanation, the lecturer on hypnotism unburdened himself in the following fashion:

"Our solution to the matter, and I, for one, would stake my professional reputation upon its correctness, is that you throw yourself into a self-induced, cataleptic trance, and, while in that condition, your soul-principle leaves the body and causes all the manifestations, "causing the pictures hung on the walls twenty feet from the 'cabinet,' to rattle and shake and the piano to sound, besides the dozens of other manifestations occurring in and about the cabinet. Your soul principle can read our minds as easily as we could read a printed book, and that is the source from whence came the names given, of our spirit friends." They expressed themselves as immeasurably pleased and satisfied with the "seance" and its results. There, reader, is an explanation of some really very simple operations, that are, in reality, more wonderful than the performance itself, even though it was produced through the agency popularly supposed to cause it. There is an explanation calculated to cause the "medium" to smile right out loud, every time he thinks of it.

Think of the aggregate of intellect there on that evening, using their every faculty to discover the true source of the "manifestations," bringing in such a verdict. It is the opinion of the "medium" of the occasion, that, in reality, they were convinced it was the work of disembodied spirits, but it would never do to admit it; hence the ridiculous explanation as the only respectable way out of it. It is only the "medium" who can enjoy these displays of brilliant ideas and profundity of the supposed profound men and women who undertake to unearth the true inwardness of our puzzling ism, for only the "medium" is absolutely certain they are wrong, and he, alone, could tell just how simple were the operations that befuddled the brainy man of science.

The first "seance" attended by the writer was one given in his native city, by a man reputed so wonderful that he found it impossible not to go him just once, anyway. Maledictions on that first seance, for it changed the whole course of his then honorable life and led to one of deception and adventure.

The "medium" referred to was a young man, of apparently twenty-seven years, of blonde complexion and slight build, with a prepossessing face and manners. His voice was soft and low, and pleasantly modulated. He was not, certainly, a man from whom you could expect anything resembling dishonesty, from his appearance.

The "seance" was held in the house of a well-known, wealthy citizen, a Spiritualist, and thorough gentlemen. The writer was accompanied by his sister, and besides themselves there were present ten couples. The fee was two dollars, or three dollars per couple. His audience on that evening netted him thirty-six dollars; quite a snug little remuneration for two hours of his time. The company numbered two "skeptics" beside the writer. At a few minutes before eight o'clock the company were ushered into the "seance-room," which was the host's dining-room. The "cabinet" was constructed in one corner of the room, by hanging across it two curtains of double-faced cantonflannel, of a dark maroon color. The curtains lapped one over the other about six inches in the middle of the front.

A thorough inspection of the "cabinet" was desired, and with several of the others present the writer did his utmost to discover the "nigger in the fence," but, after a thorough inspection was forced to admit that there was nothing suspicious in or about it. Another gentleman and himself then had the pleasure of taking the "medium" into an adjoining room and exploring his pockets, which they did most thoroughly. All they contained was a few letters, a breast pocket book, his handkerchief, pocket-knife and a few coins. As the breast pocket book could not contain any great amount of apparatus, they passed it without opening. They were satisfied that there was nothing about his person that could aid him in deception, and so reported to the audience on their return to the seance-room.

Everything now being in readiness, the "medium" seated himself in a chair, after first bringing a tambourine, guitar, tea bell, tin trumpet and pair of castanets and depositing them inside the "cabinet." After being seated he proffered some pieces of rope and stated that any one was at liberty to bind his hands and feet or secure him in any way they saw fit, in order to preclude the possibility of his having the use of any of his members during the continuance of the "seance." Again did the writer, in company with the only other skeptical gentleman in the company, exert all his ingenuity in binding the "medium" so that he felt positively assured that he would still be in the chair when the "seance" closed. After the tying was finished, the writer would have wagered any amount, that it was an utter impossibility for the "medium" to free himself. He would not take those chances with his money to-day. He has learned better. "Medium" and chair was now picked up and deposited in the "cabinet" and the curtains drawn.

We had no more than reached our seats when the guitar was seen to be gyrating around in space over the top of the "cabinet," with no visible contact with anything. The light had been shaded until you could just distinguish the forms of the sitters, without being able to discern their features. After a few seconds, the guitar was joined by the tin trumpet, and out of it came a voice, saying:

"I am the spirit father of Mr B——, and my name is J——— B———," giving his name in full.

This "test" was instantly recognized by one of the gentlemen, and there followed a common-place message to his daughter-in-law, the wife of Mr. B., who was present. While this was transpiring the guitar had disappeared into the cabinet again. As soon as the speaking had ceased and the trumpet fallen to the floor, we were requested to examine the condition of things in the "cabinet." Again the "skeptics" were permitted to do the investigating. We found the "medium" in precisely the condition in which we had left him at the beginning, it not appearing that he had stirred.

We had not reached our seats, which were distant about eight feet from the "cabinet," when the guitar again made its appearance, and began playing an air of great beauty, the entire instrument being visible, but the hands that created the music upon it could not be seen. The music produced was subdued, soft and sweet, as though the strings were being manipulated by very gentle, soft finger-tips. The "skeptics" were now very much interested. Again the horn joined the guitar, and when the latter had ceased its music, announced that its name was W——— E———, son of Mr. and Mrs. E———. The horn was correct again, and after giving a message, in which he gave some instructions concerning his pony, that the parents still kept, the horn fell to the floor of the "cabinet," and an examination disclosed everything as we had last seen it. The "medium" appeared to be in a trance, or sleep, his eyes closed, teeth set and breathing heavily. We had just turned our backs on the "cabinet" after our examination when a shapely white hand protruded through the opening in the curtains. Before we had seated ourselves there were two, three, four, all of different sizes, and doing considerable finger-snapping, thus doing away with the idea of rubber hands or stuffed gloves. Then came a bare foot at the bottom of the curtain, and in response to a request, by one of the circle, the toes were wiggled. No one was allowed to touch the hands or feet that appeared; but it was evident to any one in possession of one of his five senses that they were human hands and feet and not rubber or wax, even did we not know that nothing of the kind had been carried in by the "medium." After a few moments of these "manifestations," another examination of the "cabinet" and "medium" was made, and everything found satisfactory. Now, the tea-bell began ringing, and was soon joined by the castanets and tambourine. Ever and anon one or the other of the instruments would swoop around above the "cabinet" and disappear again. They seemed to be flying about in all parts of the "cabinet" and to be traveling with great swiftness and force; and it appeared as though the "medium's" eyes stood a very fair chance of being decorated in black. Another examination and everything found satisfactory. The writer was wavering, and was most intensely interested, to the great delight of his sister. The horn now requested that the company sing "Sweet Bye and Bye." Whilst the company were singing they were joined by the horn in a deep and powerful voice, which claimed afterward that it was at the time, John King, the "medium's" main "control." After the song was finished, a rustling noise was heard in the "cabinet" and presently the curtains were agitated, and slowly a face presented itself at the opening. Plainly, it was a face, but it was not recognized. Then other faces appeared, but without recognition. Once more the guitar strikes up its music, and during its continuance the curtains opened sufficiently to reveal to our astonished gaze a form, draped from head to foot in a dazzling white robe, in which there appeared to be a great many yards of material used. The face, in this instance, was much plainer, and in fact, was recognized by one of our number, who, however, said nothing until the form announced its name as "Mrs. E---- L-----, mother of the lady sitting next our host." The form spoke in a loud whisper, and no movement of the lips were visible. It stood stock still, and might have been mistaken for a dummy were it not that the face was so absolutely identified by the lady it claimed as daughter, and the full name it gave being entirely correct. The form remained in sight for a period of about twenty seconds, and after it had disappeared, the horn announced that the daughter carried the mother's watch, and that it contained the photo of her father. This the lady declared to be correct, and after the "seance" exhibited the watch, with the photo inside, and the name given by the spirit graven on the inside of the back lid. The lady declared that she had never before met the "medium." The props were being knocked from under the writer's materialism in beautiful shape. Other forms now presented themselves and four of them recognized. One of the faces was in exact likeness to an uncle of the writers', and he was almost paralyzed with astonishment, and ready to throw up his hands in surrender, when his sister, addressing the spirit, said:

"Uncle L——," for she, too, had recognized the face, "have you anything to say to brother? Tell him something to convince him." The writer was just about to say that it required no more evidence to convince him of the possibility of spirit return, when the apparition spoke, saying:

"Indeed, I should be pleased to grant the lady's request, but not being the spirit I am mistaken for, I cannot do so. I am the spirit of S—— W—— and the cousin of Mrs. D——."

The lady named said she had never seen him in life; but there was a resemblance to a photograph of him, in their family album. None of the forms or faces remained more than from five to twenty seconds.

Now, if this was the work of the "medium," why did he not take the opportunity presented of palming off one of his dummies on one who had already accepted it as an uncle, and make an absolute test of it, instead of denying that it was the spirit supposed to be, and make an uncertain test of it. This thought also struck the gentleman skeptic who assisted the writer in the examinations.

Occurring as it did, it certainly went far toward sustaining the "medium" as honest, and having no part in the presentation of the phenomenon. *Both* "skeptics" were, by this time pretty well *hors du combat*. All that was now required was that some spirit friend or message present itself that could be recognized, and the turn was made. The horn now made itself heard again and began announcing the names of the spirits present. In all, about twenty were given, and eleven of them recognized. Among them were four full names of the author's deceased relatives, two of them giving date of death and the cause thereof and sending messages of love to members of the family not present, in each case giving the name of the one the message was for. My sister informed me that she had never even heard of this particular "medium" before that week, and this was the first visit of any member of the family to him. The writer struck his arms and capitulated. After another examination of the condition of things in the "cabinet," which resulted satisfactorily, there was a regular bedlam of noises, begun, made by each one of the instruments setting out on erratic aerial excursion about the confines of the "cabinet." Occasionally one or two of the instruments would dart up out of the top of the "cabinet," and after executing a few fantastic movements, go below and join the general rumpus on the inside. It was, apparently, impossible for the "medium," even were he free, to put the instruments where they were seen, and besides this, the entire instrument was visible, and it was impossible to detect anything in connection with them, they seeming to float about the atmosphere as a balloon. Certain it was that the guitar could not perform on itself, and there was no human hand visible, to cause the vibrations of the strings. The only thing appearing strange, regarding the guitar, was that only one air was executed upon it. Immediately the rumpus ceased another inspection of the "cabinet" was made and everything found as it had been. The trumpet now requested that a writing tablet and pencil be placed in the "cabinet." This was done, and in a few minutes five messages of greeting, from the "controls" were handed out. One was in English, and signed by John King; another in French; another in German; another in Spanish, and the last in Hebrew, which no one present could read. It was taken next day, by the writer and others, to a Hebrew clothing dealer, who read and interpreted it with ease, and stated that it was elegantly written. The "medium" claimed to have no knowledge of any language save English and was unable to speak that correctly, which was a fac. for he did badly mangle the language every time he spoke. While we were waiting the thrusting out of the sixth sheet, the "medium" was heard to moan and yawn and move uneasily. In the course of a nunute and a-half he called for light, and stepped out of the "cabinet," freed from the repes that had bound him less than two minntes before. An examination revealed the fact that the "medium" had not only slipped out of the ropes but that every knot had been untied, and the ropes lay in a heap in the corner. Think of it. Something had untied the knots in less than two minutes that had required ten minutes of the time of two men. The instruments were handled and examined and found to be perfectly innocent of any mechanism not properly belonging to them with the exception of a small hole, about the eighth-of-an-inch in diameter, bored into the neck of the instrument, on the lower side and near the body of the guitar. The "medium" explained that it was for the purpose of attaching a music holder to the instrument, and as he was stopping with our host of the evening, he soon brought the holder and put it in position. It answered the purpose admirably, and satisfactorily explained the presence of the hole.

There, reader, is an unvarnished recital of the phenomena occurring at the first "seance" witnessed by the writer. In fact, it does not sound as wonderful as it appeared. You have probably read the statements made by Spiritualists that appeared, if anything, even less wonderful than the above narrative, and poohpoohed the idea. You said it was trickery or the Spiritualist was mesmerized, or was stretching the truth. You asserted it was trickery,—you *knew* it was; but knowing it, you could not explain the method used to produce the results, hence the conclusion is that you *knew* nothing about it. You may have *believed* it the result of legerdemain, but should have so stated. If you knew how foolish is the theory of mesmerism; how immensely it is out of the way, you would never advance it again.

Wonderful, was it? That was the opinion of the writer, especially when he had learned that the "medium" had never before been in that portion of the country and had never before met any of the parties present on that evening, save the host, and he only within two days. The "medium" had a reputation, among the Spiritualist organs as being the finest physical "test medium" in the country at that time, and well did he sustain that reputation.

Reader, how did he do these things? You give it up. So did the author, at that time.' Since that time the writer has been a celebrated "medium" for a number of years, and in due time it will be his pleasure to tell you how it was all accomplished so plainly that you can do it yourself. When the writer left that room it was as a believer in spiritual phenomenon. It is the writer's opinion that he was not more easily fooled than is any other one man in a thousand. From that time forward, he discussed Spiritualism at home and elsewhere, whenever he found anyone who would talk on either side of the question. It came about that through his talks with others and reading the accounts in the newspapers of the expose of some of the "mediums," he again found himself in a state of doubt. The printed accounts of the different exposes did not thoroughly settle the matter, for not one of them explained the *modus operandi* of the "medium," and, were it possible, they would have taken a fiendish delight in so doing. This being the case it left large room for doubt in his mind as to whether they had really been exposed, or the reporters had drawn upon their proverbially fertile imaginations for the major portion of their articles.

That which had most to do with his doubtful state of mind was due to his attending "private circles," at the houses of various Spiritualists whose acquaintance he had formed since he had become a convert. At these circles there would be assembled from six to fifteen persons, mostly ladies. There was one house in particular that was visited most fre-

SPIRITUALISTIC MYSTERIES EXPOSED. 43

quently, for the purpose of holding these "circles" where the husband was a retired doctor and zealous Spiritualist, whose wife was a "medium" for "tests" and "inspirational" lecturing. It was there he first learned to doubt that which he had so recently learned to believe was true. A description of what usually occurred will aid the reader to understand what "queered" the new convert.

Operations usually began by the hostess, becoming "entranced." This was accomplished by her seating herself in an easy chair, facing the sitters, who were ranged in straight rows across the room, each clasping their neighbor's hand. After sitting quietly a few seconds, her eyes would slowly close, her face twitch and her breath begin to come in gasps. Next her head would begin to "wobble" from side to side, and her hands begin to open and close spasmodically. Now her feet begin a tattoo on the carpet, and she is endeavoring to swallow her tongue. She was not a beautiful speciman of female humanity at best, and during these contortions of form and feature, was absolutely ugly. After a few taps of her feet on the carpet would come a mighty snort, three or four deep-drawn sighs, a gradual cessation of the spasmodic symptoms until she becomes perfectly quiet and the result sought for was achieved—she was "entranced." Slowly she would rise to her feet, with closed eyes, and deliver, at times, beautiful invocations, addressed to "Father and Mother Nature." The language employed in her prayers and lectures was invariably good, and her lectures usually eloquent. But the lady was educated beyond the point attained by most women; and she said nothing but what any one with the same education could have said, with their eyes wide open. After the invocation would come the lecture, of perhaps thirty minutes duration. During the delivery of the lecture, there were usually from two to five female aspirants for mediumistic honors in the company, twitching, jerking, gasping and snorting. By the time the lecture was concluded, one or more of the amateurs were on the floor, writhing, gasping, choking and making unintelligible gutteral sounds. They were supposed to be "personating" the death scene of some spirit who had friends in the assemblage. They would keep up their contortions until some one made a guess as to who the spirit might be. After the recognition the "medium" would regain consciousness, and the bewildered, where-am-I-and-what-have-I-been-doing looks they assumed, was acting such as is seldom seen. After "conditions" were restored, the hostess would attempt the "test" giving phase. She would open the proceedings by a liberal massaging of her eyes, and numberless finger snappings, presumably for the purpose of throwing off all earthly "conditions" from her optics. She would finally settle on the person she saw fit to open up on, and go for him in this fashion:

"I see by you, sir," if it happened to be a gentleman, old enough, apparently, to have a mother in the spirit world, "a lady. She has blue eyes and gray hair. I should say she had been a blonde in younger days, with light brown or golden hair. As I see her she is of medium height, and looks to be about fifty or fifty-five years of age—she may be older or younger. Do you recognize the spirit by the description?"

"What is the name given?" is the question put to the medium.

"I did not hear the name; but if I get it during —— What's that? A little plainer, please," breaking off in her reply and addressing the spirit.

"I get the name of Mary, Murray, Mandy, Maggie or something like that. Have you any friend of that name? Mary?"

"No, to my knowledge, I have not," answers the gentleman.

"Nor Murray, nor Maud, nor any name beginning with M? She seems to smile when I mentioned the names."

"I do not remember that I have any spirit friend by either name," protests the gentleman.

"Yes, but she comes to you and smiles. Now she lays her hand on your head and says —what is it she says—my son? Is that it? The lady must be your mother. Have you a mother in spirit life?"

"No, madame, my mother is still living."

"Are you sure? Have you heard from her lately, and know she has not passed over? It must be your mother," pursued the medium.

"I left my mother less than an hour ago, in her usual health," he replies.

"Strange—Oh; your mother-in-law, is it not? She has passed over within the past two years. Is it not so?" she asserts, with brightening manner.

"Yes, my mother-in-law lately died," assented the gentleman; "but her name was Almira," objects he.

"There! I knew I was right," she triumphantly exclaims. "She is so very much pleased that you recognize her, and has her arms about your neck. She says she brings—you have a child in spirit land, have you not?"

"No, madame."

"She says she brings your grandfather, who is pleased that you are investigating the glorious truths of Spiritualism." "Oh, my!" she exclaims, and sinks into her chair apparently very much exhausted. Her husband gives her a cool drink and fans her until she is able to tackle another, which she does thusly:

Spying a lady, dressed in mourning, one who has not been present previously, sitting on the back row, she rises and pointing her finger at the lady says:

"There is a gentleman comes to you—"

"Me?" interrupts the lady addressed, showing the feeler was a true shot, and she was probably seeking word from ner husband

"Yes," answers the medium, "and he appears to be a very near relative or friend—he comes so close—I should say, your husband," declares the seeress.

"Oh; my husband, have you come?" wails the grief-stricken widow.

"I see written above his head George, G-e-o——"

"Oh; my poor George, continues the lady, showing the medium she had struck it right."

"George A.—is it A?" queries the medium.

"Oh, yes; oh, yes. Why had you to leave me in such a dreadful way," moans the poor lady, not realizing that her words were loud enough to be heard.

"Who is it?" is inquired one of another.

Why, that is Mrs. Smith, answers some one who knew her, and the "medium" caught the name.

"Yes, it reads George A. Smith," announces the medium, and putting what Mrs. Smith had said and a recent railway wreck together, drew the conclusion that he met death in that accident, and the surmise proved correct. "He says to tell you not to mourn him—that he is happy and will watch over you. It seems, from the influence that comes over me that he was killed in a railroad accident about three weeks ago. Is that correct, lady?"

"Yes, in every particular."

"Did you ever see me before?" asked the medium of Mrs. Smith.

"No, ma'am," declares she, and another spell of exhaustion is in order, and this time quite a severe one.

But Mrs. Smith is to be further entertained for one of the "personating mediums" has collapsed again, and is lying on the floor, making all possible motions and noises to indicate that she is suffering from wounds received in a railway accident. Nobody seems to recognize the spirit, and as the hostess wants to do another act, she brings her clairvoyant powers to the rescue and announces that the spirit controlling the "medium" is Mr. Smith, and if Mrs. Smith will take the hand of the "medium" for a moment, she will aid him in getting complete "control" so that he can speak. Mrs. S. does as is suggested, but the medium being an amateur and not yet "developed" to that point where the spirits can speak through her, gradually eases up on the contortion act, her eyes open, and after the hostess has made a few mesmeric passes over her head, she sighs, arises and resumes her chair, with the look and air of one who has just achieved a wonder, and no amount of awed admiration is more than is due her. It may be remarked that she is not much of a medium, yet, but it will not be long until her shingle will be swung to the breeze announcing "Mrs. ―――― ――――, Test and Business Medium. Clairvoyant." If not too illiterate, she may, at some future time, be found on the Spiritual rostrum, delivering Spiritual discourses, at from five to twenty-five dollars per discourse. Mrs. Smith, however, has received that which will make her a Spiritualist, rank as it was. It is not that class of "mediums" that convince and convert intelligent, well-informed people. Our hostess, after the "personating" has concluded, seats herself, and proceeds to make use of her clairaudient accomplishments.

After the indispensable massaging and finger-snappings she announces that she "hears the name of Erastus." "Does anybody recognize the name?" she asks.

Nobody answers, and she continues:

"The spirit throws its 'influence' about the four persons sitting on the ends of the second and third rows of seats. It is either for one of them or somebody sitting very close to them. The spirit desires recognition for he continnes to repeat the name."

"Is the name Eras*tus*," asks one of the parties designated.

"It sounds like that, or something very similar," said the "medium."

"Can you describe the spirit?" pursues the person.

"I can not see him, at all—only hear the name," declares the "medium," "but since you have spoken, there has a beautiful spirit light appeared above your head, and from the 'influence' I get, I am sure the spirit comes to you."

"Well, I have a friend in spirit life, whose name is Eras*mus*, and it is possible that is lie." admits the party.

"That's it," quickly adds the "medium"—"Now I see the name E-r-a-s-m-u-s- written over your head in letters of white——"

"How wonderful!" exclaims the party, "Erasmus *White* was his name. How truly wonderful."

Yes, and the "medium" was as much astonished as any one present at the luck that made her say the letters were *white* ones.

"Yes," continued the "medium," "Erasmus White, and from the "condition" thrown about you, I should say a very intimate friend or relative."

"Yes, he was a very dear friend," admits the person, and the "test" was declared very wonderful. After more mesmeric business, the "medium" rises, and, pointing to a gentleman in the audience, says, in her most positive tones:

"You, sir, have lately met with a disappointment in some business transaction. I see you in very angry conversation with a gentleman of low stature, dark complexion, eyes and hair, and perhaps fifty years of age. You seem to be disputing over money matters, or the payment of money due from some business transaction between you. Have you had any such thing as a business disappointment, in the way mentioned?" she queries.

"Yes, I failed to collect some money due me, on making the attempt, lately," assented the gentleman.

"Well, I see by the brightening of the "aura" surrounding you that you will get the money after some considerable trouble. I see also that you are to be more than usually successful in your business, very soon, and prosperity, such as you never knew before, will be yours. You are to get money from an unexpected source, and by making a wise investment, this condition of things is to be brought about. You have a grandfather in spirit-life who will guide you, and you can not go astray. Am I acquainted with you, or your affairs, sir?" she asked.

"Not to my knowledge, Madam," he replied.

Another wonderful and indisputable "test" of the "medium's" wonderful gifts. But what man lives who has not had business disappointments, and bad debts to collect almost daily?

That is reasonably a safe subject to essay a test upon, with anybody. The latter part of her statements could not be denied, and stood good for an indefinite length of time. Yet, those things are looked upon as wonderful by a great many persons. Nothing was said as to whether the description fitted the debtor or not, but the admission of the truth of a part of it made the whole of it go as correct in detail. The "medium" being careful not to refer to them, after an admission of correctness of the main point. After three or four such "tests" had been given, the "medium's" Indian "control" who was supposed to be a maiden of seventeen summers, and whose name was Prairie Flower. Prairie Flower controls a great many different "mediums" in a great many parts of the United States. Prairie Flower always announced herself through the "medium's" organs of speech by suddenly exclaiming:

"How d'ze do? squaws and braves. Me's tummed zis night time to take tare of my 'medy'. "Say, chief," addressing a gentleman in the audience, "does zoo like injun dirls? 'Cause ef yoos does, me's glad, tause me like zoo. Me's glad me's peepers sees so much braves and stwas here dis night time. Oh!

such heaps of beautifulum spiritum here zis dark." She would continue this style of talk for ten or fifteen minutes, the "medium" all the time rubbing herself and making the passes that were supposed to recuperate their vitality after such wonderful efforts as has just been described. When Prairie Flower had said "dood-bye" the circle was at an end.

Men and women attended these "circles" who from manner, dress, conversation and intelligent appearance, you would suppose could not only not find anything of interest, there, but would instead be disgusted—men capable of successfully engineering the affairs of large business institutions and receiving and executing large contracts, requiring more than an ordinary education and knowledge of men and affairs. Yet you would find them regular attendants along with lady teachers and business women, deeply interested and firm believers in the genuineness of all said and done by various "mediums." As I said before, this class of "mediums" do not *convert* the man or women of brains; but after their conversion through other "mediums," they come to believe anything offered in the name of Spiritualism. This is the "bosh" that is met with at every "private circle," and which set the writer doubting what he had witnessed at the first and really wonderful "seance" of the test and physical "medium." Why the "mediums" will do these things, is a question hard to answer. They open their houses once and twice a week, allow the public to tramp out their carpets and fill the room with dirt, making extra work, knowing that the majority of their company will go away jeering at what they have seen and heard, making all manner of sport of them, besides the ridicule and "roasts" of the newspapers. They invite and receive just such treatment without one penny of money as a balm for it all. Many of those who have these "circles" at their homes are beyond the reach of want or the wolf, even did they live a thousand years. They are frauds of the most thorough description and know it. It appears to the writer that the most plausible explanation is, that they are endeavoring to work up a reputation to do business on in the future, in the case of those who are not well off in worldly goods. The other class may be self-deluded; for it must be admitted that outside their miserable mediumsbips mey are excellent persons, in the majority of cases. They give to charity freely, are honest and fair in their dealings with everybody, live upright lives, and are in every way desirable as friends. I have attended dozens of the class of "medium's circles" named, and have proven each and every one to be frauds. The friends and supporters and believers in any one of them will ask, with an incredulous sneer: "By what means did you arrive at your conclusion, my friend? I have known her for years and never knew her to be guilty of any act unbecoming a lady, or dishonest or deceitful in any way, and since she has been blessed with these powers, she has never received a cent of money through it, nor does she want any. She is doing this work solely for the benefit that will accrue to benighted humanity. I am sure that she has at no time asked pay from you, that you should thus desire to do her an injury. I myself have tested her genuineness for the past two years and have found her to be honest and conscientious."

In reply to the above interrogatory and argument, which, by the way, has been put to the writer, in the language given, he will say that the operation was simple enough, and will succeed every time it is tried. In effect, he allowed them to expose themselves. He will relate the method, as it occurred in one case, and that will answer for all, as the same principle was used in each expose. Being in attendance at one of the "circles" mentioned, wherein the "medium" was working for the benefit of benighted humanity, he was pointed out by the "medium" and the following tests given and received:

"By the young man sitting next the window, there comes the spirit of a gentleman past middle age, with light hair, having a bald front and crown, blue eyes, blonde complexion and more than six feet tall, with medium, slender form. He has in his hand one of the Masonic emblems of their order. The other hand is on your shoulder, and he says that he is your father and that he passed away about two years ago." I had, previous to the meeting being opened, stated to a gentleman sitting next me that I should be pleased to receive a communication from my father, dead about two years. I said this in the "medium's" hearing, without appearing to be aware of her proximity. I also wore a Masonic emblem on the lappel of my vest. "Does the gentleman recognize the description as being correct?" asked the "medium."

She was answered that he did, with the exception of the eyes, they being gray instead of blue, and that he was just six feet tall and not more. Otherwise the description was perfect, he having been a Mason.

She replied, "that of course she had only guessed the height, and the mistake was excusable, it being a very close guess. The gray eye would be hard to distinguish from blue at this distance," explained the medium.

This being conceded, the "medium" continued, by saying:

"He brings with him a young lady who might, from appearances, be your sister." My face brightened so perceptibly and my manner became so attentive that she was sure she had struck it right, hence she went on: "She now says she *is* your sister."

"Does she exhibit anything that might have been a present?" was asked.

"She holds out her hand, on which is two rings——"

"Right," interrupted the writer, "is either of them set with a di— stone of any kind," she was asked.

"Yes, one of them is set with a beautiful diamond," she answered.

"Right again, what is the other one like?— plain gold band?" was again asked

"It is a plain gold band, worn on the forefinger," was the reply.

A message was given by her in which she stated, *on being asked*, that she was with our brother, and had frequently met with a friend by the name of Bard. My father, also on *being asked* regarding it, stated that he was satisfied with the disposition that had beer made of the property he left, and expressed himself as pleased that I had kept his favorite horse.

I attended several of the "circles" held at this place, and my father and sister, who gave her name as Effie, and was recognized as correct. never failed to come and give me some word of love and instructions concerning the horse. In addition my brother Robert frequently came along with several friends, in cluding Mr. Bard, who is still living, while the others never had existence except in my mind and the medium's. "My father was still in the flesh, hale and hearty, and a brunette of short stature, my sisters were all living, and a brother I never had. None of my living sisters were named Effie and none of them possessed a diamond ring. My friend Mr. Bard has never been dead, and is doing business today on our earth. The five other friends who gave so many communications and described how different they found matters to what they had expected when they used to talk to me about it, when I lived in New York City with them—a place I had never visited up to that date—were merely names, that I have forgotten. The favorite horse was also a mythical one, my father or self never having owned one of any description. Yet, many were the instructions received from my spirit father and sister concerning him. They even went so far as to say, on different occasions, that they were with me on drives I was supposed to have taken since last they communicated with me—behind this favorite piece of horse flesh that had no existence.

As to the argument that their friends had never known of their being guilty of a dishonest or deceitful act in long years of acquaintance, it is only necessary to say that the most hardened criminal committed a *first* crime at some time, in order that it be possible to commit a second. Again, many women have lived for years with loving husbands, who would strike you dead at their feet did you even hint that their wives were not what they should be, yet was grossly untrue to them every week of those long years. They did not discover it, and probably went to their graves believing their wives as stainless as the lily. All deceptions and crimes, in fact, a very small percentage of either, or the perpetrators are ever detected. Another argument is that the writer was, himself, under the eye, and in the pay, as medium, of a gentleman investigator for three years, not only not being detected at any tricks but making a firm Spiritualist of him. I will guarantee, too, that of all the phenomena produced in that time, that the writer was the sole proprietor thereof, not being in league with the devil, as has often been said of him, by ignoramuses, nor yet having any special pull on the spirit world. More than this, the writer during his mediumistic career was never heard to claim that his phenomena was the work of spirits, always dodging the question. However, he never objected to persons other than himself, calling it whatever they chose. His little speech, before taking his seat in the cabinet being in these words:

"Ladies and gentlemen: You are here tonight, and pay your money, to witness and pass judgment on the phenomenon presented in my presence—phenomenon that have been occurring through *me* since I was eighteen years of age. I am not here to proselyte any one to Spiritualism, simply to present to your notice the phenomena that is described as wonderful by all who have witnessed it. I make no claims for it, and you are welcome to explain it in any way you choose after witnessing it. I will say that it is not the work of the Devil."

If, after hearing that, they persisted in claiming that he was a medium and the phenomena the result of spirit work. I fail to see that he had any business to do anything but "saw wood and say nothing." It was left entirely to their judgment, and no claim made for it except that it was not the work of the Devil. There were no pretenses of any kind --- simply a case of non-committal cunning. It is a fact, though, that, without a solitary claim being heralded, he rose from a disgusted backslider Spiritualist to an individual mentioned and written of as the finest "medium" for "physical manifestations," materialization and independent slate-writing in the United States. Did the hundreds who have visited his "seances" but know through what simple means they were deceived they would make grimace at themselves every time they caught sight of their reflections in their mirrors. Especially would this be true of the scientific gentlemen and other top-heavy investigators, as well as the "expert" committees of the Spiritual Societies throughout the country before whose august presence he had to appear and demonstrate his "mediumistic" qualifications, before he had the indorsement of the organized Spiritualists of their city. Oh! ye *experts*! You have been given a description of the style of Spiritual work that "queered" the writer, and if you are a Spiritualist, of very long standing, you will know, by the perusal, that he has been there. The description will answer for many an experience of your own. He will now relate an experience with the *other* kind of a medium, and the experience that started him on the highway to "mediumship."

There came to the writer's city, during the year of '71, and after the time of visiting the circle just described a professional, traveling "test medium." In this instance I will give the name, for there is nothing to be said concerning him as a reason I should not. His name was Frank T. Ripley. A glance at the "Movements of Lecturers and Mediums," in the pages of the *Banner* of *Light*, today, will disclose his name. He is still doing business in the old line. He was to occupy the rostrum at the Spiritualist's hall four Sundays, afternoon and evening. A lecture at 2:30 p. m. and "tests" beginning at 8 p. m. The writer visited each lecture and "test" tournament. Mr. Ripley's professional work did much to strengthen his weakening faith. The particular meeting that made a "medium" of him was on Mr. R's third Sunday evening. A description of the proceedings on this evening will suffice for all, as they were all very similar. The festivities would open with singing by a choir, then Mr. R. would offer an invocation; then more singing. During the singing of the second song Mr. R. would make passes before his face and eyes with his hands and his hands, limbs and body twitch and jerk convulsively.

As soon as the singing ceased, he rose from his chair and came hesitatingly forward to the front of the rostrum with one hand spread open across his forehead and the other raised aloft and seemingly feeling for some object. Arriving at the front of the platform he stood some seconds in silence and then with a start his hands dropped to his sides and he began to speak, saying:

"I feel an influence, as though I were sinking in salt water. I am drowning. I have fallen from the yard of a vessel that is moving before the wind in mid-ocean. I had been sent aloft to make fast a brace that was playing through its thimble, lost my footing and fell.

I have a brother in the audience. My name is—— ——, Does my brother recognize me?"

"He does, beyond any doubt," answered a gentleman in the audience having the appearance of a working man. "If you are not my brother, you are some one who knows me and and all the circumstances of my brother's death."

"Now", said Mr. R, "I see standing in the aisle, beside you, sir," addressing a gentleman, "an old gentleman, with gray hair, gray eyes, one eye being sightless; he is bowed with age and has a cane on which is inscribed, 'From —— —— to —— ——, his father, on his sixty-fifth birthday. He says you are his son and the donor of the cane. He passed away about three years ago, of paralysis. Is what I have said correct, sir?"

"It is, sir, in every particular," declared the gentleman.

"Now," continued the "medium," "there stands by you, sir," addressing the writer, "a gentleman of apparently thirty years of age, tall, slender and lithe of form, with light hair, blue eyes, fine features and even, white teeth. He served a few months in the army and came home sick. He did not pass over through the sickness but was accidentally shot. He says his name is L———A———, and that he is your uncle. That you mistook another spirit for him at a "seance" not long ago. He says to tell you that if you will sit for developinent, in the "cabinet" you will get "manifestations" as wonderful as any you have witnessed. Do you recognize the person as the one he claims to be?" The author could not have told the story better himself, and as everything he had said concerning him was correct, there was nothing to do but admit it as a fact. After from ten to twenty of such "tests" the meeting would close. What would you think, reader, to sit in a public audience and have a man single you out and tell you all about some loved spirit relative, when it appeared impossible that he should know even yourself and much less your spirit friends. The writer had been careful to take a seat in some remote part of the room, and never to enter or leave in company with his sister. He avoided an introduction to him, and had never exchanged a word with him, arriving at his meetings at the last moment and taking his departure during the singing of the closing hymn. It was very satisfactory to him; but the memory of those private "circles" would present itself and he was in a quandary. One hour he would feel that there was a truth in it and the next he would declare to himself it was all "bosh". Had the writer never came in contact with other than finished, professional "mediums" the chances are excellent that he would not have become an adventurer. It finally struck him, that, in order to make certain of the truth of the matter, it would be the proper thing to sit for the development of a "mediumship" of his own. He would use every endeavor to obtain some "mediumistic" gift, and if he succeeded, that would finally and indisputably settle the matter. If he did not succeed he would, of course, have the same uncertainty about it as before he attempted his development. It would cost nothing but a small portion of his time, and even if it was a failure there would be no loss. Accordingly, after seeking for the proper instructions until they were obtained and he had been assured that if they were carefully observed, there was no such thing as failing, a "cabinet" was erected at the home of the writer and the attempt begun. The instructions were obtained through a "trance medium" and were as follows:

Construct a cabinet in the corner of one of your rooms by hanging across it a pair of heavy curtains, fastening them to the walls of the room where they touch at the sides but leaving them open in the middle of the front. Put into the cabinet a guitar or banjo, tea-bell, tambourine, pair of slates and tin trumpet. Have four or six persons to sit with you, equally divided between the sexes. They are to sit in a semi-circle about the front of the "cabinet" the sexes alternating, clasping each the other's hand. You are to sit inside the "cabinet" alone, and remain one hour, in as passive a condition as it is possible for you to attain. The sitters, those outside, should sing about four songs during the hour you are sitting. You should sit twice per week, always on the same evening and hour, Tuesday and Saturday evenings, and from eight until nine o'clock. These instructions are all that will be necessary until you are able to get further advice through your own "mediumship." There is no such thing as failure if you persist in following out these instructions, and you will begin to receive demonstrations within three months.

That was satisfactory, and he began his "development" sittings in as handsome a "cabinet," and as good instruments as the purses of his friends, who would not allow him to go to any expense, would permit. Those who sat outside were Spiritualists, six of them, all interested in seeing the prospective "medium" developed to the fullness of his capabilities, whatever they might be. They were friends of his family, and the writer found the developinent business quite pleasant. The "sittings" continued the three months named as the time that the "manifestations" would begin, but none had put in an appearance, neither had the would-be "medium" experienced anything that led him to believe that any progress had been made. He was abjured to be patient, by the "sitters," who told him that it was an easy matter for the spirit to be mistaken as to the length of time required to bring about results, but that they were probably not *far* wrong, and possibly the next sitting would see the first of the "manifestations." Thus encouraged, he continued the "sittings" until the sixth month had passed into the months that are gone. Nothing had occurred, except a healthy desire on the part of both "medium" and sitters that the "manifestations" be forthcoming, begetting in the "medium" an inclination to cause some phenomena on his own hook. The more he thought about it the stronger became the desire to practice a little deception on his friends, then, after telling them of it, drop the matter entirely. After turning it over in his mind for some time, he concluded he would see what effect a few spurious "manifestations" would have on his friends. It would be easy, they having unbounded confidence in him. His mind made up to do it, he hardly knew what to try, and finally concluded he would wait until the "sitting" came around and, after getting into the "cabinet" see what suggested itself. This was the course he pursued, and on one Saturday evening, after the first song had been sung, the "sitters" were delighted to hear sharp raps, seemingly on the walls of the room, within the "cabinet." Of course, the "medium" had to be happily surprised, or appear so, which he did, and his first act of deceit was done. He was forced to deny the authorship of the raps, also, and the first lie had been given birth. The "sitters" endeavored to get answers to questions; but did not succeed, for the rapper did not care to go to that length with his deception, and, besides, did not know what answer to make to the inquiries. Nothing occurred but the raps, although every eye and ear was alert to catch anything that might transpire. The "sitters" also displayed a tendency to connect any noise occurring to Spiritual agency. Noting this the "medium" could not help reflecting with what ease one could deceive them. It also gave him an idea that the average "medium" had pretty smooth sailing when he had none but Spiritualists in his "circle." If he could not readily offer an explanation for anything occurring, some one of the "sitters" would do it for him, thus educating him in the business. When nine o'clock had struck and the medium come from the "cabinet," you may rest assured he felt strange. He was sure that every time one of the "sitters" looked upon his face they knew he had not only made the raps, but had afterward lied about it. A dozen times was he on the point of *peaching* on himself, but as many times did a sense of shame overcome his resolution, and he told himself he would tell them one at a time, as he met them, laugh it down and dismiss any further "sittings." The "sitters" were so delighted, and offered so many unselfish congratulations and encouragments, shaking his hand and patting him on the back, it is no wonder he felt his smallness. One of the ladies remarked:

"There! I am sure none of us need ever have any doubts regarding the 'physical manifestations' after this. I am sure Mr. ———— would be guilty of no act of deceit."

Think of it, reader. A respected lady friend offering such an expression of perfect confidence in him regarding the very thing in which he had just been deceiving her. Would you have felt perfectly at ease in his place? I think not. He was glad when his "sitters" had departed and thought long and deeply on his deception of the evening and concluded not to say a word to any of them about it, but just shut down on any more "seances." His wits were at work the entire time that elapsed between the regular "sitting" nights, trying to concoct some plausible reason why he discontinued the development course. The evening came however, and no excuse that the "medium" could offer without exciting the suspicion that the "manifestations" of the previous "sitting" were a fraud, had been formulated. After the "sitting" had gotten under way, the requests by the "sitters" for phenomena were so frequent and entreating that the "medium's" conscience smote him again and again for his previous deception. However, he soon found himself rapping again. This time he essayed answers to the questions regarding the progress made in the "medium's" development, rapping an affirmative answer to the question:

"Is the development proceeding satisfactorily, and will he develop good physical powers?"

Nothing but raps occurred at this "sitting," and the "sitters" were much pleased that the raps had been made to answer their questions. This was looked upon as a decided improvement over the preceding "sitting." The "medium" was not so much abashed at their compliments and encouragements as on the previous occasion, and during the week actually caught himself wondering what new thing he could do, that would create more interest and enthusiasm than the raps. The only things he could think of, was to produce "spirit lights." This he tried with match-heads. It was successful, and the sitters delighted. The lights and raps were all that were produced for some dozen or more "sittings," for the reason that the "medium" could think of nothing more wonderful. On one evening he went to sleep in his "cabinet," and on waking found that he was supposed by the "sitters" to be entranced, and it struck him as the proper thing to allow them to remain undeceived, which he did. Now, the sitters were sure that some new phenomena was about to occur. It did not, however until one evening he found about twenty feet of rope that had been concealed in the "cabinet" without his knowledge. He found it nicely coiled and tied with thread to the under side of the cane chair seat in which he sat. He had no knowledge of rope tying feats, but undertook to bind himself with the ropes, which he finally succeeded in doing. He now essayed his first speaking under "control" by exclaiming, "Look, look, look," until the "sitters" understood that the spirits wanted them to examine the "medium's" condition. They were delighted beyond measure at finding the "medium" apparently so securely bound. The light was so dim that it was impossible to detect anything wrong with the knots or manner of tying. The "medium," though, was fearful all through the examination that some of them would discover his deception, and only breathed freely when the examination had been completed and he was admitted to be "most securely bound, and in a way that it was impossible to have accomplished himself." The "medium" realized, however, that the absolute confidence of the "sitters" in his honesty had as much to do with the successful termination of his rope-tying "test" as anything else, and that, with a "circle" of skeptics, it would have been an entirely different matter. It was also his intention to stop his "sittings" and deceptions after he had satisfied himself as to what length he could go in the deception of the persons composing his "circle." We shall see how he succeeded. It now became a study with him to invent new phenomena or duplicate that which he had witnessed. He could not account for what he had witnessed nor evolve a satisfactory theory as to how it was accomplished. Nevertheless, it was becoming more of a certainty in his mind each day that it was all the clever work of the "medium." His success in deceiving his "sitters" as to the rope tying feat, crude and incomplete as it must have been, compared with the finished and expert work of the "medium," led him to believe that with practice he could become expert to that degree that he could deceive the elect. This impression led to the spirit's writing on the slate, at the next sitting, that one of the gentlemen should bind the "medium" at the next following "sitting," and they would see what they could accomplish. This was done, as he thought, at the time, in a tolerably thorough manner. His hands were tied to the top of his knees, as he sat in the chair, and the rope continued down, binding his ankles to the legs of the chair below the bottom rung. He was put into the "cabinet," and while the circle was engaged in singing, he found it very little trouble to free the right hand by putting his knees close together, thus making the use of the left hand possible in securing the release of its neighbor. But, could he get back into the ropes again so as to avoid detection? He made the attempt, and found he could get back easily enough, but, the best he could do, the ropes were not so closely drawn as they had been before he had released himself. Here was a pretty state of affairs, surely. Just as certain as the gentleman examined the ropes, just so surely would his efforts be discovered. What was to be done? He did not see any way out of his dilemma until it occurred to him that he could remove the rope entirely, if he could do no better, thus removing the evidence of having unsuccessfully attempted any trickery. He concluded to do so, but the thought struck him, why not go on and attempt to put himself in the condition in which the gentleman left him, until he had either succeeded or proven to himself his inability to accomplish it. It was inky dark in the "cabinet" and the sense of touch was his only mode of ascertaining the condition of things. The song was concluded and the "medium" found it necessary to discontinue his experiments, until the second song was began, on account of the creaking of the chair at every move that was made. Questions were put to the spirits to which no answers were obtained, the "medium" still having his hand in the ropes, hence it was inpossible to produce the raps. He can get raps today, no matter how he is secured or watched. Such are the advantages of experience and practical education in any line of business. The failure to get raps was accounted for on the theory that the spirits were working to overcome the "condition" of the ropes. They were correct in regard to at least one spirit, closely related to their "medium." The second song was started and again the "medium" essayed to complete his task. After a few minutes he struck it. Later on he will explain, in detail, just what he struck. Now, that he accomplished it once it was an easy matter to do it again and again as he discovered by experiment. It was his intention, now, to stir things up lively—to make as much of a noise and rumpus with the instruments as possible, and call for an examination of the ropes. On a second thought, however, he concluded it would be better to do but very little, as the development might be considered too sudden to be of a healthy variety, and, in comparison with the time required to obtain the raps, it certainly would appear bad. Therefore, after a few raps, a light or two and two or three very light thrums on the guitar, an examination was called for, and the gentleman expressed himself as very thoroughly satisfied that not a rope or knot had been touched or tampered with. This statement created quite a murmur of pleased satisfaction among the "sitters," and the prognostication of two or three of them that the "medium" was destined to become one of the finest and most satisfactory "physical mediums" in the world. This was calculated to cause the "medium" to "feel his oats," and he declared to himself that he would furnish them more food for thought ere another year had passed, and would endeavor to fulfill their predictions. He had no idea why he came to any such conclusion, it not being, as yet, his intention to follow anything of the kind as a business. Nothing more was seen or heard at this "sitting" and at its close the "medium" was found freed of the ropes, all knots being untied and the rope, neatly coiled, lying in the corner. Great was the speculation indulged in regarding the probable results of the next "seance." He was now, since the success of this "seance," firmly convinced that the "physical

SPIRITUALISTIC MYSTERIES EXPOSED. 79

medium" he had visited was simply an expert manipulator of ropes, and had means of his own to cause the "manifestations" he had witnessed, notwithstanding the seeming impossibility of such being the case.

The one thing that puzzled him most, was the source of the information he had regarding persons who were absolute strangers to him. How came he to know that Mr. and Mrs. E———— had a son Willie E————, and that he had owned a pony that the parents still kept and that the pony was called "Midget?" From when came the faces that were recognized in every feature and spoke so certainly on subjects the "medium" could not possibly know anything about? How came he to know the names of my spirit friends and the names of members of my family not present? Even if he *did* know them, how came he to know that I was their relative? I had not had an introduction previous to the "seance." When he would think of these things he would be fearful, for a time, that he was perpetrating these deceptions on his friends, and under the eye of his sorrowing spirit relatives, and was inviting all kinds of catastrophies to blight and ruin his prospects and life. Again he would explain the whole proceeding, to his satisfaction as the result of mind-reading, and determined, within himself, to acquire that power if it were a possibility. He has since learned how to accomplish those same feats, and if the reader will peruse this book to its close, he or she will know enough of the methods employed to become, in a very short time, one who can work the same wonders and become a celebrated and much sought after "medium." At the next meeting of the "developing circle" each one was in a state of pleased expectancy, and some very intemperate predictions made as to the wonderful nature and vast amount of phenomenon that would be presented. From the expressions of what was expected to occur, the "medium" was positive that there would be some disappointed "sitters" present after the "seance." By no possible means could he fill the bill they had prepared in their minds, and was so confident would be produced at this "sitting." They appeared more anxious than the "medium" had ever been, even in his most impatient moments. However, after being bound, and this time in a manner different to the previous occasion, and in a way that created a healthy doubt in the "medium's" mind as to whether or not he would be able to free himself, the singing was begun. This time his hands had been tied to the front legs of the chair, at his sides, and there was no possible way to get them together. However, after a dint of hard work and much experimenting, he found his right hand free, and that the tactics employed on the previous occasion would restore the ropes to their original condition. He had been careful to place in the "cabinet" a chair that was sound in all its parts and would not creak with every movement, and he was enabled to work when the "sitters" were not singing. At this "sitting" raps were produced, the guitar twanged, louder than before, the tea bell was heard to skip across the floor of the "cabinet" with considerable force, lights appeared at the opening in the "cabinet," three or four at a time, and a message written, declaring that the "development" was progressing favorably, and signed Jno. King, control. At the "seance" previously witnessed by the "medium," Jno. King was the "control" and seemed to be quite well appreciated by the Spiritualists present, therefore the "medium," in this case, concluded he might as well have a "control" of favorable mention, as not, as all that was necessary to procure him was to subscribe his name to the communications written This he did and great was the pleasure expressed by the "sitters," all of whom had attended the "seances" of the aforementioned "physical medium." They were now positive that full-form materialization would be the ultimate outcome of the "sittings," as Mr. King was identified with nearly every "medium" getting that phase of "physical" phenomena. On the gentleman entering the "cabinet" to inspect the ropes, he declared he smelled phosphorus, brimstone or matches. The "medium's" heart jumped, and he was sure that his manner of making lights was about to be exposed. However, it was passed by as probably being an odor induced through some chemical proceedings on the part of the spirits in producing the "manifestations." That theory was accepted and restored the "medium's" peace of mind, but he swore to never make any further use of matches in producing spirit lights, but would find some safer way or dispense with them entirely. After a few more "sittings," of substantially the same "manifestations," except the lights, and being secured with the ropes in a different manner each time, the lights were missed by the "sitters" and their absence remarked. The "medium" saw that he must either furnish lights, in some way, or lay the previous ones open to suspicion. An idea struck him. He procured a flat, two-ounce druggists' bottle, and filling it about one-fourth full of water, cut the heads off about one hundred parlor matches and dropped them in. When the composition was dissolved he poured off the water, saving it, and threw away the bits of pine left in the bottle. He now returned the brown fluid to the bottle and corked it. After labelling the bottle "Cough Medicine," he put it in his pocket and sought a dark closet to see how his "cough medicine" would work. Getting into a dark place he took the bottle from his pocket and was not disappointed to find that it was not at all luminous, and of course a failure. However, he thought he would smell of it and see if it would have passed for a cough mixture in odor as well as appearance. What was his surprise, on admitting a little air, in the effort to extract the cork, to have the bottle become a beautiful yellowish luminous shape. Ha! now he could furnish all the lights they wanted without any betraying odor being able to fill the "cabinet'" or escape into the room. He actually exulted over the success of his experiment and was as pleased as though it was an invention for some useful purpose and would win for him fame and fortune.

Really, it has won fame of a certain kind, and money enough to travel and live comfortably upon. But he did not yet know of the possibilities of his "cough medicine," and in the course of a few months had discovered a way in which to produce a great deal of interesting phenomena with its aid that was new to most Spiritualists. Try it, reader—you will be astonished at the results you can obtain from a bottle of this "cough mixture," a white handkerchief and a dark room. More concerning it presently. After having been tied in several different ways and easily freeing his right hand and replacing it again so as to present the appearance of not having been removed or tampered with, the "medium" began to have a pretty good opinion of his abilities to deceive, and a feeling of pride in his deceitful work took possession of him. By this time it had become noised about the city that some wonderful "manifestations" were occurring through him under "test" conditions, and many persons were clamoring for admission to the "circles." It was denied them on the ground that to admit strange "magnetisms" at this juncture would have a tendency to retard the progress in "development." So many of them importuned so lustily and incessantly that it was finally agreed that the "sitters" would ask Mr. King, the "control," and be guided by what he said. Accordingly, at the next "sitting" Mr. King was approached on the subject with the following question:

"Mr. King, do you favor the admittance to our "circle" of persons other than the regular members thereof?"

"The medium" being anxious to see what would be said of the "manifestations" by others than his "developing sitters" caused Mr. King to reply that they could admit four at the next "sitting," two ladies and two gentlemen. They were to sit by themselves, in a row back of the regular "sitters." One of the strangers would be permitted to do the tying. One of the ladies then asked Mr. King if he did not think it would be the fair thing to charge them an admittance of twenty-five cents for wear and tear on the carpets. Mr. King, after thinking a few moments, said he thought that would be about right. The "medium" knew his "manifestations" did not compare at all with those he had witnessed, but that they were worth one-eight what was asked for the better ones, besides, since burying his conscience, he was of the opinion some one, other than himself, should pay the funeral expenses. The night arrived and with it the four persons privileged to attend. They were Spiritualists, all of them, but exercised the privilege granted of making an examination of the "cabinet." As the "medium" did not invite an investigation of his pockets, none was made. A twenty-five cent "medium" could not be expected to submit to such indignities and reflections on his uprightness. The hour for the "seance" to open arrived and the "medium" seated himself with the ropes in his lap in front of the curtains. One of the regular "sitters" assumed the management of the "seance" and announced that either of the gentlemen strangers would be permitted to bind the "medium" in any manner he chose. After some hesitancy and protestations that neither of them cared whether the "medium" was tied or not, one of them came forward and undertook to make him fast. The "medium" had learned a thing or two about this time about stealing some of the slack of the rope for future use, while being tied. By sitting well forward on his chair when the ends of the rope were made fast to the back rung, he could, by sliding back in his seat afterward have the use of as much slack rope as any ordinary, unselfish "medium" could wish. The coat falls close up to the back of the chair, thus hiding a move of that kind. When the wrists have been tied and are being drawn down to the knees, to the chair-legs or together at the back, one twist of the hand, and, consequently the two ends of the rope, and by a reverse twist, when the time arrives, you have all the slack you need, or you should go out of the business. There is never any occasion to free but one hand. It will astonish you to know what a number of things you can accomplish with one hand, your mouth and elbow. If you fail to get in the twist do not allow it to disconcert you, and result in your being helplessly tied. But, if they proceed to tie your hands to your knees, sit up straight, thus compelling them to tie around the fleshy part of the leg. All you have to do to obtain the coveted slack is to lean forward and force your hands toward your knees where the leg is much smaller and the slack is yours to command. If they proceed to tie your hands to either the front or back legs of the chair and you do not have an opportunity to twist on them, without their observing, which sometimes happens, sit very erect and shorten your arms by not allowing them to entirely straighten and by elevating your shoulders as in shrugging, thus making the distance from the point on your wrist where the rope is tied to the top-most rung about four inches. It will always be their endeavor to tie below the top rung around the leg. By slipping down in your seat you ought to have all the slack you could possibly make use of. If they are tying behind you, turn the inside edges of your hands together, and when they make the ends fast to the bottom rung, or any point below the hands, sit up straight, drawing the hands up just far enough to avoid it being observed, and there will be plenty of slack. You can, by reversing the tactics used to free yourself, get back and leave every rope taut and drawing by giving an extra twist to the ropes where they pass around the wrists. Never furnish a soft, cotton rope or you are a "goner" except your hands will permit of your drawing them out of any loop as large as your wrist. Even if you succeed in doing that you cannot possibly get back again. The fact of the matter is, if you practice a few weeks, it will be an exceedingly difficult matter to tie you so that you cannot readily get out. More on this subject later on. As a matter of course, there are very few experts at tying and the gentleman who tied the "medium" on this particular evening was no exception to the rule, and before he had finished his undertaking to his satisfaction, the "medium" was as good as free. Before he reached his seat the tea-bell was violently ringing and the guitar sounding. Now a hand was thrust out at the opening and the fingers snapped. The trumpet was thrust out and an unintelligible sound made through it. One of the gentlemen strangers mistook the sound to be the word William and exclaimed.

"William, is that really you come to see your old father?"

"Yes, replied the horn, and the old gentleman stated it was the first time he had been able to get his son's name through a "medium."

Once more the "medium" made a noise through the horn that could be mistaken for Charles or Clarence or almost any name beginning with C, and again was it recognized as a son, this time of one of the lady strangers. She mistook the sound to be Clarence. The horn was dropped, and a communication written from Clarence to his mother. It proved satisfactory, and the "medium" concluded that was "tests" enough for the initial "seance." An examination was now made of the condition of things in the "cabinet," and the gentleman who did the tying stated that he was positive the ropes were in precisely the shape he had left them. Mr. King now requested that the room be made dark, as they desired to illuminate their hands. The lights were turned down and a screen put between it and the "cabinet." The "medium" brought forth his "cough medicine," and, after wrapping his handkerchief about it to conceal the shape of the bottle, gave it a dash up and down the front of the "cabinet." This light was different from the former ones, being the size of a man's fist, while the first ones had been only small specks. The lights were the hit of the "seance," and drew forth many expressions of wonder and delight. Especially were the regular "sitters" delighted. After showing the light three or four times, always in motion, he loosened up the handkerchief, making it stand away from the bottle on all sides, thus producing a light about the size of a human head. This he slowly pushed through the opening in the "cabinet" and allowed it to stop a few seconds and then he drew it back and put it away. The "sitters" now claimed that the last light was a human head and face, the features being distinguishable. It was set down as a case of etherialization, as they declared they could look right through it, and see the curtains behind it. One gentleman, a doctor, declared he could see the whole convolutions of the brain. Thus they helped out the show with their imaginations and made a reputation for the "medium." Another examination was made of the ropes and all pronounced satisfactory, another song, the "medium" is untied and the "seance" is at an end. Many were the congratulations received by the "medium" over the progress made and the wonderful "manifestations" just received. The strangers paid their admission fee and expressed themselves as well pleased that so wonderful a "medium" was being developed right there in the city, and they should not have to depend upon the traveling "mediums" when they wanted communication with their friends. After his visitors had departed, the "medium" took the dollar from his pocket and wondered what he should do with it. He had made up his mind, now, to become a professional "medium," and concluded he would keep it for the purchase of articles he would require in his business. Since his "sitters" had mistaken his handkerchief for a human face, he had an idea that he could provide something that would not require so much of the imagination to make it appear a face, and to that use was put the dollar received at his first public "seance." Repairing to a toy and novelty house he purchased one of those wire gauze masks, which would permit a light to shine through it. This he trimmed down until it could be put into the breast pocket, and yet enough remained to make quite a good spirit face. By putting this mask in front of the luminous handkerchief a luminous face and head was presented. It was bald of course, until he discovered that with a small piece of black cloth he could put hair on the gentleman. That wire mask has been recognized by dozens of persons as fathers, mothers, sisters, brothers, cousins, sweethearts, wives, husbands and various other relatives and friends. None but the "medium" knew that it was only a fifty-cent wire mask, hence none but the "medium" could enjoy the humor of the occasion. His fame rapidly spread, now, and the people became even more clamorous than before to get in. His first "sitters" had gone away and told wonderful stories of the strange phenomena they had witnessed at the "seance," and it went from one to another until it appeared the whole city knew of it and wanted to witness it for themselves. The "medium" concluded that now was the time to make it pay in that particular city if he ever intended to attempt it. Accordingly Mr. King was made to say that he would admit eight persons in future, and that the fee for admission should be fifty cents. He would also advise holding an additional "seance" on Thursday evening, each week. He also selected one of the regular "sitters" as master of ceremonies, who was to have charge of the "seances," without other recompense than the glory he could get out of the position. He was much pleased at the confidence manifested in his ability, and all that kind of thing, and accepted the position. Our "medium" was now in the business for what there was in it, in a financial way, and for several months he had all he could do. By that time, not having been detected at his tricks, he was fully persuaded to undertake his "mediumship" as his profession and make his living with it. Articles had appeared at different times in the various Spiritualistic journals from the pens of those who had attended his "seances," descriptive of what occurred and the "conditions" under which the "seances" were held, and, the "medium" was in receipt of a number of letters, the writers of which were desirous of engaging his services as a "medium" in their respective towns. He gave up his position, had some cards printed and set out on his career of travel and adventure. He has been continuously on the road ever since that day, stopping nowhere more than a few days at a time, and having never as yet figured in an expose. To be sure his "seances" are much different to what they were when he started out, they improving each time he sat. He met many "mediums" the first year and from each one gained the admission that they were frauds. They would also tell him who to look out for in the towns from which they had just come. His "manifestations" were pronounced "out of sight" by every "medium" who ever witnessed them, and many were the entreaties to tell them how it was done. He would not reveal the simplicity of his operations, however, as he did not want any opposition in his particular line, and having the reputation, now, of being one of the finest "physical mediums" in the country, did not care to have to share it with any one. He made it a point to learn all possible from the "mediums" which he met, but to give up nothing himself but what they already knew. By following up this plan, of taking all the information possible and at the same time keeping a still tongue, he came to know the methods pursued by a great many "mediums" which was of much use to him in his own work. He will say, just here, that of all the "mediums" he has met, in eighteen years, and that means a great many, in all phases, he has never met one that was not sailing the very same description of craft as himself. Every one; no exception. Of course, the lecturers he has met, who do not lecture under "influence," and who have no phase of "mediumship," are probably honest in what they teach. They are not different to any other convert to Spiritualism who does not lecture. There may have been a few of the "inspirational speakers," too, who were honestly mistaken as to the inspiration. It is a fact that he has "developed" inspirational speakers, for a financial consideration, who have taken to the platform, and who believed themselves inspired. It is true too, that in some cases he was not very proud of the quality of inspiration he had developed. He was proud of no part of it, save the financial consideration which reposed in his wallet. Reader, if you become a "medium," be very careful to give the female professional "mediums" a wide berth, and no possible knowledge of the methods of your work. They are universally selfish and jealous, and will leave no stone unturned to do you an injury. When you meet a female professional who is a lecturer and "test medium," and who has a hall rented in which she gives her alleged "tests" and the harangue in poor English, that she dubs a lecture, and advertises herself and her clairvoyant powers in her "test and business sittings" at her home, look out for her. She is as rank a fraud as you can possibly be, but is jealous of your powers to obtain "physical manifestations," and although she may not say anything against you in public, be sure that every individual she meets will have a "bug in his or her ear" concerning the genuineness of your "manifestations." Her "tests" usually are very rank, and all resemble the "tests" given by a married professional in a northern city, whose reputation was anything but savory, and whose "tests" ran something like the following:

"To the gentleman sitting there," indicating the individual she referred to by pointing to him, "there comes a condition of prosperity. I see that his business will be prosperous in the future, and he will not meet with certain unpleasant conditions that are troubling him. Now I see a white dove that circles about his head and now it has alighted on your shoulder, indicating a condition of peace for you. I see that a change in business will be the cause of

your prosperity, and that change will be in—
But, if you desire to know more about it, you must come to my rooms, as there is so much of it that I can not take the time in my public meetings."

If he goes it will cost him one dollar and that is the purpose of the hall meetings. This same woman is supposed to be "controlled" by one of the ancient sun worshippers, and while under his control she is supposed to be fire-proof. Anything she holds in her hands is supposed to be fire-proof also. She handles heated lamp chimneys in her bare hands, holds her fingers in the blaze of a lamp for a few seconds, passes her little son's hair through the blaze, also a handkerchief, and borrows a gentleman's neck tie, which also withstands the ordeal. During this performance, she throws back her head, rolls her eyes upward until only the whites are visible, and contorts herself in various other ways, besides giving tongue to some outlandish gibberish, supposed, and claimed to be, the language of the aforementioned sun worshipper in his adoration of the sun. I will wager, that if a sun worshipper should happen to hear the lingo she claims as bis language, he would never again open his mouth and give utterance to an audible sound

In order to duplicate this woman's performance prepare the following:

Dissolve one-half ounce of camphor in two ounces of aquavitæ; add one ounce of quicksilver and one ounce of liquid styrax, which is the product of the myrrh, and which prevents the camphor igniting. Shake and mix well together. Bathe the inside of the hand and the fingers in this preparation, allowing it to dry in and you can duplicate the performance with the lamp chimney and hold your fingers in the blaze quite a while without any bad effect. You will also be able to accomplish it without any grimaces or gibberish or rolling of the eyes.

For the remainder of the performance, dissolve all the salt a tea-cup of water will contain. In another cup dissolve a tablespoonful of soda in warm water. Now pour the two together, and after they are well mixed wash the little boy's hair, or that portion you intend using in your experiment as a sun worshipper, combing it until dry. Now take the neck tie of a gentleman friend, and your confederate, and after washing it allow it to dry. You are now ready to accomplish the feat in its entirety, the only other thing needful being to roll your eyes, throw back your head and make sounds that would shame a Siwash Indian, with your voice. You could go the lady one better by adding to the first preparation two ounces of pulverized red stone. After stirring it well together rub the bottoms of your feet with it and you can walk several steps on a bar of red hot iron. Usually, these women have only "clairvoyant" and "trance mediumships," which require no skill of execution, and which, as a matter of course, you cannot expose. You can state that nothing they have said is correct, and that mistakes of magnificent dimensions have been made in what they have told you, but what matters that? They will say that "conditions" were not good, or that you came in a "condition of deception" yourself, and that they only told you what they saw and heard.

They have not the nerve, or what is more probable, are not smart enough to attempt anything in which there is more risk, and decidedly object to anybody else doing it. Female mediums" of the description just mentioned are generally the most depraved in their tastes, and life behind the scenes. Many of them who have had much to say in opposition to the writer, were themselves recking with fraud and morally rotten from center to circumference, and if any of them discover the identity of the writer and want him to specify, he will do so in another book, in which names will be given, and most of the scenes laid in San Francisco, and the cities on the railway lines between that city and the Eastern States. The writer has not, up to date, met a female "medium he would trust, nor has he yet met one who was not as fraudulent as himself. There are a few who are lecturing and giving "platform tests" who attend their own business and are laying up something for a rainy day. But none of them give the satisfaction that the male "mediums" give, in the same line, for the very reason that they cannot be entrusted with anything, and are continually wondering how *Mr.* so-and-so, manages to give so many positive and undeniable "tests"—full names, dates, incidents and places, instead of doves, "conditions of prosperity" and symbols; being able to dispense with psychometric handkerchief readings and to give tests that are counted as such.

Be wary, I say, of the female, professional, "medium." She is as full of deceit as you are, but has not the good business sense that ought to keep her mouth shut when her jealousy is aroused. She will lay herself open to suspicion in order to excite a feeling against you. Not so among the boys. If they have a grievance they punch each other's noses, but do not go and give away any professional secrets, thus lessening their opportunities for getting a livelihood, easily and comfortably.

The writer's "seances" had, by this time, grown to be quite wonderful exhibitions, and attracted much attention and comment wherever he gave them. To be sure the newspapers cried trickery and humbug, but forgot to explain how he accomplished it, hence they only made more business for the "medium," the people visiting his seances to verify, if possible, the newspaper statement that it was all a trick. The part of the "seance" that puzzled the "sitters" most was a new idea the "medium" had worked up. It was like this.

After he had finished the work in the "cabinet" and had untied himself, he would come outside, and, seating himself to one side, the left, of the middle, with his back up close to the curtain, he would request that two of the audience sit with him. This would make three persons, sitting in a row, with their backs against the curtains forming the "cabinet" front, the "medium" being at the left hand end of the row. He would now allow the middle man to take his left hand in his left, while he would take firm hold of the "sitters"

left arm above his elbow, with the right hand
He would have the "sitter" at the opposite end
place and dispose himself similarly. It will be
seen that as they now sat the middle "sitter"
would know if either of the others made a
movement of any kind. After getting in this
position in the sight of the audience and
instructing the middle "sitter" to report if either
of the others moved, the "medium" would
have a curtain drawn across the front and
pinned to the "cabinet" behind thus hiding all
of the three sitting there with the exception of
their heads. The man in the middle held both
the other "sitters" and was requested to report
if either of them let go or moved. "Manifestations" would now occur in the "cabinet" back
of the "sitters." Tunes would be played upon
the guitar, the tambourine, tea-bell and other
instruments would fly about the "cabinet" as
though possessed of life. Hands would appear
at the aperture between the curtains and also
over the top of the "cabinet" which was six
feet high. Those sitting next the "cabinet"
would be patted on the back and their hair
and ears pulled by a hand through the curtain.

The middle man, on being asked would
invariably reply that the "medium" had not
stirred, and that he still had both his hands.

Many would say that the "medium" might produce the "manifestations" while he was alone in the "cabinet" but it was an impossibility that he caused the "manifestations" while being held on the outside. Certainly, that appeared to be the facts in the case, but the righthand of of the "medium" did all the work nevertheless. How did he get it away without the gentleman knowing it, Easy enough.

You will remember that they took their positions in view of the audience and are not supposed to have moved until the close of the "seance" and the taking down of the curtain. But they *have,* just *once.* While the curtain was being pinned, the "medium" let go the gentleman's arm to indicate to the person putting up the curtain where to put a pin. His hand was away only an instant. The gentleman knew when he took it away also when it was returned again. But, when it was returned it contained a thin piece of sheet lead, cut about the size of the "medium's" hand. When the "mediums" hand closed on the gentleman's arm, the lead was inside it and as his fingers closed it was bent around his arm giving the impression of the grip of a hand. You can see, now, how easily the "medium," could have the entire use of his right hand and yet have the sitter declare that his hand had not moved.

As this "medium" had not yet arrived at that state of perfection in which he could allow himself to be searched, he went into his pocket for a small article resembling a lead pencil, but when rightly manipulated transformed itself into a tapering steel rod about four feet in length, with a small hook and a slot in the end. Into the slot he slips a pasteboard hand that he has also fished from a convenient pocket, and the next you know it is visible just over the top of the "cabinet," where, as the astonished spectators admit, the "medium" could not reach, even were he free. Next a hand is seen at the aperture and the fingers move and are filliped. The fingers of the hand seen at the top of the "cabinet" did not move nor were not filliped, but the last hand did, and if asked about it afterward ninety-nine times in a hundred either one of the "sitters" will declare that the fingers were moved and snapped in each case.

There *is* a way to make the fingers on a painted, pasteboard hand appear to spread out sideways and close again. To accomplish this, paint on a piece of cardboard an open hand with the fingers spread out. Do not cut out on the outline of the hand, but fill in between the fingers with black, just trimming off the card that is in excess of the width or length of the hand. Now turn the card over and proceed to paint the same sized hand with the exception that the fingers are not spread apart. Paint all the card remaining, black. Now, put it into the slit of your reaching rod, and by quickly turning first one side, then the other to your audience, in the dim light, it presents the appearance of one open hand with the fingers spreading and closing. By the same means you can make a hand appear to be opening and closing.

It is the same principle that causes a series of drawings in different positions in the act of climbing a ladder, appear to be *one* image, going through all the motions and actually climbing the ladder, when seen through a narrow slit, and in rapid succession.

After putting the pasteboard hand into view in different places distant from himself and snapping the fingers of his own hand, thus giving the impression that the fingers of the pasteboard hand were snapped, he hooked the bell to the end of the rod and it was rung and shown in distant parts of the "cabinet." After closing the rod and concealing it as well as the hand, he proceeds to shake up the guitar, tambourine and bell, to present the hand in different positions giving the impression of different sizes of hands. It is wonderful what a number of "manifestations" you can produce with one hand and not disclose your connection with it by a perceptible movement of head or body.

If you think these are only *theories* of one who never made use of the ideas, try them and see how beautifully they will work, and the amount of astonishment they will create among your friends.

The "medium" now requested some one to hold a slate up to the front of the "cabinet." On its being held as directed, a hand appears from the "cabinet" and writes "Good Night."

This ends the "seance," and after the curtain is taken down disclosing the "medium's" hand just where it had been when he sat down, and the gentleman states positively that it has not been removed during the "seance," the "medium" removes hand and lead, palming the lead, and, reaching into his side coat pocket drops it, brings out his handkerchief, innocently mops his brow, replaces the kerchief, and it is done.

There are no really smooth, expert and finished female "mediums" for "physical manifestations," notwithstanding the fact that they are eminently fitted to carry a great many articles about them without discovery, in their clothing or hair. They are universally hunglers, which accounts for so many exposes. It is not the male "medium" who has his "materialization" exposed, one time in a hundred.

The sharpest, quickest and most expert female "materializing medium" the writer ever met is a resident on the Pacific coast, not at this time in the business. She did her work without the aid of a confederate, and work good enough to fool everybody who visited her "seances." People were there who could not believe it was the work of spirits but who could not offer any other solution.

It was during the third year of the writer's travels that he became a member of an organization of "mediums" that discovered to him the manner in which the first "medium" visited by him came by the information he possessed regarding the writer and the writer's family. It was made clear to him, how, without any mind-reading powers, he could probably have given a "test" to every spiritualist or investigator in the city who had ever received a "test" prior to his visit to the city.

The writer was asked how he was fixed for

"tests," and had to admit he had none that he had kept track of. Well, the organization was for the purpose of keeping each other posted on "tests" in the territory in which we traveled.

The writer was not long in discovering that it was an excellent organization to belong to. He was supplied with all the "tests" known by from one to twenty "mediums" who had done the territory he intended covering, and was expected to make notes of any new "tests" he should discover.

You can see, reader, what an impression a "medium" so prepared could make in Cincinnati. He would have, say, five hundred tests for Spiritualists and frequenters of "seances" in a city of that size, and could give three or four to a dozen wonderfully accurate "tests" each night so long as he remained. Here is what a page of those note books look like:

FOR CINCINNATI, OHIO.

G. A. WILSON, (Merchant).

Spt. Dau. Elsie—Died '76, age 14 mos. diphtheria, blonde, blue eyes.

Spt. Moth. Elenor Wilson—Died '67, consumption, age 56, dark.

Spt. Fath. Nathan E. Wilson—Died '71, pneumonia, age 64, light.

Spt. Friend. Andy Nugent, schoolmates at Oberlin, O.

SPIRITUALISTIC MYSTERIES EXPOSED. 109

S. O. WILBUR, Shoe Dealer.

Spt. Son. Albert E., '74, lung fever, 19 years, blonde, only child. His parents keep his books and clothing. He is always described as a student, with book in hand. Good mark for private sittings.

R. B YOUNG, rich.

Spt. Dau. Alice E., aged 19, pneumonia, '79, upper front teeth gold filled. Extraordinarily long hair. Quite an artist, and one of her landscapes hangs in parlor in gilt and plush frame. Spirit painting of her in the sitting-room, that is kept curtained. She is an artist in spirit world. Supposed to have a son in spirit that had no earth life named Egbert O.

Spt. Son. Egbert O. never had earth existence, an inventor in spirit life and supposed to work through Thos. Edison. Is especially interested in electrical work.

Spt. Fath. Robert B., Died '69, paralysis. Manufacturer of machinery, two fingers off left hand.

Spt. Moth. Sarah—Died when he was a child.

Spt. Broth. James and Samuel.

Spt. Aunt. Lucy Wilkinson, Mary Wilkinson and Eliza Shandrow.

Remarks—A good mark for private seances at his home, and will pay well. Dead gone on physical manifestations and materialization. Will get up lots of seances. Agree with everything he says and you are all right.

A. T. YOUNGER.

Spt. Son. Albert F., drowned under suspension bridge, May, '87. Sends message of greeting to Aunt Mary and Cousin Harry.

Spt. Fath. A. O. Younger, died '84, railroad accident in Illinois. Is looking for private papers supposed to have been left by him. Sends love to his wife Kate in Covington.

There, reader, is one page out of sixty-three similar ones all relating to Cincinnati Spiritualists and investigators.

Could you not go to Mr. Young, having arrived direct from Denver or the Pacific coast, and never having previously visited Cincinnati, and astonish the gentleman as to your knowledge of his family and affairs? Would it not be possible to give him a number of absolute pointed tests?"

Suppose you were giving a "seance," and should put out a face. Nobody recognizes it. Mr. Young is in the audience. All that is necessary to have a grand "test" out of the unrecognized face is to cause it to announce in a loud, labored whisper the name "Egbert O. Young. My father, R. B. Young, is present."

If, as is sometimes the case, Mr. Young desires to make a still stronger "test" he is likely to ask:

"How old were you when you passed over?"

The spirit now replies, "I had no existence on the earth plane."

"What are you engaged in on your side," continues Mr. Young.

"I am still working on electrical problems through Mr. Edison."

The spirit might now *clinch* the proof of its identity by saying:

"Grandfather Robert B. Young, and great aunt Lucy Wilkinson are with me to-night. Uncle James Young has something of importance to say to you at first opportunity."

It may be that Mr. Young has heard nothing of the spirit Egbert for a year or a greater length of time. and on your causing him to "manifest his presence," it being the first time you have met Mr. Young, and your first visit to his city, it is likely to place you high in the esteem of that gentleman.

As he is rich and in the habit of having "private seances" at his home and paying well for them, as you will learn by referring to the Y's in your note book, it is quite desirable that you make an admirer and champion of him. Many will be the twenty dollar "seances" given at his home by yourself, and frequently will you be called upon for slate-writing, if you are doing that "phase" at two dollars per writiog.

If you are a close observer you will manage

to pick up many new "tests." In looking through the family album you will probably find the faces of many of his friends and relatives.

It is your duty to yourself and brother "mediums" to be at all times armed with the twenty-five cent cameras. These cameras are made of paper or pasteboard. In order to obtain a copy of a photograph, pull the two ends as far apart as they will go, which is the proper focus for an object one foot distant. Now place the photo to be copied in position and tear the small square of black paper from the aperture, retaining the end that hung loose. Count fifteen, and stick the piece of black paper over the aperture—it was already mucilaged, all you have to do was lick it—press the ends together, put it in your pocket, and you have a fair copy of the picture.

Copy all the pictures of which you can get the names and relationship. What for? For the money there is in it.

In order to get your money out, you must take them, with their names and relationship to a "spirit photographer," tell him all about it and give him the cameras. He finishes the work you begun by developing the copies and again copying them on his own plates, leaving them undeveloped. Of course he does not copy all of them on one plate, but perhaps one and then four or five other faces, including an Indian or two, that may or may not be recognized.

If they were all copied on one plate, there would be only one "sitting" necessary, and of course, only one five dollar bill in the transaction. As it is there are from one to five plates with one and two faces that can be positively identified. He will take "sittings" as long as faces are produced that he recognizes, and, at times will pay for several after the "medium" operator has ran out of material. It is now the slate-writing medium's play to cause the Spiritualist's spirit friends to declare that they want to furnish him with their spirit photographs, and if he will visit Mr.—— ——, "medium"for that phase, he will get them.

Of course he is delighted with the idea, and is soon in your friend's studio. He sits. The first plate developes two of his spirit friend's faces. He is delighted, but all that promised to appear are not there. Another "sitting" is suggested by the operator, who declares that there are others present who are frantic for an opportunity to be photographed. He sits again. Another face appears that he recognizes, and, more than likely he will sit from four to six times.

If he has fout sittings, at five dollars per sitting, he is indebted to the operator in the sum of twenty dollars. Now, on the next day, you visit the photographer and receive ten dollars as your share of the results of the transaction.

We will presume that the Spiritualist becomes enthusiastic on the subject of "spirit photography" and sends to another "spirit photographer" in a distant city to see what success he will have. He sends his own photo, and the fec. The "medium" applied to writes to the "medium" living in the city and asks if he has anything for Mr.——— Of course he has and forwards them. He gets one-half of the profits of the transaction, and, in the language of the "medium" the Spiritualist is again "nailed to the cross."

Another benefit to the "medium" is a copy, life size of one or more of the faces in water-color, that will answer to present from between the curtains at one of his "seances." It will be recognized as a matter of course, and great will be the wonder and surprise. It is possible to palm off these paper faces in the dim light. When you quit the city, leave them with the photographer for the use of the next brother "physical medium" that stops in the city.

The writer was now "in it" all over. His "seances" were equally as wonderful as the one he had first witnessed. He could now have the instruments floating about in space over the top of the "cabinet" without visible support. He had, also, a guitar that would *play on itself* and was a wonderful instrument in more ways than one. It had, also, the small hole bored in the neck, for the music-holder. It *would* contain a music-holder, but was also useful for other purposes.

He could, without any danger of detection, permit a thorough search of his clothing and person for apparatus that might be accessory to his "manifestations." He could produce "full-forms" with faces that could be recognized beyond doubt by various visitors to his "seances." He could clothe his "spooks" with robes that appeared to have a great number of yards of material used in them, and still no piece of white larger than his handkerchief could be found about him. It had been long since his last lingering doubt, but what there *might* be something in it, had disappeared.

His guitar was an innocent appearing but wonderful affair. It was decorated by dividing the sides into small panels by gluing strips of ornamental molding from top to bottom. The panels thus formed were further decorated by inlaid designs in pearls. One of the panels on the large end of the instrument could be displaced leaving an aperture sufliciently large to comfortably insert the hand an fore-arm. Inside it was arranged for holding various articles, in such a way as to be impossible of discovery except through the defective panel. Besides this the machinery from a small one-tune spring music box had been affixed to the wood forming the top, just under the strings. Wind this up, set it in motion. take your reaching rod and insert it in the hole in the neck of the instrument, raise it into view, slowly turning it round and round and waving it back and forth and you present the strange phenomena of a guitar floating in the air and performing a tune upon itself. It does not sound exactly as though the the music was produced on the strings; but near enough so that the true explanation, or any explanation other than the one the "medium" is supposed to offer has ever been advanced for it.

In this guitar was kept the flowing robes with which the "spooks" were clothed. The robes were of white netting so very fine that enough of it could be compressed into a space no larger than an ordinary tin blacking-box to furnish a full evening suit for the largest spirit. Enough more can be carried in a hollow boot-heel to dress up a couple more with an abundance of clothing. In the other boot-heel can be carried an assortment of netting-masks with which to transform your own face half-a-dozen times. In the envelopes supposed to contain letters you have the water-color faces for completing the forms, when their relatives are in attendance. If the reader is a Spiritualist, who has attended "full-form materialization seances" in New York, Brooklyn, Cincinnati, Chicago, Denver, San Francisco, Los Angeles or New Orleans, he or she will say:

"Oh, pshaw! that don't explain it at all. I have never seen any "materialization" in which the explanation given would answer, in any way. In all the "full form materialization" I have seen, the forms have come out from the "cabinet," walked and talked with the "sitters," and the "medium" could be seen sitting in his chair. I have seen as many as ten "spirit forms" out at one time and of different sexes and sizes. They were not all dressed alike by any means. You can not stuff that down me as an explanation."

118   SPIRITUALISTIC MYSTERIES EXPOSED.

It may be possible that you have not visited the writers' "seances" in years past, but he gave scores of them just as have been described and he is personally aware of several others who gave the same "manifestations," making use of the same apparatus and methods. However, he will come, in due time, to the class of "seance," you *have* seen. He has participated in many a one. Mission St. in San Francisco, at one time harbored some very fine "mediums" for "full materialization." It is possible you have shaken the writer's hand at some of the full-form "seances" you have visited, and called him husband, father, brother, and, possibly sister. Many rich stories could be told by various "mediums," did they dare open their mouths

The apparatus just described is quite costly for the reason that you must go to the manufacturer to have your guitar made. It would be a very simple matter to remove a piece of the guitar so that it can be replaced, but it is entirely another matter to so accomplish it that the instrument will not be ruined as to its musical qualities, and in such a manner as to avoid detection of the defect.

It must be so arranged that the apparatus concealed inside will be immovable and will not rattle, in handling the instrument, thus disclosing the fact that it is "loaded." Seventy-five dollars will pay for an instrument that will be perfection in its way and defy detection under a most critical examination.

The shoemaker, for twenty dollars, will make you a pair of congress gaiters with hollow, steel heels veneered with leather, by raising the insole of which discloses quite a roomy "cellar." Of course these shoes are to be worn only while at work.

The writer has also carried effective apparatus in his elegant gold watch. The watch was without a movement, and a watch only in appearance.

At one time in his career the writer ran afoul of one of nature's sharp newspaper men, in a southern city who proposed to stop all the "horn manifestations" given during one of his "seances." He did not succeed in it, but tried to the best of his ability.

In order to stop the voice through the horn, he brought one of *his own*, and after the "medium" was tied, he produced a flask of wine and had the "medium" fill his mouth. After the "manifestations" on the horn, if any occurred he was to spit out the wine, thus showing conclusively that the "medium's" voice was not the one heard.

Here is the means by which the "medium" beat the reporter's game. Freeing his hand, he obtained possession of the tea-bell. Turning it upside down, he emptied the wine into it and held it between his knees. It is needless to say that the horn put in its "best licks," and in addition a quick tune was performed on a mouth-organ. The wine again taken into the mouth and spit out in the presence of the "sitters," including the reporter.

His "conditions" would not hold, and he went away wondering what *did* do the talking through the trumpet, anyway.

The writer, after some three years of "physical seances," concluded that the phase of "independent slate-writing" would be an additional source of revenue that would possibly be easily worked. He proceeded to investigate and soon he was "in the swim." He did not confine himself to any one method; but in the course of time came to make use of a great many systems of obtaining it. The most successful for a long time was obtained through the use of acid. He will give the explanation, and you can try it, yourself.

Procure one ounce of muriatic acid and into it drop about one-half ounce of pure zinc shavings. When the zinc has been dissolved, write your communication upon a slate with a gold or quill pen. When it dries it will resemble writing done with a pencil. Once the writing is on the slate there is no such thing as getting it off.

When your "sitter" comes, wash the slate containing the writing and it appears a perfectly clean slate. Allow your "sitter" to examine it then hold it with one hand under the top of a kitchen table, keeping the hand in view. When the slate has dried, take it out and hand it to your "sitter," who will be pleased with the beautiful, even writing thereon, and astonished that the full name of one or more of his relatives or friends are inscribed thereon.

In order to give these "tests," you must prepare in advance of the coming of the "sitter." This is easy enough as you have your "sitters" make an engagement on their first visit. Look at your note-book and see what you have in the way of "tests" and names on the gentleman or lady, and prepare your slate accordingly. If you have nothing, visit any other "medium" or "mediums" in the city and perhaps they can fix you. If not, write for him in one of the different ways that will be described or dismiss him by saying his friends cannot make use of your organism and refer him to other "mediums."

Another way is to make use of a silicate flap. To prepare for this method procure a silicate slate, and a pair of ordinary slates four by six inches inside the frames. Cut, from the silicate a piece that will fit snugly inside the frame of one of the slates. Paste on one side of the silicate flap a piece of newspaper.

In operating with this apparatus, you write your communication on the side of the ordinary slate that the flap fits. Now place the flap in position with the papered side next the writing. Have a newspaper lying on your table. Pick up the prepared slate and wash first the flap and then the opposite side of the slate. Now lay it down on the newspaper, the flap side down, and proceed to wash both sides of the remaining slate. As soon as you have finished, pick up the first slate, being careful that you leave the flap lying on the newspaper. As the papered side is uppermost, one can stand quite close and not observe it. Now put the two slates together, writing inside, and request your "sitter" to assist in holding it. When you see fit, allow the "sitter" to take the slates and open them. While he is reading them carelessly fold up the paper and put it safely out of harm's way.

Another system is to exchange a clean slate

for one that is written upon. The apparatus consists solely of a chair with a wooden seat, underneath which has been fastened two pieces of grooved wood, such as is used for sliding tills and small drawers. These pieces have two grooves, into the bottom one has been placed the prepared slate.

In operating this system the "sitter" is given a seat on one side of a small square table. The "medium" takes a seat on the opposite side. Both "sitter" and "medium" are sitting with their sides next the table, the "sitter's" left and the "medium's" right side. The "medium" now takes the clean slate in his right hand and thrusts it under the table. There is a cover on the table that falls about a foot below the edge. The "medium" now engages in conversation with his "sitter" and carefully slips the clean slate in the upper groove and pulls out the prepared one. After sitting a sufficiently long time he withdraws the prepared slate and delivers it to his "sitter."

This, and other change acts is the system principally used in getting "variegated writings" or writings that are written with different colored crayons. Female "mediums" have convenient pockets in their skirts for effecting the change of slates.

Another feat that is astonishing and convincing is accomplished with two clean slates. They are thoroughly cleaned and laid side by side upon a table, on one side of which sits the "sitter" and opposite him the "medium." The "sitter is now furnished with a small square of soft white paper and requested to write the name of some deceased friend or relative and with it a question. This being done he is requested to fold it up small, similar to the physician's powder papers. The "medium" has a blank one, folded in the same way and palmed between the index and middle finger of the right hand. When the "sitter" has folded his pellet, the "medium" reaches forth his right hand and takes it between the thumb and index finger and carries it to his forehead. While raising the hand to the head, he slips the written pellet down and the blank one in view. After holding it to his forehead a few seconds he requests the "sitter" to take it and hold it against his own forehead for a moment. Of course the "sitter gets the blank pellet and the 'medium's" hand drops to his lap. He now opens the pellet and reads it. We will say it reads—

"John Smith. Will my business succeed? George."

Having read it and palmed it again, he now requests to hold the pellet to his forehead again. He effects the change and says to the sitter:

"You now hold the pellet in your left hand and I will write the answer."

This time the "sitter" has the pellet he wrote and holds it while the "medium" takes up a slate and leaning well back holds the slate with his left hand and body and writes with the right hand in such a position that the "sitter" can not see the writing. He writes:

"Dear George: Your business is sure to succeed beyond your expectations. John Smith."

He now states to the "sitter" that he does not feel at all sure that he has written the correct answer, and reads aloud:

"The papers will never be found. Harry White."

Of course it is *not* an answer to the question and the "sitter" so states. The "medium" requests that he open the pellet and see if it is plainly written with no omission of words.

While he is doing so the slate is deftly turned the other side up. When the "sitter" reports that the question is properly and plainly written, the "medium" *apparently* rubs off the line of writing and lays the slate on the table, writing underneath. He now announces that he will let the spirits do their own writing, and putting the other slate on top of the one containing the writing lays his hands on top of the slate a few seconds when he opens them, and of course there is no writing.

He now states that he does not believe he can get anything——but, wait, he says, we will put the pellet inside——*that* may help them.

The pellet is placed on the blank slate and the one containing the writing laid on top. Now the writing is between the slates. In picking up the two slates together, he turns them over, and the writing is on the bottom slate. He now allows the "sitter" to hold the slates alone, and indicates when to open them. They are opened, and much astonishment created by the pointed answer to the question inside the pellet.

Another method that appears very wonderful is to produce writing between slates that are locked together. It is usually accomplished by placing a marked sheet of blank paper between the slates and the writing occurs on the paper, after the slate has been locked shut.

The slates are prepared by getting two of the same size. Around the frame of each slate nail a strip of wood one-half-inch thick and three-quarters-of an inch wide, so that when they are placed together there will be a space between the slates of about an inch-and-a-half. Now precure a three-quarter-inch draw lock and staple. The lock is fastened to one of the slates and the staple to the other. You can put on the lock, but the staple must first be "doctored."

"Doctor it by filing the staple until it will come out of the flat piece of iron it was fastened in. Save the piece it came out of and solder a piece of soft iron to the shank of the staple, about one-half an inch in length. This will make the shank about five eighths of an inch long. Taper the point of the shank so that it will readily enter a mortise prepared for it. Now drill a hole large enough to accommodate a half-inch escutcheon pin, about three-sixteenths of an inch from the point of the shank. Now take the flat piece of iron from which you took the staple and be sure that the shank will go through easily but *fit snugly*. Cut a mortise for the flat piece of iron in the frame opposite the lock. Screw it down and so mutilate the screw heads that they cannot be taken out again, for should the investigator take off that bit of iron he would immediately see through the whole business. You will now bore a hole in the frame through the hole in the flat piece of iron you have screwed to the frame, large enough to accommodate the shank of the staple. You will find, when the shank is pushed into the hole until the staple comes snug up against the flat piece of iron, supposed to hold it in place, that it appears an ordinary staple, fastened in the ordinary way. Now that you have made the staple fit properly, you will bore a hole from the ends of the piece containing the staple to and in a line with the hole in the shank of the staple. The diameter of this hole must be the same as the one in the shank. The corners of the slate are to be strapped with thin sheet brass nailed in place with half-inch brass escutcheon pins. Take one of the pins and solder to the end of it a piece of brass wire of the same diameter as the pin, thus making it long enough to reach through the frame from the corner and through the hole in the shank of the staple. Put the hinges on your slate and lock it. *You* can now open the slate by forcing the thumb nail under the head of the pin at the corner and drawing it out until it frees the shank of the staple. *Others* will find it necessary to first unlock it. This description of slate will admit of a most

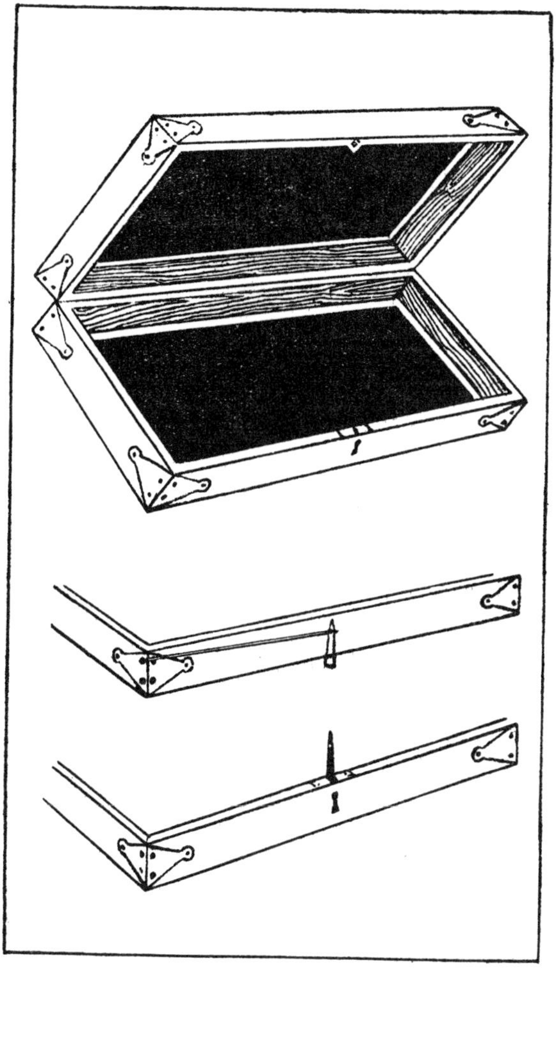

critical examination at the hands of the scientific or professional exposer.

The writer has a sentiment of deep disgust for the scientific, the reverend and the newspaper exposers. The scientist may be versed in certain lines of scientific subjects, but their knowledge in those lines will not be of service to them in their investigation of the "medium."

In what way is the chemist better fitted to discover the defect in the slate just described than the ordinary clerk or day laborer?

The writer has a double slate of the style just described, and it has passed scores of critical examinations at the hands of scientific and other investigators, and came through them all with its secret undiscovered.

The slate just described is suitable for private "sittings," where you have made an appointment with your "sitter" previous to his visit for obtaining a communication. Its greatest value, however, lies in its peculiar fitness for public work. A description of the methods pursued in its employment in public Spiritualistic meetings for the purpose of advertising the "medium's" powers will be interesting.

After the regular services the "medium" announces that he will now give the audience an exhibition of his "independent slate-writing" powers He produces his double slate and passes it to the audience for their inspection. After a thorough examination has been made one of the audience is invited on the rostrum to assist and keep both eyes open for fraud

After the investigator has been seated, the "medium" produces a pencil tablet about four by six inches in size. He tears off a leaf, and tearing an irregular shaped piece from the corner hands the sheet to the investigator that he may satisfy himself that it is a clean sheet and perfectly clear of writing.

After the investigator has satisfied himself that the paper is clean, he is instructed by the "medium" to fold it, place it in the slate and lock it, keeping the key. This he does, besides stuffing the key-hole full of paper and sealing it over with letter wax. He is now handed the piece torn from the corner of the sheet, which he holds for the purpose of identifying the paper or demonstrating that it is the same sheet he put inside the slates.

The "medium" now takes the slates between his open hands and holds them out in front of him, and a curtain is thrown over both hands and slates. After standing thus a moment or two, he instructs the investigator to take the slates and open them.

He complies, and is astonished to find the sheet written full on both sides.

It is possible, and more than probable, that the communication will be signed by some one well known to several of the persons in the hall, or it may contain a message to some particular one of the audience, in which from one to a dozen positive undeniable "tests" are given.

To the investigator and the company assembled this is a very wonderful feat. Admitting that the "medium" could open the slate otherwise than through the lock, how would it be possible that he write the communication standing in full view of the audience and without a perceptible movement of hands or arms. More puzzling still is the "tests" given, and the full name of the spirit signed. The "medium" is careful to cause the recipient of the message to admit the truth of the statements made, the correctness of the signature and the relationship claimed. He also draws from him the admission that he has at no time in the past met the "medium" or had any communication through him, from any spirit friend or relative.

These being facts the "medium's" performance is certainly wonderful. The skeptic will probably say:

"Oh; that's easy enough. He exchanged the sheet of paper for a prepared sheet; or the sheet was prepared with chemical writing that was developed after placing it inside the slate."

How about the "tests?" How did the "medium" know that the one receiving the communication would be in attendance? How does he know all about his spirit friends when he has never before met the gentleman? Those are the questions that puzzle the "skeptic."

He may satisfy himself with the thought that the recipient of the message was a confederate, and will probably continue to flatter himself that that is the correct solution of the matter until he receives the same experience himself, when he will be forced to drop the confederate theory. If he becomes a regular attendant at the meetings he is sure to get a similar dose of "skeptical antidote."

It is just such persons that the "medium" labors to convert, and once they undertake it, you may be sure there will be some fine "tests" given him, and no stone left unturned to bring him into the fold. Especially will this be the case if he be rich or has a good business. The more difficult it is to convert a man the stronger will be his faith in Spiritualism

As to the medium's having exchanged the sheet for a prepared one, that is an impossibility since the investigator held the piece torn from the corner, and when the writing was taken from the slate the piece he held fitted exactly, thus proving conclusively that no exchange had been made. You must admit that the "medium's" work was wonderful, but wonderful as it appeared it was, in reality, very simple.

His result was attained through an exchange of sheets of paper. You will probably say:

"Why, certainly. I *knew* that."

But *did* you *know* it? I think not. You may have *thought* so, but did not *know* it. *Knowing* would imply your ability to explain it, and, after fitting the torn corner to the sheet you would be at a loss to account for the exchange. Scores of persons have felt sure they knew the means by which the writer produced his "manifestations" but on attempting to put their theories into actual use they found they could not make them work.

An explanation is now in order, and after reading it you will be able to tell the "medium" how he effects the change of sheets.

Here is the way the medium does it. On his arrival in town he gets out his note-book. On one of its pages he finds the following:

JOHN CORDRAY (Publisher).

Medium size—wears black clothing always—silk hat—dark complexion—brown eyes and hair—index finger off left hand at first joint and middle finger of same hand is rigid. Skeptical but inclined to believe —Solitaire diamond ring on right hand.

Spt. Fath. John W. Cordray. Died in Baltimore, '67, bilious fever. Manufacturing chemist. Age 54 at death. Gave his son John his diamond ring and his brother Charles his watch and chain. They are wearing them. Charles lives in St. Louis and is in the drug business.

Spt. Moth. Mary J. Cordray. Died in Cincinnati, '74. Was living with John. Aged 66. Had been blonde.

Spt. Dau. Mary——Died '87. Croup—three years of age—blonde.

Remarks—Has a son living four years of age. His wife affected with rheumatism. Mediums all tell him he will make a materializing "medium."

Our "medium" now sits down and writes the following message:

"My dear son, John: It is with great pleasure that I meet you at this place this evening. Continue your investigations of this philosophy and you will find the truth. We *can* and *do* return to earth and visit the loved ones we left on the earth plane. Your mother is with me and bids me give you her greeting. Little Mary is also here to see her papa. She is progressing nicely on this side of life and although she loves her parents she has no desire to return to earth life again. I am pleased to see that you still wear my last gift to you, as does your brother Charles in St. Louis. My dear son, the "controls" of this "medium" tell me you would make a fine "materializing medium," and I would advise that you get instructions from some "medium" and develop the phase. Your wife will have her rheumatism cured through Spiritual healing if you will have her visit a "medium" for treatment. Good bye dear son, I, and all your spirit friends will be continually with you, guarding you to the extent of our power. Do not give up the investigation of this subject, but go on until you have all the proofs of its truth. Your affectionate father and mother,

JOHN W. CORDRAY,
MARY J. CORDRAY.

P. S. Send our love to St. Louis.

For fear Mr. Cordray may not be present at the meeting the "medium" prepares another communication, purporting to be from his "controls" in which a knowledge of different members of the Society is disclosed, that it is not supposed possible the "medium" can know of. If Mr. Cordray is not present the "control's" communication will be given instead. If Mr. Cordray is present, the "medium" tears a small corner from the communication. The small piece he places in his vest pocket. The communication he folds in convenient size, usually two folds across the sheet, and places it in his shirt cuff where it is out of sight but very convenient when the cover is thrown over his hands and the slates. When the time arrives for him to give his demonstration he takes the small corner from his pocket and palms it in his left hand. He now tears the sheet from the tablet and tears out of its corner a small piece and hands the sheet for inspection. When it has been examined and put into the slates he hands the investigator the small corner from his *left* hand. He now puts his right hand into his pocket bringing out a nail to stuff the keyhole of the slates with and leaves the corner torn from the sheet of paper contained in the slates.

After the slates are covered with the cloth he opens them just wide enough to admit his fingers, extracts the sheet and places it in his sleeve. He takes the prepared sheet from the other cuff, places it in the slate and locks it, and all is ready.

When the investigator takes the paper from the slate, he finds the corner fits and must admit that it is the identical sheet he placed inside. Besides this Mr. Cordray has received some very fine "tests" outside the "physical" part of the operation, thanks to the note-book of the "medium."

Another method, but a very bungling one, is to lock a pair of slates together with a small pad-lock. The slates are then held beneath a table and unlocked with a duplicate key and message written on slate. It is so simple that it is scarcely worthy of mention.

Another dodge of the "medium" to advertise himself or herself, that is effective, is this:

The "medium" advertises to give independent slate-writing in the hall, and instructs everybody to bring a pair of slates, fastened together.

After the usual exercises the "medium" announces that he will now attempt "independent slate writing" in public, but does not expect that more than one out of all who came up will get anything.

Those having slates are now requested to step upon the rostrum, one at a time. As they come the "medium" will grasp one end of their slates in both hands, and stand a moment with closed eyes. If the owners of the slates are to get any writing the "medium" will begin to writhe and twist and moan. This will be kept up for perhaps thirty seconds when the "medium" will sink into a chair, as though he was much exhausted. On opening the slates they are found written full, and many extraordinary "tests" given.

Out of twenty attempts the medium will have produced perhaps four to six communications between the sealed slates.

It is needless to say that he would not have succeeded in obtaining a solitary communication were it not that his confederates were present with their communications, self-written and sealed between the slates.

A very effective and astonishing method of obtaining slate-writing is through the carpet trick. We will say you are seated in the "medium's" presence after having stated your desire to obtain a written communication from your spirit friends.

The "medium" seats you at a small table on which is a damp sponge and dry towel. He now goes to the opposite side of the room, and from a pile of slates that are stacked up against the wall he takes up six of them. He now stands at your side and partially behind you and hands you one of the six slates with the request that you clean it thoroughly and return it to him. When you have done so he hands you the second one to clean and so on, until you have washed the six slates. He now throws them, one at a time on the carpet in different parts of the room, and, sitting at the table opposite you, takes your hands in his. He now proceeds to do the snorting and jerking act for the space of from five to ten minutes. When he has "snorted" a sufficiently long time he releases your hands and allows you to pick up the slates which he had thrown on the floor after you had carefully washed them, and which have, since then, been under your eye.

In picking them up you discover that one or two of them are written full, the writing having been done between the carpet and the slate. It may have been written with a slate pencil or written with several colors of crayon, one line red, the next one blue, the next yellow, and so on, until ten to twenty colors appear on your slate. From whence came the writing, reader?

I know what you will say. You will account for it through the acid writing, but not so. You will please remember the "sitter" cleaned the slates himself, and they were *dry*, when he received them, hence it could *not* be produced either by the acid or flap method.

Some of my readers may have ran afoul of this method and have been unable to account for the writings through other sources than spirit power.

That "phase" or method has made many a convert to Spiritualism through the writer However, he now has no further use for the secret and here it is:

Prepare your communication, and if on one slate let it be on the fourth slate from the top of the pile, with the writing on the undermost side. Seat your "sitter" and pick up four slates from the top of the pile. The bottom-most slate will contain the communication. Standing at the side of your "sitter" and a little behind, hand him the top-most slate to clean. When that one is cleaned pass the second one, putting each one on the bottom as it is cleaned until you reach the third, while he is cleaning that one slip the fourth on the bottom again. When the third is cleaned, take it, put it on the bottom and hand him the top one. He has cleaned it before but does not know of the change you made in the position of the slates, hence he cleans it as the last of the four Now scatter your slates on the floor and sit for a few moments, doing any amount of "snorting" you may think the occasion requires. Allow your "sitter" to pick up the slates, collect two dollars, and you are ready for the next.

If the communication is written in colors you account for it by saying that the spirits wrote with a substance extracted from the colors in the pattern of the carpet.

Of course you must know in advance of the coming of your "sitter" in order to give satisisfaction in this "phase." However, when you become a "medium" your visitors will be amazed at the amount of business you *must* be doing, for they will find, that, in order to get a "sitting" with you they must leave their name on your book and call in a day or two, your time is so fully occupied. This he will do, and if he has ever visited a "medium" before, it will not be very long until you know enough about him, through your note-books and the brother and sister "mediums" of your diocese to give him quite a "testy" reception.

If you can find nothing regarding him you may fix up some kind of a communication regarding his future affairs, which, of course, he can not deny; also write him that he will develope into an extraordinarily strong "materializing medium," that his financial conditions are to change for the better, (that will always be a pleasant bit of information) that he has incipient heart trouble, but by bathing his chest with salt water when the moon darkens, his life will be spared, etc., elaborating and polishing off each piece of information until you have quite a lengthy communication.

After witnessing the marvelous manner in which the writing is obtained he will, more than likely, go away believing the whole thing true.

Spirit pictures obtained on slates bring the "medium" many dollars. To get them you visit a "medium" who is "gifted" with that "phase," pay him or her two dollars and he or she will produce the pictures of your "spirit band," and, possibly, some of your relatives or friends that have passed over.

They will do so by seating you on one side of a table and taking a seat on the opposite side themselves. They will now hold, underneath a table, a slate that you have examined and found to be clean. After sitting a few moments the slate is taken out and handed to you.

It is not clean, now, but will have from five

to twemy faces drawn upon it, with the names under *some* of them. The names are omitted from the balance for the reason that it is possible you may find a resemblance among them to some relative or friend, and a name written under it would show clearly you was mistaken, and the slate be less satisfactory.

When the slate comes from under the table, it appears to have been covered with a white powder and the faces are produced with black lines on this white surface instead of white lines on the black slate. From whence came the pictures? You can not believe the "medium" could execute the drawings under the table without seeing the slate. Yet they are there and well executed, too. It may be that you know for a certainty that the "medium" can not draw or make a picture of any kind.

Well, reader, it is another case of exchanging the slates. Any child can execute the drawings if they will follow these instructions:

Wash your slate clean, and, with a pencil rub it all over until it is white, then with the ends of the fingers rub lightly until the powder is evenly spread. Now cut from newspaper or magazine the faces you desire to copy. You must not cut out the face on the lines, but cut out a piece of the paper with the face on it leaving a margin of about an inch all around. Wet the side of the paper opposite the picture with the tongue, being careful to wet it evenly. Lay the paper on the slate, wet side down. Hold it firmly in place and with a round pointed pencil trace over all the lines of the face, putting a good pressure on the pencil. Now take off the paper, and when the slate dries you will find an exact reproduction or copy of the face on your slate.

The picture is made by the powder on the slate adhering to the wet paper wherever your pencil touches, and the surface of the slate shows where the powder is removed, making a black line through the white powder. Proceed as above until you have all the faces wanted on the slate, slip it in the slide on the bottom of your chair and wait for a "sucker."

The writer knows of one woman who is laying up something for a "rainy day" from this one deception. She is called the "picture medium."

It would astonish you, reader, to know what a large number of the faces are recognized as friends and relatives by the people who receive them. The writer knows of at least five people who have recognized Lydia Pinkham's newspaper cut as relatives, after it had been transferred to the "medium's" slate.

Another phase of slate writing that has puzzled and converted many an investigator was the finger-writing or "materialization" of a pencil on the finger of the "medium."

These "seances" were given to "circles" of from five to thirty "sitters" and investigators at one dollar per head. He would arrange his "sitters" in a circle in a room, and request each "sitter" to write a question addressed to some spirit friend on squares of paper furnished by himself. They were instructed to fold them into pellets. When this was done he would have one of the "sitters" collect them in a plate, take them into an adjoining room and empty them out on a table. He would now work the "dummy" pellet until he had read three or four of them, when he would go to the door opening into the "seance-room" and announce the answers to half the pellets he had read giving the names they were addressed to as the one answering. The ones he did not answer he would jot down in his memory for use later on. He would now take a different watcher into his "cabinet-room," and repeat the above performance until he had read all the pellets and answered one-half of them. The watchers would invariably report that the "medium" had not seen the contents of any of the pellets, nor had he taken any of them out of their sight for a single instant. He read them all by the method described before.

After he had read all the pellets he would come into the room with the "sitters" and seat himself in the center of the circle with half-a-dozen clean slates on the floor at his right and a pitcher of water on his left. Taking one of the slates on his lap and holding it in place with his left hand he would offer his right hand for examination.

When all were satisfied that his right hand and fingers were perfectly clean and innocent of any apparatus, he would close all the fingers but the index, and, after swinging it above his head for a few seconds he would bring the end of his finger down on the slate and proceed to write a message in answer to one of the pellets that had not been answered during the earlier part of the "seance." When the message had been completed he would give to some one of the "sitters" the small bit of pencil, about the size of a pin head that would be found clinging to the end of his finger. They were in great demand, for had not the lucky possessor seen it materialized from the air? Another examination of his hand would be made and another message written. This would be repeated until all the pellets had been answered, and, when there were those present who were mentioned in his note-book a few "tests" independent of the pellets would be given.

This "medium" had been repeatedly "tested" by investigators, but his trick was never detected. His fingers had been washed with acids so frequently that the nails were almost eaten off. He converted a great many to a belief in Spiritualism.

His trick was simple enough, the trouble being all with the investigators. They invariably searched in the wrong place for the bits of pencil. There was no use in washing the fingers of his right hand for his pencils were not kept in that hand.

The pencils were made by pulverizing a slate pencil and mixing the powder thus obtained with ordinary mucilage, forming a thick paste. This was cut into small squares about the size of a rice grain. These squares were allowed to dry perfectly hard. He also kept a few of the pencils made by simply breaking small bits off a piece of slate. When he seated himself to give the writings he would deposit about a dozen of the mucilage pencils on his left knee. His pants were black, hence they were not visible; besides, the slate was nearly all the time over the knee. They could not fall off, for he held them a few seconds in his closed hand before sticking them on his knee This warmed them and made them sticky so that they stuck where he put them. Four or five of the pencils not made with mucilage he put into his mouth.

In picking up a slate with his right hand, he stoops over with his left hand on his knee. When he takes up his left hand one of the pencils is sticking to his thumb. He grasps the slate with his left hand in such a way that the thumb is across the frame on the uppermost side.

He now offers his right hand for inspection and while everybody's attention is attracted to it he scrapes the piece of pencil off his thumb on the slate. Both the pencil and slate being black the pencil is not seen in the dim light. All he needs do, now, is to place the index finger of the right hand on the pencil and proceed to write. But, suppose he drop the pencil and has no opportunity to get another from his knee. He will simply do a little snorting and contorting and drop one from his mouth and go on with the message. The reason he does not put the mucilage pencils in his mouth is because they would melt. The reason he does not use his mouth altogether is because he is too liable to detection. In order to add to the appearances of his act, he would usually drink a gallon of water during the hour and-a-half that his "seance" required.

This man traveled all over the country on the one deception and always had all the money he required. He is now dead, and his phase is being worked by others.

He used to often remark to the writer that he wondered what there was for man beyond the grave if anything, and what kind of punishment, if any, the "mediums" would receive. He is dead and it is the writer's turn, now, to wonder whether he knows any more about it than he did when he was playing his tricks in the flesh. Oh, for some *absolute* proof of a future existence, if there is one.

The writer has furnished positive proof of life everlasting to scores of skeptical minds that the church did not reach. It was very satisfactory proof to them but the writer knew just how much it was worth, and for his own satisfaction it did not fill the bill.

It is very pleasant to *believe* that you do not

stop in the grave, if you can; but a large majority of the people do not want to believe it any longer—they want to *know* it.

Many persons will tell you that they have obtained slate-writing from the "medium" and, besides furnishing the slates, which were screwed together, they were not out of their own hands a moment from the time they entered the "medium's" room until they reached home. They will also tell you that a list of questions secured between the slates were answered. Your informant will believe that every word he is telling you is the truth, for he has *himself* been deceived. Don't laugh at his seeming gullibility for were you to have the same experience he has passed through, it is more than likely you would be telling the same story. There are many men and women in the Spiritualistic fold who are just as intelligent as you may imagine yourself to be. It is only the fool who will deny the truth of any proposition when he is utterly ignorant on the subject.

The writer has had men, who were *supposed* to be intelligent, say to him that they "would not believe in Spiritualism if they *knew* it was true." Others have said it was not true "because *I* can not get "manifestations."

SPIRITUALISTIC MYSTERIES EXPOSED. 153

There is not much intelligence displayed in a statement of that kind. He might as well say there is no such thing as a watch because, being a car-driver, "*I* can not make a watch."

No man ever received "independent slate writing" between slates fastened together that he did not allow out of his hands a few seconds. Scores of persons will tell you that they *have* received writing under those conditions through the "mediumship" of the writer; but the writer will tell you how he fooled them and how you can do so if you see fit.

In the first place you will rent a house with a cellar in connection. Cut a trap-door one foot square through the floor between the sills on which the floor is laid. Procure a fur floor mat with long hair. Cut a square out of the mat and tack it to the top of the trap-door. Tack the mat fast to the floor, for some one may visit you who will want to raise it up. Explain the presence of the fur by saying it is an absorbent of magnetic forces, through which you produce the writing. Over the rug place a heavy, pine table about four feet square, and over the table a heavy cover that reaches the floor on all sides. Put your assistant in the cellar with a coal-oil stove, a teakettle of hot water, different colored letter-wax and lead pencils, screw driver, a pair of nippers, a pair of pliers, a pair of scissors and an assortment of wire brads. You are now ready for business.

When your "sitter" comes in you will notice his slates, if he brings a pair, and see if they are secured in any way that your man in the cellar can not duplicate. If they are, you can touch his slates with your finger and say to him that you can not use his slates on account of the "magnetism" with which they are saturated. He will know nothing of "magnetic conditions," and will ask you what he is to do about it.

You will furnish him a pair of new slates with water and cloths to clean them. You also furnish him paper to write his questions on and the screws, wax, paper and mucilage to secure them with. He will write his question and fasten the slates securely together.

You now conduct him to your "seance-room" and invite inspection of your table and surroundings. After the examination has been made you will seat the "sitter" at one side of of the table with his side and arm next it. If he desires to keep hold of the slate a signal agreed upon between yourself and your assistant will cause the spirit in the cellar to open the trap door, which opens downward, and to push through the floor and into a position where the "sitter" can grasp one end of it, a pair of dummy slates. This dummy your assistant will continue to hold until the "sitter" has taken hold of it after the following performance:

Your assistant lets you know everything is ready by touching your foot. You now reach and take the "sitter's" slate and put it below the table, and under it, telling the "sitter" to put his hand under from his side and hold it with you. He puts his hand under and gets hold of the dummy slate held by your assistant.

Your assistant holds on until you have stood the slate on end, leaning against the table leg, and have got hold of the dummy. He then takes the "sitter's" slate below and closes the trap. He proceeds to open it, read the questions, answer them and refasten it.

You will be entertaining your "sitter" by twitching and jerking and making clairvoyant and clairandient guesses for him.

When your assistant touches your foot you will know that he is ready to make the exchange again, by which the "sitter" will get hold of the slates he fastened. When you get the signal you give a snort and jump that jerks the end of the slate from the "sitter's" hand. He is now given the end of the slates held by your assistant, and you will allow the assistant to take the dummy. After sitting a moment or two longer, you will tell the "sitter" to take out his slates and examine them if he chooses. Many times they do not open the slates until they reach their homes.

This, reader, is the man who will declare that he furnished the slates and did not allow them out of his hands a minute.

The usual method of obtaining the writing is for the "medium" to hold the slates alone. When this is the case, the "medium" passes the slates below, and receives in return a "dummy" which he is continually thumping on the under side of the table for the purpose of showing the "sitter" that the slates are there all the time.

It is not necessary that you should use a cellar to get this "phase" of "independent slate-writing." You could place your table against a partition door and by fitting one of the small panels with hinges and bolts, would have a very convenient way of obtaining the assistance of the "spirit" in the next room. It

SPIRITUALISTIC MYSTERIES EXPOSED. 157

is also possible to make a trap in a room that has a wooden wainscoting.

Another way is to have in the room a bureau and place the slates in one of the empty drawers, locking them in. Of course the bureau stands against the wall, and a sliding trap gives access from the next room.

You must keep both eyes wide open if you would avoid all the impositions practiced by the slate-writing "mediums."

The very latest "fake" that is being worked on the Spiritualist as the evidence of the power of disembodied spirits is the work of Lulu Hurst, the Georgia Wonder, and Mrs. Abbott, the electrical woman. Her feats have recently been demonstrated very easy of performance by anybody strong enough to carry a three-gallon pail of water, once they know the law of mechanics governing her feats.

Preliminary to describing the tricks, attention is called to certain points. It is claimed that Mrs. Abbot cannot exercise this strange force when standing on the ground or on metal, and but slightly when on carpet. The surface must be dry (not wet) wood or other similar substance. The reason is apparent when the tricks are understood. On earth, smooth metal or carpet, the surface is unyielding and proper purchase cannot be obtained; the feet slip and the conditions of muscular rigidity are rendered impossible or precarious. On wood, rubber, or other similar yielding surfaces safety is secured. This is of great importance. Again, she cannot work except with animate matter. Why? Because without animate matter she cannot get that concord of action, that unconscious or involuntary aid necessary to a performance of the tricks.

"The pushing of a man while holding a chair in his arms is a trick older than this generation, having been performed by all the old "mediums." If the holder allows all the muscles of the body to become lax or limp, and merely stands and holds the chair without attempting to resist any external force, the trick cannot be performed. He is requested to hold tightly, which he does; he braces himself to resist some strong force. She, by a slight, and to him imperceptible pressure, takes deft advantage of his straining and he is thrown about (by himself) at will. Any one can do it with a person not familiar with the two causes.

"The lifting of a man in a chair is equally simple. She presses the fingers against the sides of the chair and is supposed to raise it by her force. By gently pressing upon the back of the posts with the ball of the thumb, the chair rises—apparently lifted. No pressure need be exerted by the fingers, in fact the hand of a third person may be placed between hers and the chair, and no pressure be felt, or an egg may be placed there and not be broken. The thumb which is behind the interposed hand does the business. In doing this, certain conditions are absolutely indispensible: First, that the sitter lean back so as to throw the center of gravity exactly over the hind legs of the chair; secondly, that the toes be braced in front of the chair and as near it as possible; and thirdly, that he grasp firmly the hind legs of the chair in order to bind the body down to the seat. If the chair rests on all four legs, if the man's feet are not on the floor, if they are on the floor—but back of the front legs—or if his grasp on the chair is relaxed or is on the front legs, or his body bent forward, the trick is impossible. The center of gravity is shifted or the mechanical conditions so altered as to render it impossible. The toes are the fulcrum and that cannot be moved. If the force as represented were real, these changes would not be material. The following modifications might be suggested and could not reasonably be objected to, were it not a fake, for they retain all the elements of contact and circuit claimed as essential:

Let the sitter lean back as requested, and on the floor in front of him place a board resting on two wooden rolling pins, and on the board let him rest his feet. Notice now that the toes, the fulcrum are not stable; as soon as any pressure is thrown on that point it rolls away, proving conclusively that it is upon that point she throws the whole weight of the body, and that there is no "unknown force" operating to lift it. It lifts itself and is self-supporting. The trick of pushing her off her balance, while more complicated, mechanically considered, is only mechanical. If she stands squarely on both feet any child can push her over, or if on one foot or heel, with the other in front instead of behind the leg upon which she stands, then she can be easily pushed over. The raised foot must be thrown back and used as a counterpoise to maintain the center of gravity at the proper point. If her force were real, she could hold the cue horizontally and prevent it being pushed up or down, or she could hold it behind her and resist being pressed forward, but these changes alter the mechanical conditions, and, of course, will not be entertained by the manager.

"The pressing of a cue downward through

her open hand is the simplest of all. You must grasp the cue at some point between her hands and press hard. She then presses up at the lower end thereby bending the cue and neutralizing your force. She will not submit to any of the following modifications since they destroy her mechanical advantage. Reverse the cue so the small end is up and it is less easily done, or use a rake handle which will not bend. If the one pressing grasps firmly, but does not bear down—just pressing gently so as to create no leverage, its movement cannot be prevented, nor can it if pushed at the top with one hand or with both, or if merely pulled at the lower end. In order to be resisted successfully one must press hard at some point between her hands.

"The trick of lifting her from the floor is that upon which they put special value as indicating the operation of the force, but, as in all the other tricks, there is a mechanical advantage taken by the lady which renders it impossible to lift her. The trick lies entirely in the position of the body. The elbows are thrown slightly out and back, the shoulder blades are slightly drawn together, the spine elongated to its full extent and the body slightly inclined forward. In this position no man on earth can lift her or any other lady or person who will practice the trick until the proper position is learned. The trick of holding her after the chair on which she stands has been drawn from under her is likewise dependent entirely upon the position of her arms. Her elbows are thrown either forward or backward sufficient to permit of her easily dropping to the floor. Those attempting to hold her up are thrown out of balance and all power of lifting is lost. She will not submit to a straight, fair, vertical lift, but invariably drops out of the vertical line. In lifting her from the floor she will not permit any but one certain hold. If the lifter could put his arms around her, grasping her left wrist with the right hand and her right wrist with the left hand, then she could be easily lifted, for her power of squirming would be killed. All the element of flesh contact may in this case be preserved, but she will not permit it. So, too, in holding her up, if the lifter could have one hand under her arm at the shoulder joint, any two boys in the land could lift her up.

The tricks where a boy places his hands on hers, or where he holds one end of a silk handkerchief and she the other end, while a person tries to lift the boy just as she is lifted, are the same as trying to lift her. She deftly manages to get the boy's arms into position so he cannot be lifted. In this trick she must use excellent judgment but as a safeguard against possible failure she announces that she cannot operate on all persons equally well.

The trick of pressing her against the wall when her fingers only touch it, her hands resting on those of committeemen, is purely mechanical and one of the easiest tricks to do. Let any lady try it aright and no man or combination of men can press her against the wall if she supports herself by but the tips of two fingers.

The trick of lifting a man on top of a billiard cue is purely mechanical. The more men you have to hold down the cue the easier one can lift it, for when a man is on top each holder lifts up although he intends to bear down and thinks he is doing so. Take the man off the top and the trick fails as it will, too, if a short cue is used, or if but two or three men grasp it, or if they grasp at the middle point of the cue.

Finally, there is the tumbler trick, which is the greatest fake of all, and the easiest to perform. It will be noted that at each performance Mr. Abbott steps out prior to this trick and gets a fan for Mrs. Abbott, who thereupon holds it but does not use it. From contact with its handles, which have probably been covered with resin her hands are coated so as to stick to a vibratory surface, such as glass. When the glass is held between both hands note that the axis of one hand is at right angles to the axis of the other, and that then, by an imperceptible twist in a rotary manner, the faint rappings are produced. When a glass is beld in a silk handkerchief the sound is still easier to produce by merely pressing the tips of the fingers on the glass and gently drawing them in a succession of pulls. A noteworthy fact is that Mr. Abbott always says that the vibrations of this force are irregular and less rapid than the pulse. This trick may be blocked in any of the following ways. Let the committeemen watch the hands closely and see that she does not move them. or hold them, or have the glass held by a companion.

Read the explanation just given carefully, so as to thoroughly understand the ideas the writer meant to convey, and do a little experimenting on your own hook. See if your wife or sister cannot exhibit feats of wonderful strength or "magnetic" power without a very great outlay of muscular energy. You will be astonished at the apparent great strength she has suddenly acquired.

It is possible there may be some virtue in animal magnetism as an agent for healing the sick and diseased. but of all the Spiritual and "magnetic" healers the writer has become acquainted with in fifteen years, they were all as deep in the "faking business" as the writer himself.

The most successful one he ever met did business in an Eastern city. He was more than usually sucessful for the reason that he was more than usually clever in his methods of deception. His deception lay in his ability to cause his patient to feel the magnetic current during his treatment of them. He accomplished it in this way:

Procuring a sheet of zinc about eighteen inches wide and three feet long, he placed it under the carpet, just back of an adjustable reclining chair. The arms of the chair had strips of copper along their under side. The foot-rest was also covered with a sheet of copper fastened in place with large brass tacks. To the zinc beneath the carpet was attached the positive pole of a small electric battery, and the copper strips on the chair arms were attached to the negative pole of the battery.

The battery was charged with some five or six grains of the bi-sulphate of mercury.

When a patient was in the chair for treatment the "doctor" would step into the battery room, drop the zinc into the solution, start the vibrator to buzzing, slip on a pair of slippers, the soles of which were paste-board and dampened with water. Taking up a wet sponge and entering the treating room he was ready for business. He would proceed by slyly wetting the carpet over the zinc sheet, and instructing the patient to lay out straight in the chair.

In doing so the arms of the chair were so convenient the patient invariably grasps them. If, by any chance he does not, his feet, from which the shoes and stockings have been removed, at the "doctor's" request, are touching the plates on the foot-rest.

You will see that the instant the "doctor" touched his patient, he would experience a tingling sensation under the doctor's hand. The current was always a very mild one, so that the patient could only just distinguish the prickling sensation and no more. It was enough, though, to convince the patient that there was something in the "doctor's" hand not common to every one.

Spiritualistic Mysteries Exposed. 167

If there *was* something there not possessed by others, it was possible that it might result in the cure of the disease afflicting him, and he would generally give it a pretty thorough trial at two dollars per treatment in advance.

At times the "doctor" would catch a patient by absently lighting the gas jet with the end of his finger while the prospective patient was looking his way. This act would generally excite some remark giving the "doctor" an opportunity to explain that the agent that lighted the gas was "animal magnetism," the same force that overcame disease in his patients.

This doctor also gave alcohol baths and massage treatments. In massaging his patients he would pour into his hand from a small phial about a teaspoonful of alcohol in which was two or three drops of the essential oil of mustard. He would now place his hand on the bare back of his patient, and by holding it there and excluding the air for twenty or thirty seconds his hand would appear to the patient to become almost red-hot.

Our friend, the "doctor," would explain this as a "manifestation" of his wonderful "magnetic" and curative powers. The patient must believe it, for he knew nothing of the transaction with the phial of the oil of mustard, supposing that the hand was wetted with plain alcohol, which he had been using.

It may be there is something in magnetic healing but the writer's experience would lead him to think not.

He has made some wonderful cures himself in a magnetic way, when he knew for a positive certainty that the agent in the cure was the patient's own faith, imagination or mind.

There is no doubt that many persons become sick or diseased through continually thinking they are, or dreading some certain disease. That being the case it would naturally follow that the imagination or mind might be a factor in the cure of disease.

It appears to the writer that gaining the confidence of the patient would be the difficult part of the transaction. It is a hard matter to *talk* yourself into another's confidence; but when you are prepared, as was our "doctor," to demonstrate undeniably that you are gifted with some power out of the ordinary, it would seem that you are armed with a very effective advantage.

Another source of profit to the "magnetic healer" is the sale of magnetized paper and belts for the cure of disease. These things are magnetized and kept in stock for sale to those who do not think they can afford the money for a course of treatments, for they come much cheaper than the treatments.

Tissue paper is generally used, and it is supposed to be saturated with the healer's magnetism, so that if you have kidney trouble you can have a magnetic treatment by binding on the small of the back one of the sheets, wear it about ten hours and replacing it with a fresh sheet.

Treatments are two dollars each while the paper sells six sheets for a dollar. The belts are usually made by folding a piece of white canton flannel until you have a belt two inches wide, three or four folds of the cloth in thickness and thirty-six inches long. Quilt this and magnetize it and it is good for five dollars.

"Table-tipping" is accounted for by some persons on the "magnetic" theory. They can not stuff that explanation down the writer, for he has tipped too many tables in his career as a "medium." There is *one* strange thing about "table-tipping." It is this:

You can *hear* wonderful stories as to how the table floated in mid-air or walked across the floor with no human being touching it. You can hear these things, yet you are never lucky enough to be present at a "table-tipping seance" where anything of the kind occurs, although you may be in attendance on those "seances" almost nightly.

It has been reported of the writer's "tipping seances" that the table walked without human aid when he knew better, although, for business reasons he did not deny the entire correctness of the report.

In a company of ten or twelve "sitters" even when there are no "mediums" present, it is no trouble to get "table tippings." If there are not two or three who will do all in their power to produce the "tippings," the whole company will unconsciously make the "manifestations."

Is is possible the reader has read the *scientific* explanation offered for the "rappings" of the Fox girls. It was claimed that the "raps" were produced by snapping the toe joints and by throwing small shot against the walls and ceiling. The claim was also made that the ladies suspended leaden weights with elastic braids beneath their skirts, and by a slight movement of the limbs these weights could be set bobbing up and down, striking the floor on the downward movement, thus producing the mysterious "raps."

It is possible that such tactics would answer

the purpose, but, in view of the fact that there are much more simple methods, the writer is of the opinion that the learned gentlemen were entirely wrong, in fact it has been demonstrated by the Fox girls that their theories were wide of the mark.

When the writer desires to produce "raps" for the investigator he does not find it necessary to make any special preparations in order to do so. He merely seats himself at the table, spreads his hands on the top, and the "raps" come without the least particle of trouble. You, reader, can perform the feat just as easily as the writer if, in spreading the hands on the table you will be careful to bring the thumbnails in contact, one with the other. Press them together tightly and slip them a little at a time. You will find that every time you slip them, one against the other, quite a loud "rap" will be the result.

Another way is to place your shoe against the leg of the table, and by slipping it backward or forward "raps" will be produced that will appear to proceed from the table top. Your knee will also furnish "raps" if pressed against the table leg and moved slightly one way or the other. You can produce "raps" on a slate or book by holding it in such a way that the nails of the forefingers are in contact, one with the other, and slipping them as in "rapping" on a table.

In your own room it is an easy matter to so fix a chair or table that by wrenching it one way or another you can get an elegant variety of "spirit raps." However, "raps" are rather out of date now, since the "medium" has evolved so many other more wonderful manifestations.

If you intend to become a professional "medium" the most agreeable and remunerative "phase" is that of answering sealed letters. A few hints as to the manner in which others have "got to the front" in that "phase" may be of use to you.

Sit down and write an article describing the wonderful phenomena you have witnessed at your own "seances" for "physical manifestations." In this communication or article for publication by one of the Spiritual Journals, you will describe yourself as having been very skeptical previous to your having visited your own "seances" and witnessed the wonderful proofs of "spirit return." After describing the wonders of your "physical seances," you will mention the fact that you are a "medium" for answering sealed letters and describe some wonderful "tests" you have received from yourself in that line. Lay it on thick and be sure to get your name and street number incorporated into the article so that people will know where to address you. Now sign any name but your own and mail it to one of the leading Spiritual Journals.

If your article is well written and you have described the "phenomena" as unusually wonderful, besides giving them to understand that you are now, through what is described in your manuscript, a firm believer in Spiritualism, your article will surely be printed.

As certainly as it is printed just so sure will you be overwhelmed with letters of inquiry from all over the United States. The letters will be asking information as to your fee for answering sealed letters and the method they should pursue in communicating with their spirit friends in that particular way. You will receive hundreds of letters to answer at one dollar each. You will receive letters sealed in all manner of curious ways, in order to prevent your opening them. If you will exercise plenty of patience no letter will come to your hands so securely sealed that you can not readily open and replace it in its original condition so as to defy detection.

The writer knows of a "medium" who, at one time, received a letter to answer that required him to earn his dollar before he had it in shape to return to the writer without danger of detection.

This particular letter was enclosed in three opaque envelopes. The letter itself was folded to fit the smaller of the three envelopes, and the edges glued together. It was now stitched with silk thread, red in the needle and blue in the bobbin or shuttle. It was put into the first envelope, with two or three spots of glue on it causing it to stick to the envelope, and the "medium" to swear. Not being content to let this end their precautions they now stitched through envelope and sheet, and, after putting mucilage all over the side on which the seams were, inserted it in the second envelope. This envelope was mucilaged and placed in the third envelope which was sealed with furniture glue, besides being waxed with letter wax and stamped with some kind of die that the "medium" could not duplicate without going to more expense than it would be worth.

The "medium" succeeded in getting the letter out and back again. How did he manage it?

He began by prying the wax off the outside

envelope with a thin knife-blade. It came off in pieces from the size of a pea to pieces as large as a five-cent nickle. He took good care not to break the wax containing the impression of the die, the balance did not matter, for it could be melted again. Now he got up steam in the teakettle, and after first dampening the seams soon steamed off the outside envelope. When it came off it was put carefully to one side to dry. The second envelope was disposed of in the same manner. After examining the third envelope and finding he could duplicate it he steamed and cut it from the letter. He now had a good hour's work to pick the silk thread from the letter. It was finally accomplished, and the letter read and copied. The letter was folded on the old creases, and taken to the sewing machine and stitched with red and blue silk in the same needle holes from which the thread had been taken. He now gets a duplicate for the envelope he had destroyed and after gluing the sheet it was inserted in the envelope. It was necessary to put the thread back into this envelope by hand for the reason that it must be held between himself and the light in order to see where the holes were in the letter inside. These could not have been seen with the envelope under the machine needle. You can imitate machine work very nicely by hand. The last envelope was now folded over it, after giving it a liberal coat of glue, so that it would be impossible to do much investigating without destroying the evidences, if any were left, of the "medium's" having tampered with it. Now comes the fine work. The wax has left a stain on the envelope which will guide you in putting back the pieces of wax on which are the impressions of the die or seal. Give them a good coat of glue, stick them in place, being careful not to allow the glue to show beyond the edges of the wax. Allow the pieces to dry on before replacing the remainder of the wax. After they are fast, melt the remainder of the wax in a vessel and pour it where it had been before, being careful to make it cover all the stains and marks made by it in the first instance. See to it that the wax you have melted does not show a joint where it joins the pieces that you glued on. This can be remedied by heating a knife blade and holding it close to the wax until the two edges melt together.

This letter came from what is called a "Bundyite" Spiritualist, viz: one who believes that all "mediums" are frauds and all phenomena fraudulent until they have demonstrated it differently to their own satisfaction. His questions were satisfactorily answered and quite a complimentary letter was received by the "medium." This, though, was not the only complimentary letter he has received from persons who had received entire satisfaction through the sealed letter "racket."

To be sure, he has received letters on the other side of the question, but the "medium" was entirely blameless in the matter. No "medium" can be blamed for not giving satisfaction when questions are asked that it is impossible that he can answer.

Such questions as: How old am I? Where did my father die *if* he is dead? Did my father or mother die first? Have I any children, and if so how many? Where was I born? Have I any children in the spirit world? is calculated to "knock silly" *any* "medium," especially when those questions are insisted on, and there is nothing outside of them to talk or write on. If you think that you can do it, try it.

But in this case the "medium" had notes on the gentleman, and his questions were not only answered but considerable information given on private matters that he had not mentioned, besides three or four names of his spirit relatives being given.

Those note-books are a grand institution.

It is the writer's intention, now, to leave two or three of them at the office of the publisher of this book, that the curious or Spiritualist who doubt the existence of such books may go and examine them and wade through the endless bits of information contained in them regarding persons and their deceased relatives in various parts of the United States.

But the smoothest thing in the sealed letter reading and the one that has puzzled the people for years, is usually done in connection with "slate writing." The "sitter" is furnished a heavy white envelope, of small size, and a white card of the size of an ordinary visiting card. He is requested to write the name of a spirit friend on the card and to write one or not more than two questions with it. After he has written as requested, he is instructed to place the card in the envelope with the writing next the smooth side and away from the glue. This being done, he is furnished with letter-wax with which he seals the seams to prevent the envelope being opened.

The "medium" now takes his seat at the table opposite his sitter and near a window. Placing the envelope on a slate he thrusts it beneath the table. After sitting long enough to do his work, raps are heard on the slate and withdrawing it he hands it to the "sitter." The envelope still lies on the slate and there is no evidence of its having been touched. The seals are intact and there is not a mark or mar on it.

On the state is written the replies to his questions and the name of the spirit addressed is signed at the bottom of the message. There is a "manifestation" of spirit power that is generally admitted to be a "corker."

Really, it *is* wonderful, or would be were not so simple of performance, once you know how. This is a feat performed by only a few "mediums," as but few know the secret. It has captured many a dollar for the "mediums" who have worked it.

In order to perform this trick, do just as the "medium" did up to the time he placed or held the slate beneath the table. Instead of holding it there with your hand, slip one corner between your leg and the seat of the chair. Thus you are holding it by sitting on it. Your hand is now free to do as you choose with. Your "sitter" can not see your movements for the table is interposed. Put your fingers into the ticket pocket of your coat and bring out a small sponge that is saturated with alcohol; dampen the envelope over the card and you can easily read the name and question. Write the answer and sign the name addressed, and your "sitter" will be "paralyzed" with astonishment.

Nothing will serve to dampen the envelope but alcohol. Nothing else will allow of your reading the writing on the enclosed card and nothing else will dry out quickly enough and leave absolutely no traces of any manipulation. Water will not dry out quick enough, and when it *does* dry leaves the envelope shrunken where it was applied, thus leading your "sitter" to suspect that you have not played fair.

This deception is also useful in giving "clairvoyant sittings," for by its use you can learn what particular thing has brought your "sitter" to your presence.

There are other methods for learning the contents of a sealed envelope that is written in your rooms. The next best one is accomplished by furnishing your "sitter" with a tablet of *soft* pencil paper and an extra *hard* lead pencil. You instruct the "sitter" to write the name of a spirit friend on the tablet, together with one or two questions, in a plain, large handwriting. When he has done so, have him tear off the sheet and seal it in an envelope. You will now hold the envelope between your fingers, just in front of your "sitter," and proceed to answer his questions by "clairvoyantly" seeing the answers written on the wall. You will know what questions he has written by examining the tablet from which he has torn the sheet. The paper being soft and the pencil hard, you will find that his questions are impressed quite plainly on two or three sheets of the paper.

When your next "sitter" comes, you must tear off all sheets having the impressions, else it may puzzle you somewhat to read his questions.

Here is a good place to give the blood writing test. Do it in this way: Wet the forearm with strong salt water, allowing it to dry. Now, after having answered his questions, give him the envelope and begin a nervous walk up and down the room, behind him. Take a sharpened stick from your pocket and write the name on the arm, pressing hard on the skin. Wait until the red lines have disappeared and then announce to your "sitter" that the "controls" will write the spirit's name on your arm. Allow him to examine your arm. When he has satisfied himself that it is not fixed, rub briskly over the writing a few times with the open hand, and the name will appear in bright red letters. It makes a good finish to a sitting and the "sucker" gives up his money with more satisfaction. Try it, in the way of a joke, on some of your friends, and see the amount of wonder and surprise it will create.

Another way is to write the name on your arm with varnish that has been made very thin with alcohol or turpentine. Now have the "sitter" burn his envelope, and, taking up the charred paper, rub it over the writing. It will not stick to the skin save where it has been written on; thus giving the name in black letters. A sponge and a few drops of alcohol will remove it.

Reader, have you ever attended "dark circles?" If you have, and were not convinced it was the work of the spirit world, the writer would enjoy hearing your theories as to how the "manifestations" were produced. You have probably explained them to your own satisfaction in a hundred or more impossible ways. It is the simplicity of the operations that protect the "medium" from exposure; for the reason that you will think that such wonderful "manifestations" can not be the result of any but the most complex manipulations.

You will accuse the members of the household where the "seance" is held of being accessories, and imagine that the room is strung with wires so fine as to be invisible and worked by some one in an adjoining room or closet, or even in a house next door or half-a-block distant. You will think that electricity or mesmerism is at the bottom of the whole affair. It does not appear possible to you that the "medium" can, alone and unaided, cause the "manifestations" you have witnessed. A description of a "dark seance" as given by a celebrated medium" for that phase of "manifestations wil be given and explained afterward You will recognize the description as substantially the same as you have heard from others, if you are not a Spiritualist, and set it down as a fabrication or the narrator as the most consummate fool you ever encountered. If the narrator happened to be a respected friend of yours, you concluded he had been mesmerized, hypnotized or bamboozled in some way that he could not exercise his senses, and only *imagined* he saw the things he described.

If you are a Spiritualist and have ever visited a "dark circle" you will realize that the writer is not guessing at anything in the description, and if you will read the explanation and experiment on the methods exposed vou will be forced to admit that he is correct as to the causes and had probably been there himself as the "medium." You will be amazed at the simplicity of the means used to produce the phenomena that had seemed so marvelous, and astonished that you can so easily produce the same results. It is possible that you may feel disposed to hire a large, strong man to pound you on the head with a rail-splitters' maul for a few hours, or exercise himself by kicking you all over a ten-acre field.

Do not swear vengeance on the poor "medium" who has fooled you out of fifty or a hundred dollars; but give him the credit due him in having so completely deceived you. Do not come the baby act and ask the law to restore to you the money you had not brains enough to keep. Be a man and catch even by beating some one else. The best man is he who wins, and if the "medium" has beaten you doff your hat to him and be careful in the future.

There are few persons who will read this description, but will recognize to what particular "medium" the writer refers. He is celeebrated and his "seances" have been given and written of all over the United States.

Into a room that has been darkened so that not a single ray of light can penetrate is placed a large dining table and chairs sufficient to seat the persons in attendance. On the table is placed a guitar and a tablet of pencil paper. The investigators are now seated in a circle around the table, male and female alternating. The person sitting on the medium's" right, for he sits in the circle, grasps the "medium's" right wrist in his left hand, while his own right wrist is held by the "sitter" on his right, and this is repeated clear around the circle. This makes each "sitter" hold the right wrist of his left-hand neighbor in his left hand, while his own right-hand wrist is held in the left hand of his neighbor on the left. Each one's hands are thus secured and engaged, including the "medium's."

It will be seen that no one of the "sitters" can have the use of his or her hands without one or the other of their neighbors knowing of it.

Directly behind the "medium's" chair is placed a musical instrument, usually a dulcimer, on a stool. There is also a tin trumpet, tea bell, tambourine and accordeon. The "medium" cannot use them for his *hands are held*.

The light is turned out and after a song has been sung, lights are seen darting about near the ceiling. They fall toward the "medium" and disappear, raps are heard on the table and the guitar is twanged. The "sitters" are permitted to ask questions that are answered by raps on the table. Should you ask those sitting next the "medium" they will tell you that they still have his hands. Presently the trumpet is felt by those sitting farthest from the "medium." It is traveling about the circle where the "medium" cannot possibly reach. Out of it comes a voice announcing a name. The name is recognized by one of the "sitters" as belonging to some friend or relative. The voice may or may not give a message, but after the horn has been heard scraping along the ceiling it falls on the floor behind the "medium's" chair. Touches are now felt by the "sitters" and the table jumps up and falls down several times in succession creating quite a noise. More lights are seen darting about and keeping time, in their motions, to a air being *whistled* by the "medium."

After the music or whistling has ceased, a light is seen over the table and the sound of writing is heard. Presently the sheet of paper is put into the lap of one of the "sitters" who will keep it until the "seance" closes before he can read it. Usually every member of the circle gets a message before the close of the "seance." Some of them contam "tests" of an indisputable nature, while others are merely a name or some advice as to mediumship or business from the "medium's" "controls." The teabell is heard ringing in different parts of the room, against the walls and ceiling from eight to ten or twelve feet from the "medium."

It touches the "sitters" on the shoulders and head and skips about from one locality to another with remarkable quickness. Now a luminous hand appears above the heads of the "sitters." Hands of different sizes are seen, and finger snapping heard. The "medium" now begins whistling and the guitar strikes up an accompaniment, and travels all about the room, apparently. When the guitar stops its accompaniment the delcimore takes it up and continues to play as long as the "medium" will whistle. When he has stopped it strikes up a tune on its own hook and executes it in admirable style. At different times during the "seance" the person sitting on the "medium's" left has been exchanged for another, so that no claim of their having been a confederate would stand

The changes would be rang on these "manifestations" until an hour and-a-half or two hour's time had been consumed, when the "medium" would announce the close of the "seance."

On turning up the lamp the instruments that had been placed behind the "medium" would be found piled up on the table in the middle of the circle.

From what you have read regarding the "cabinet seance" you could understand how the "medium" accomplished these things if he only had the use of *one* hand. As each hand was held by a separate person, you can not understand how he could get the use of either of them except the one on his right was a confederate. Such was not the case and he *did* have the use of one hand, the right one. But how? He took his place before the light was turned down and those holding him say he did not let go for an instant during the "seance."

He did, though, after the light was turned out for the purpose of getting his handkerchief to blow his nose. After blowing his nose he requested the "sitter" to again take his wrist, which is done, but this time it is the wrist of the left hand instead of the right. He has crossed his legs and there is but one knee to be felt, hence the "sitter" on his right does not feel that she is reaching across the right knee and thinks the left knee which she *does* feel to be the right. He has let his hand slip down until, instead of holding the "sitter" on his left by the wrist he has him by the fingers, thus allowing him a little more distance, and preventing the left-hand "sitter" using the hand to feel about and discover the right hand "sitter's" hand on the wrist of the hand holding his. You will see, now, that although both "sitters" are holding the *same* hand each one thinks he is holding the one on his or her side of the "medium."

The balance of the "seance" is easy. His hands are made of pasteboard, painted black on one side and with luminous paint on the other. He fastens a hand to his reaching rod, and elevates it. As long as the black side is toward the "sitters" they do not perceive it, but on turning the luminous side toward them it is immediately visible. The guitar is, so tuned that the accompaniment to his whistling can be performed without any fingering of the strings being necessary. This is not impossible, for who has not seen the artists at variety shows play accompaniments and airs on his guitar and banjo with one hand. The music on the delcimore was easy enough of production after he had secured the release of one hand.

The "seance," you will observe, depended entirely on the one feat, that of getting the use of his right hand. He has his note-books and if any are present at any of his "seances" who are mentioned in it, he will be sure to get some fine "tests." One or two good "tests" in a circle is enough. Of course, if you have more it is well enough to give them. The more the better, although two or three is sufficient to demonstrate your wonderful powers in that line as well as helping out the "physical" portion of your entertainment.

There are other descriptions of dark circle that are not so difficult of performance, and, of course, not so wonderful. There is the circle in which the "medium" sits in the center of the circle and is secured with ropes. There is no use to describe the operations in this description of "seance" for the reader has already read the methods pursued in regard to rope-tying feats. Then again, instead of the "medium" being tied she or he is continually clapping their hands to show that it is not the hands of the "medium" that is being felt by the "sitters" in different parts of the circle.

All that is necessary is to pat your cheek instead of your hand when you have use for one or the other of them.

Another plan is to put a certain number of small shot in each hand and count them after

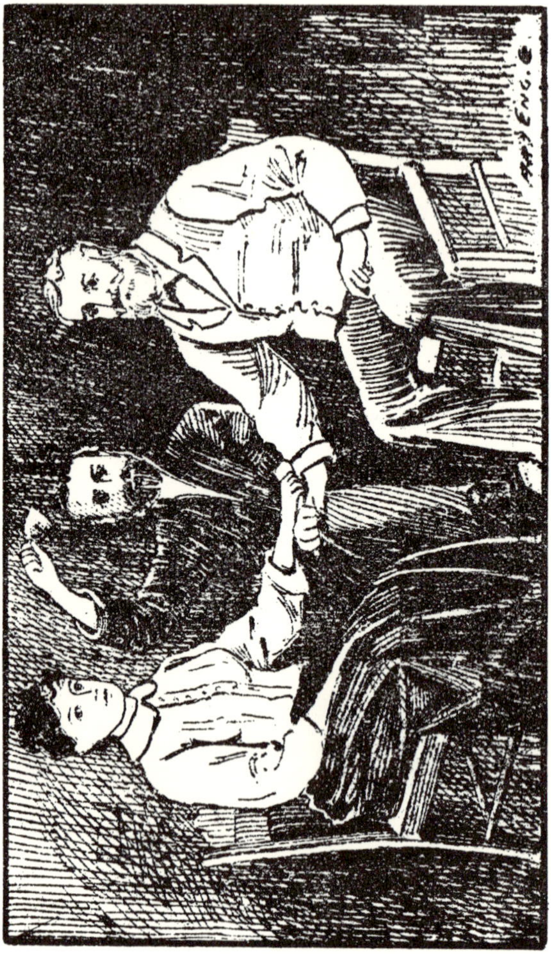

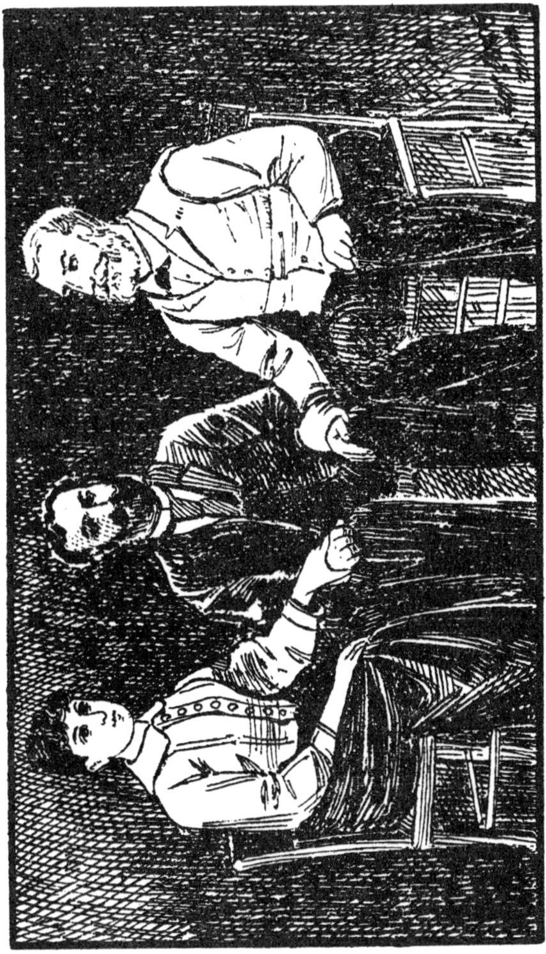

the "seance is closed. Put the shot of one hand in your mouth and go on with the show. You will have no use for *both*.

Again, the "medium's" hands are filled with flour. Put all the flour in one hand and divide it again when you are through.

Another plan, and a very satisfactory one, is that the "medium" allow one of the "sitters" to keep their two hands in contact. The "medium" seats himself, facing the one who is to watch him, and allows the "sitter's" knees to be placed one each side of his own. He now has the "sitter" spread his hands on his knees, palms downward, and places his own hands on top. If he should remove either hand it is supposed the "sitter" will know of it and expose him. The deception lies in the fact that the "sitter" does not get *both* the "medium's" hands on his, but has only one turned so as to lay across both of his.

The "medium" accomplishes this by making passes downward from the "sitter's" shoulders to his hands with his own hands. After three or four such movements, he turns the left hand so that it will cover both the "sitter's" and when he has reached the hands he allows it to rest lightly across them. The "sitter" now *thinks* he has both hands and will so state on being questioned. This is a "test condition" that gives general satisfaction, for no one is supposed to be so stupid he can not tell when a weight is removed from his hand. Yet he is!

Under cover of darkness many apparently wonderful "manifestations" can be produced by one who has been practicing for a year or longer time. Where one is not a member of the "medium's" brotherhood and finds it necessary to "rustle" for "tests," there are many ways open for obtaining them. You know the names of a large number of the Spiritualists of the city in which you are stopping and by a dint of careful questioning, can learn the names of a great many persons who are regular attendants at the "seances" held by the traveling "mediums."

Armed with a list of such names, make it your business to visit the cemeteries and it is more than likely you will be able to pick up considerable information that will be useful to you before you leave the city.

It is always a fruitful piece of work to buy the back numbers of the newspapers of the city and carefully read all the funeral notices. The State Library will usually furnish you with much information regarding the old settlers and their history. Besides this you can usually pump "tests" from one Spiritualist or another by a little fine work on your part. We will say you are in search of information regarding the friends, in spirit life, of Mr. Brown. You meet Mr. Smith, who is an intimate friend of Brown's, and after a little general conversation, say to him:

"The gentleman who was in company with you at the social last Tuesday evening, would make a fine 'medium.' I saw a great number of bright spirits about him. He must have a large number of friends or relatives in the spirit land. I think his father and mother were both with him the evening of the social. Have they ever told him he would make a 'physical medium,' do you know?"

"I believe the 'mediums' do tell him occasionally that he could develop a fine phase of mediumship. I do not know what particular spirit furnishes the information, although it is probably his father, who was quite a strong Spiritualist for many years previous to his death, and was the cause of many persons investigating it in his town in Ohio," replies Mr. Smith.

"Why, you don't mean to say Brown is a native of the Buckeye state?" exclaims the "medium."

"Yes; born and raised in Dayton, where his father died and his mother still lives with his sister," replied Mr. Smith, who is "pumping" wonderfully easy.

"I think I have heard of him or read articles from his pen in the Spiritual papers. His name was Ebenezer Brown, was it not?" queries the pumper.

"No; his name was Elijah," corrects Mr. Smith.

"Oh, yes; now I remember! Ebenezer Brown was from Pennsylvania," says the "medium," but Mr. Brown certainly has a host of friends on the other side, and death must have many times bereaved him."

"Yes; he has many relatives over there. He has four sisters and two brothers that I know of, and a great many uncles and aunts," states Mr. Smith.

"That is quite a number from his immediate family," remarks the medium; "there must have been some hereditary disease running in the family."

"I believe they all went with lung trouble," assents Mr. Smith, and the "medium" has learned enough regarding Mr. Brown to make it interesting for him when he visits his "seance room" or calls on him for "slate-writing." He can now pump Mr. Brown regarding his friend Smith, with possibly just as fruitful results.

The "medium's" ear is always open for "tests," and not one escapes him. Family bibles and albums are very interesting books to him, and if there are any children in the family he is visiting, he will await an opportunity and learn all the child knows regarding the portraits in the album.

A good way to keep posted as to "tests" on the Spiritualist is to subscribe for the Spiritual Journals and keep an alphabetically arranged scrap-book for the clippings you cut from them.

The writer will probably bring down on his head the curses of many hundreds of "mediums," for, if this work is very widely read, there will be few "mediums" save the lecturers who can do business, with any degree of safety from exposure. However, we will now explain to you the manner in which the "lecturer and test-medium" give their wonderful "tests."

We will say that Mr. Stevens, a wonderful platform "test medium" has arrived in the city and is to give "tests" for the month at the Spiritual Hall, wherever that may be, on each Sunday evening, beginning at eight o'clock.

This description will describe work that was

recently performed by a "medium" in a certain city; but no names will be given. It will also describe work done by scores of other "mediums" although they may, and some of them do, have different methods of arriving at the same results.

Mr. Stevens arrived at a certain city in which a "materializing medium" had been holding "seances" for a month. The society had engaged his services at twenty-five dollars per Sunday. He was to deliver a lecture in the afternoon and give "tests" in the evening. The first move Mr. Stevens makes is to hire two parlors in a good hotel. He is so fatigued on his arrival that he does not make or receive any calls for two days, but confines himself to his room. He receives *one* caller, however, and that one is the "materializing medium" who makes his calls in a very stealthy way, no one seeing him go or come.

When they get together, they get out their note-books and begin the work of editing the "tests," getting them in shape. The first thing they do is to take the note-book of the "test-medium" and verify what is written therein. The "materializing medium" runs over the names and "tests" and sees to it that the "tests" agree with what he has learned of the party in the month he has been among them. If they are all right, they are copied on a sheet of paper in alphabetical order. If any of the parties have left the city a note is made of the fact, giving his new place of residence. After the "test-medium's" book has been made all straight, the "materializing medium" adds to the list all the "tests" he has been able to get together.

The "medium" for "tests" will now have probably one hundred *sure* "tests." That will make twenty-five for each night.

But this does not end the preparations, for these "tests" must be committed to memory for it is not always convenient to have notes to refer to, and it is impossible to tell which of the subjects will be present on any given night. When everything else is arranged our two "mediums" repair to some previously named rendezvous and meet from two to ten men that the "materializing medium" has made friends of, and each one is told what name will be announced for him to recognize, and they are told to admit all that is said; but to do it in an unwilling way and rather make the "medium" force the admissions from them.

Everything is now ready and the "test medium" repairs to the hall early, while the "materializing medium" puts in an appearance at a later time. When the "materializing medium" arrives he seeks an introduction to the "test-giver" and then proceeds to introduce him to those on whom he has "tests." Each one is anxious to be introduced, and the "medium" comes to know just how many of his subjects are in the room.

If any come who avoid an introduction the "materializing medium" points them out and gives their names. *They* are *sure* to get "tests."

The confederates have all arrived and stationed themselves in different parts of the hall and the time for operations to commence has arrived. The "medium" requests the choir to sing, and while they are doing so he is snapping his fingers and massaging his eyes. When the song is finished he steps off the rostrum, and with his hand above his head, snapping his fingers, he paces up and down the aisle looking to the right and left, occasionally halting in an undecided or faltering way, until finally he stops in front of a person he has singled out, before he left the platform, and says:

"Madame, your husband, J—W—D—," giving the full name, "is here and bids me say to you that you will find the papers you have been seeking. I now see a child standing beside you. The child is apparently five years of age, of blonde complexion, with long golden hair, blue eyes, and she says she is your daughter, A—D. She says to say to you that she is happy with papa. This child passed away about ten years ago and would have been fifteen years old, had she lived. She died of lung fever in Cincinnati. Now I hear the name of J—W—who says he is your brother; the one who died in the mines along the American river in California in 1852. He says he is accompanied by your father L—W—."

In each case he gave full names. When he had finished he would say:

"Did I ever meet you before, madame?"

When she had replied, he would continue:

"Is the names and relationship given correct?"

After she had admitted the entire correctness of his statements he would resume his walk up and down the aisles. Without stopping in his walk he would announce:

"There is the spirit of a young lady here who says there is, in this hall, a young man to whom she was engaged to be married, but who is so prejudiced against Spiritualism that he will not admit the "test" when it is given.

I will give the lady's name and if the party does not admit the "test" I will hunt him out and let the audience see him. The lady's name is Gertrude Spinner. Does any one recognize the spirit?

No one answers, and the "medium" says:

"I will find the man!"

He goes through the audience, touching first one and then another with his finger tips, until he suddenly stops before one of his confederates and says:

"You are the man. Do you know Gertrude Spinner?"

"I do not think I do," answers the man.

"Well, *I know* that you do, and I propose to make *you* know her before I am through. Gertrude Spinner, who was your affianced, died in Chicago two months ago to-day. She died of heart failure, and you attended her funeral. She was interred in Lakewood Cemetery in the afternoon of the third day after her death. You have a photo of the lady in your inside vest pocket, cabinet size, that was taken in a studio on West Madison Street, Chicago. "Do you know Miss Spinner, now?"

"Yes, sir," he answers, apparently very much agitated.

"Have you a photograph of the lady in your vest?" continues our "medium."

"Perhaps," sullenly answers the gentleman.

"I want no *perhaps* about it," roars the "medium," take that photo out and let the audience see that I am *not* mistaken. You must not attempt to make a monkey of me, for when I tell you anything, I *know* I am right. Bring out the photo' or I shall do it for you!" howls the "medium" apparently in a rage.

The gentleman appearing very much astonished and frightened produces the photo and replaces it in his pocket.

"There!" said the "medium," you *did* know the lady, after all. Ladies and gentlemen, when your friends announce their names, you will confer a kindness by recognizing them without compelling me to drag it out of you.

I say nothing but what I *know* to be correct, and must have your admissions."

The gentleman with the photo gets up and leaves the room with a scowl on his face, as though he had had a very unpleasant experience. The "medium" follows this with two or three "tests" from his note-book in which he invariably gives full names, dates, incidents, and places, and then rings in another confederate by suddenly stopping in front of one of them and saying:

"Your trip last week did not pan out as you expected, did it?"

"What trip?" asks the confederate.

"Shall I tell you before these people about that trip you made one night last week?" he replies.

"I did not make any trip last week in the night time," protests the man.

"*I* say you *did*," roars the medium. "Yourself and two companions walked about eight miles up the river and dug several holes in the ground searching for buried money that some one has told you is buried there. You did not find anything and never will."

"I have never tried to," asserts the man.

"What?" howls the "medium," I say you *did*, and will make *you* say so, too. One of you was slightly hurt by falling off a fence when you was returning to town. You told your wife that you had been with a fishing party. You were all drunk before you got home. You are a drinking man and have been drunk before and will be again. A fortune teller told you there was money there and you went to find it. Was you out looking for money last week?"

"Yes," meekly assents the man, and he to leaves the hall.

There was evidence of the "medium's" wonderful "clairvoyant" powers that was calculated to be a "clincher."

His next "test" was for an old gentleman who was in the hop-raising business. He was down in the note-book as G—— S——, hop raiser, very comfortably fixed. Lost last crop of hops by not selling to buyer and shipping to a Jew in London, England. Spt. Daughter Clara S. musician and fine pianist, twenty-two years of age, killed by being thrown from a horse. Spt. Daughter Anna, died at two years of croup. Spt. Son, Albert drowned when nineteen years of age. Was drowned while visiting away from home. Approaching the old gentleman, he raises his hand to his ear and says:

"I hear beautiful music about you. It is made on a piano, and I hear the name Clara S——. She says she is your daughter and was killed by being thrown from a horse. She appears to be about twenty-two years of age. Do you recognize the spirit?"

"I do, and you are entirely correct," he answers.

"Now I hear the name of Albert S. He

says he is your son and was drowned while away from home on a visit. He says you had best sell your hop crop to the home buyers this year and not take chances on the English Jews in London. He says his sister Anna, who died with croup when very young, is with him. Is this all correct, and did I ever meet you previous to this time," asks the "medium."

"It is correct in every way, and this is the first time I ever saw you," answers the gentleman.

After two or three more "tests" he would tackle another confederate, by announcing a name when the confederate would recognize it. After a message in which business instructions were given he would say: "I see on your back a scar made by your having been struck by a sign that had blown down. Have you such a scar on the small of your back?"

"Yes, sir," replied the confederate.

"I see also that you are a sufferer from inflammatory rheumatism, contracted in the army. Have you the inflammatory rheumatism?"

"Yes, sir, and I contracted it in the army," he replies.

"I see a tall gentleman, with blue eyes, and gray hair, bald on the top of his head, who says his name is Doctor James R. Hayes. He says further that he was your father's family physician when you lived in New York State twenty years ago. He instructs you to procure a quart of whisky and into it put one ounce of gum guieacum and one ounce of poke berries. Take a tablespoonful before meals and your rheumatism will disappear. Did you know doctor Hayes, and was he your father's family physician?"

"I do know of the doctor, and he was our family physician," the confederate replies.

"Have you ever met me before or is there any way in which I may know these things," asks the "medium."

"I do not know how you could possibly know of them except in the way you claim," he replies, and the "medium" tackles another. When he comes around to another confederate he brings it about so as to make some startling "tests" out of him. He has been prepared before hand and it is an easy matter to make the audience think the "tests" are very wonderful indeed. He gets at it in this way. Stopping in front of his man he says:

"I see for you, sir, an agreeable and remunerative change in business. Your business will be traveling in some capacity or other. You have been contemplating this change for more than a year, and now your desires are to be gratified."

"How do you know, or how may I be certain that you know, *certainly*, what you are saying?" asks the sitter.

"I know by the same power that tells me that in your left hand pocket there is three silver dollars and an old bronze coin pocket-piece besides a white-handled pocket-knife with three whole blades and one broken one," answers the "medium." "You have in your breast pocket a letter from the parties for whom you are to work telling you to come East at once and enter on your duties. You intend to start to-morrow morning, and in the pocket-book in your hip pocket is a railroad ticket to Cincinnati. Your father, George W. Haskell, is here and says you are wearing the watch that was his in life. Your sister, Alice Haskell, is here and bids me tell you she has just left your mother in Louisville, Kentucky, and that she is quite well. You have a scar on the calf of the right leg made by your burning yourself with concentrated lye. Do you think I know anything about it, now, or have I told you nothing that you know anything about," asks the "medium."

"I am entirely satisfied," replies the confederate; "and every word you have said is correct. I do not believe in Spiritualism, but you are a remarkably gifted man in some way that I know nothing about."

"Thank you," says our "medium," and he proceeds to "paralyze" somebody else.

This business is kept up until he has given from twenty to thirty "tests," when he closes his entertainment. He now leaves the hall, loaded down with floral offerings from his admirers and goes to his room.

After leaving his flowers, he goes out and meets his confederates, and a general good time is indulged in. Perhaps our "medium" may get a little mellow before morning, but that is no harm if the Spiritualists do not discover it. He gives his confederates a couple of dollars each for their work, this often causing an outlay of more money than he was paid for his services. What does he get out of it, you will ask.

He gets some elegant advertising, and his parlors will be crowded from ten o'clock until six with persons who pay him two dollars each for a "clairvoyant sitting."

It is not the Spiritualist that he gets his big money from, but the investigator who happened into the hall through curiosity.

On entering his parlor for a "sitting" you will find one corner of the room draped with curtains of black, and a small table standing across the corner also draped in black. On the table is a wax candle and around the base of it is scattered powdered lycopodium. There is also an empty plate on the table. To the curtain that drapes the corner is pinned various mysterious packages, tied around with black tapes. Photos are also fastened to the curtains, some of them upside down, some with the face to the wall, and all with black tapes tied about them in different ways. This is his charm working department for working the "sucker" that he can convince of his powers to "weave spells" and "work charms" that will bring about any kind of conditions that are desired.

He catches many a man and woman in that corner of the room. The men are generally after buried treasures, mining claims, luck at the gaming table, or to beat some man in a business transaction, or to obtain lottery numbers. Women usually want conditions that will straighten out their love affairs. They sometimes want a "condition" brought about that will cause the death of their husband or lover, or an "influence" set to work that will result in certain ones giving to them money or jewels or remembering them in their wills.

All classes of people go against this corner of the "medium's" shop, from the poor, ignorant laborer, who wants only a job at a dollar a day, to the female members of wealthy and aristocratic families, who leave their carriages around the corner and make a "sneak," heavily veiled, and who want to know all manner of things about husband or lover, or how they can get rid of rivals or disease.

His charges for these things are on the sliding plan. If the person wear diamonds and rich apparel, he is liable to name one hundred dollars as the price for discovering whether she has a rival or not, and a larger price for bringing about a "death condition." The man looking for work is "touched" for from two to ten dollars, according to appearances of prosperity or his ability to take care of himself.

Such "mediums" often find their work for one week to run up as high as from one to five hundred dollars. He must, of course, make the culmination of the charm he works far enough ahead to give him six or eight weeks in which to work, and leave before any of his "suckers" get around to "kick" because of the failure of his "spell" to work. None of these operations are attempted on the Spiritualist, for it would not only not go, but might result in his being driven from the city.

The female "lecturer and 'test' medium" are satisfied to get ten dollars per Sunday and get a dozen or two "sitters" during the week, at one dollar each. Their "private sittings" consist of visions of doves, crosses, bright or dark clouds, water, ships, and a hundred other things which they interpret so as to best please their "sitter." They do not give general satisfaction —for the reason that they do not give full names, but "see" only first names and wait to see if they are recognized.

One of the easiest "fakes" to work is the "development" of mediumship. Of course, you must have a "physical" or "slate-writing mediumship" yourself, in order to interest any one in "developing" their own mediumistic powers. You strike every "sitter" that visits you; or rather have their spirit friends do it for you. If you are giving a "slate-writing sitting," and your "sitter" is very much interested in your wonderful powers, the balance is easy. After you have answered the questions he has asked of his spirit friends, write something like the following:

"My dear son," presuming he has addressed

his father, "within you lies the power to become one of the finest "mediums" for "materialization," "slate-writing" and "physical manifestations" that the world has ever known. You should "develop" those powers by all means, for you would not only be the means of affording comfort to thousands of afflicted mortals, but would earn a comfortable competence for yourself during life. Your mediumship would be so satisfactory that no "test condition" could be imposed that would at all interfere with the "manifestations." Your name would be celebrated throughout both continents. You would also be of great value to the spirit world, for, through your organism, the spirit world will find it possible to accomplish many things for the benefit of humanity that they can not consummate through any other. If you will promise to develop the powers you possess, I will give you instructions that will bring about that end in a few weeks. Your father,

John Douglas."

We will say that he agrees to undertake his "development." His father now writes:

"Arrange with this 'medium' for 'development. He knows the method to pursue up to a certain point when I will take charge and see you through."

He will now turn to you for information, which you will give in about the following language:

"It will cost you twenty-five dollars. You will come to me twice a week for "sittings" in the evening. You will get further instructions at each sitting " He is likely to ask:

"How is the payment made; in advance, or after I am developed?"

"My terms are cash in advance," is your reply. Now is your time to tell him of the wonderful "mediums" you have "developed," and the large amount of money they are making. You want the money in *advance* for you know that if you wait until he gets "manitestations" you will never get your pay. You will be surprised at the number of "development sitters" you will get that will pay you from ten dollars to two hundred each.

The writer knows of one "medium" who has had forty persons "sitting" with him for "development" at the same time. When the time arrives for the first ones to begin to get "manifestations" the time has arrived for you to pack your grip and "skip for new pastures."

If the reader has ever sat with a "developing medium" can he or she say that they developed to any alarming extent, and did you not lose your "medium" through his "skipping out?" It was either that, or you tried until you was disgusted and gave up in despair.

As a great many Spiritualists imagine that the work of the Steens' is the result of spiritual agency an expose of their work will not be out of place, besides the means used by others to obtain the same results. The Steens have been seen in the dime museums and their work has puzzled many a man. They call their work mind reading.

Mrs. Steen is seated in a chair on one of the platforms of the room and Mr. Steen stands beside an easel on which is a small blackboard, the back of which is toward Mrs. Steen. He hands the board to any one in the audience who will take it and requests that they write four rows of figures on it, as though to add them. Mrs. S. has not seen the figures for she has been thoroughly blindfolded. She is now asked to add the first column of figures which she does and annouces the figure to set down beneath it and the number to carry to the next column. This is continued until the sum has been added. She is now asked to name the figures as he touches them. He now touches each figure with the chalk, touching them at random. She correctly names each figure as she hears the chalk touch the board. She now tells the number formed by drawing a chalk line through any two figures on the board. This concludes their act, which is admitted by all who witness it as being very wonderful.

However, wonderful as it may appear, it is, in reality very simple of performance once you know the secret, and any three persons can perform it as well as the Steens. You will notice that the board is close to, and facing the Punch and Judy cabinet. If you could look inside you would find the man who does the adding and communicates to Mrs. Steen the numbers touched, for he has a small peep-hole from which he can see the board and figures. How does he communicate with her? Electricity. A jar of battery fluid containing the necessary zinc and carbon is kept in the cabinet. A wire from each pole of the battery is carried beneath the floor to the leg of the platform upon which she sits, up through the leg and terminate in two nails, the head of which are on the top of the platform. The nails are close enough together so that the bottom of a chair leg will cover them. In this chair-leg is two more wires that run out in the side of the chair to a point near the front and terminate in two tacks driven into the chair frame. On Mrs. Steen's forefinger of the left hand is a ring and on the third finger of the same hand another. These rings, when she grasps the side of the chair come in contact, each one with one of the tacks, thus making her hand a part of the circuit of the battery. Inside the Punch cabinet one of the wires is cut. So long as those ends are apart, Mrs. Steen will not feel the current, but every time they are touched together it will cause a shock to her hand. Mr. Steen touches the figure four and the man in the cabinet touches the wires together four times. Mrs. Steen feels four shocks announces four. A line is drawn through a three and a five; the man in the cabinet completes the electric circuit three times, a short pause and he completes it five times. Mrs. Steen announces thirty-five as the number, which is correct, of course.

The chair in which she sits must be so placed that the leg containing the wires is over the two nail-heads in the floor of the platform and the two wires each in contact with one of the nails. This is telegraphy by shock instead of by sound.

After the act is finished Mrs. Steen can arise and change the position of her chair, thus showing that she is not in any way connected with wires.

These things are not practiced by the mediums, but are given because the writer imagined they would be interesting to the reader. No medium could use them in a private house. They are fit only for theater work.

Another mind-reading feat that appears wonderful is worked by the operator taking down one of the aisles of the room a small table and two chairs. Placing the table on the floor, and a chair each side of it, he requests the assistance of any one of the audience who desires to "test" the experiment. When one has been secured he is given a seat on one side of the table and the operator sits opposite him.

He now produces a slate and the gentleman is instructed to write on it the number of a bank bill or the number of his watch. When he has done so, the slate is laid on the table and the operator and the person join hands across the top of it. The operator instructs the "sitter" to keep his eyes on the number written on the slate and to think of nothing else. He calls the trick transmission of thought. The mind reader stands on the stage before a blackboard, blindfolded, and with his back to the audience.

Without a word having been spoken or the operator having made any movement, the mind reader raises aloft his left hand and with his right slowly copies on the blackboard the numbers on the slate. The operator and his subject may be fifty feet apart. Any number written on the slate is copied by the mind-reader.

This is considered a very wonderful performance by hundreds who have witnessed it. Let us see just how wonderful it is.

From the stage to the dress circle there is laid a strip of aisle carpet, the edges of which are bound with carpet binding. Across the end of this strip is a copper binding that is broken in the middle. Under this binding on the edges of the carpet runs a copper wire, the ends of which are soldered to the copper strip across the end. At the end on the stage the wire leaves the strip and is conducted to the room below the stage to the battery jar and a telegraph sounder. On the toe of the operator's shoe has been fastened a strip of copper long enough to reach across the broken place in the copper strip at the end of the carpet. It will be seen that every time the operator bridges that space with the copper on his shoe the telegraph sounder will speak, the same as messages are sometimes sent by cutting a wire and tapping the ends together. The operator makes and breaks the current with his piece of copper instead of using a more convenient telegraph key. An assistant sits beside the instrument and every time it clicks he pushes on a wire which passes through the floor of the stage just under the mind reader's foot, thus conveying, by tapping on his shoe sole, the number the instrument has ticked to him. Extraordinarily wonderful, isn't it?

Another mind-reading feat that has astonished its thousands and sent them away in quite a state of mind is performed by seating the mind reader on a chair near the middle of the stage, and, after he has been blindfolded a large sack of heavy material is thrown over him. A number of gentlemen are now invited on the stage. After a screen has been placed between the gentlemen and the mind reader the operator announces that the subject will tell the name of any article placed in his hand or held by others where he could see them. The investigators now hand him different articles from their pockets, and, without a word being spoken the mind reader calls out just what they are, as:

"That is a knife."

"Now it is a tooth brush."

"You have a watch."

"Now a button hook."

"A tobacco pouch."

"A piece of money."

"A card case."

"One of the gentlemen's hands."

"A handkerchief," etc.

If the mayor, chief of police, president of the board of trade, or other prominent citizen happens to be on the committee it is very likely the mind reader can tell him all about his watch, the number of movement and case and makers of each, the composition of the case, number of jewels in movement, etc.

You will admit that if not a wonderful performance it is at least clever. So it is, but so simple it will almost make you sick.

The chair the mind-reader sits in is not an ordinary chair. It is a high-backed affair, and one of the hindmost legs is hollow its whole length. The tops of those legs have an ornamental turning, or knob. In the hollow leg this knob is used as a cork to conceal the hole, and the chair appears an ordinary one. When the mind reader has been covered with the sack he pulls out the plug and in its place puts an ear piece. In the floor under this leg is a small hole through which and into the leg of the chair is pushed a section of tin tubing. To the other end of this tubing is fastened a rubber hose. This leads across the stage and up through the floor behind the scenery where an assistant is stationed at a peep hole where he can see all the articles handled and whisper them to the mind reader. How about the watch number? He could not see that at the distance he is away from it. True enough; but it is not necessary that he see it. He has been around among the jewelers of the city and on pretense that he wanted to buy a watch like the mayor's found the jeweler who sold it and from his book got a full and complete description of it and other watches of prominent men. Of course, if none of them attend or if he cannot get them on the stage he has his trouble for nothing.

When the act is finished the mind reader conceals his ear-piece, and replaces the ornamental knob. The man below takes down and out the tube and inserts a plug in the hole in the floor. The sack is taken from about the mind reader and the bandage from his eyes;

the chair carried off, and you might guess a year without striking the proper solution to the mystery.

The writer can not explain the work of Bishop, the mind-reader, but is of the opinion that he too, was "faking" although he may be mistaken. Confederates are always useful in mind-reading entertainments, and in the last described exhibition one or two could be used to very good advantage, for the extraordinarily wonderful portions of the "tests."

Another feat that drove the people almost wild was performed in the following way:

Performer shows slates clean and washes them to insure against having been prepared. He now binds them tightly together and coming down into the audience has some gentleman hold them above his head, in full view of the audience. He then produces a book of poems and allows one of the audience to open it at random by pushing his pencil or knife blade between the leaves. The book is opened and the performer reads the first two verses of the poem on each page, after requesting the spirits to write what he reads between the slates. After the reading is finished the slates are opened and the verses just read are found copied between the slates.

"There!" you will say; "your silicate flap or acid writing will not work in this case, for the writing is done after the book is opened and read, which is done after the slates are fastened together."

The writing was done through the flap method, just the same. How did he know where the book would be opened? He did not care where it was opened as the book was specially made for him and every page was *exactly alike* with the exception of the number. Not very wonderful now, is it?

The writer has heard all manner of impossible solutions offered for this trick. Some said he exchanged the slates as he came from the stage; but the question "by what means did he know what to write in the first place," was always a silencer to that theory. Others have said that the man who opened the book was a confederate, and there was no way to convince him he was wrong except the trick was explained, which the author did not care to do. The writer once paid a four days hotel bill for three persons by convincing his landlord that the man who opened the book of poems was not a confederate. The landlord contended that had anybody else opened the book my trick would have failed and said:

"I will bet you your bill at my hotel against five dollars that if *I* open the book your slates will be wrong."

His bet was taken, and that night found him in a front seat. When the slates had been securely fastened together they were handed to the landlord's clerk to hold. On this night a different book was used, six being kept, so that no repetition of the verses may occur in six nights. The landlord was instructed to push three or four cards in different parts of the book and then choose at which one he would open. He used three cards and took some time to decide at which one the book should open. When he had decided and opened the book the operator read the verses on each page, and, when the slates were opened the verses he had read were found copied within.

To say that he was astounded, is putting it mildly. He was frantic to have the trick explained to him and offered one hundred dollars to be shown the secret. He did not learn it, and is probably still figuring on it. This was one of your cute men that know more than half-a-dozen ordinary men, and who had several persons present to see him stop the slate-writer on that night. After all his boasts he must have been considerably mortified at his failure, and his friends will probably salt his stories in in the future.

While the writer is about it he will explain the remainder of the stage-people's Spiritualistic illusions, at least the most mysterious of them. Table-lifting is one of their feats, and there are various ways of accomplishing it.

In order to lift a small, round-top table the performer drives into the center of the top a black pin, allowing the head to project a quarter-inch. On the middle finger of his right hand he has a flat band ring. This ring has a slot filed into it from the edge wide enough to admit the shank of the pin, but will not allow the head to slip through. After making a few "magnetic passes" over the surface of the table he slips the pin into the slot in the ring, and, spreading the fingers, bracing the table with them, he easily lifts it, apparently on his finger tips. The same means are used to lift chairs, blocks of wood, etc.

In lifting large tables at which is seated a commitee from the audience, the performer must have a confederate among the committee. The apparatus used consists of a small steel hook fastened to a piece of metal whichs fits and is strapped to the forearm under the clothing, so that the hook will catch the underside of the table when the hands are spread on the top. Both the operator and confederate is supplied with this apparatus, worn on the right arm. They sit opposite each other in the middle of the long way of the table. They get the hooks fastened, and, after first moving the table a few times backward and forward between them, they rise to their feet and the table rises with them. They now get the table turning round and round, and trip up or push over one or two of the committee, thus showing to the audience the great force the table is exerting.

Another, and more easy and convenient apparatus for the same feat is made by fastening a strong hook to a strap which is placed around the neck and hangs down in front under the vest in such a way as to make it possible to cause the hook to project from below the vest. When you are seated the hook is released and when you rise it will catch under the edge of the table causing it to rise also. You require a confederate opposite you, and you will balance the table with your hands.

These persons do the sealed letter reading also. In this act the performer takes into the audience twenty or more small cards and envelopes. These are given to those wishing to write a question. The question written on the card, it is sealed in the envelope. These are now collected by the performer and placed on a table in view of the audience. The operator takes up one of the envelopes, and after holding it against his forehead will say:

"This card reads, 'what will be the price of wheat in May.' Who wrote it?"

"Here," answers some one in the audience. He now opens the envelope and reads aloud: "What will be the price of wheat in May?" thus showing to the audience that he had read it correctly.

He now takes up the second envelope and announces what it contains as before, and some one in the audience will acknowledge having written it. This he continues until the last one has been read. He has read them without a mistake and all have been recognized by the writers. They were all read before being opened. By what means did he read them? If some one has not told you, you will never guess it.

When the performer emptied the envelopes on the table he placed with them a marked dummy envelope. He has a confederate in the audience who answers for the first envelope. When he picked up the first envelope he merely said anything he thought of as the contents and his confederate acknowledges it. He now tears open the envelope and apparently reads what he had stated it contained. But instead of "what will be the price ot wheat in May" being written on it he finds that it reads:

"What is my age?"

After reading it he throws it to one side, and taking up the second envelope announces that it reads, "What is my age?"

Of course some one wrote it, who was not a confederate, and will signify that it is his envelope. The performer tears it open and reads aloud:

"What is my age?" But instead of that, he reads:

"Where was Moses when the light went out?"

The next envelope taken up he announces that it contains the question:

"Where was Moses when the light went out?"

This is repeated until all are answered, he taking up the dummy envelope for the last one. You will understand the use of the dummy. Without it he would be compelled to stop before he had answered all the envelopes. You can do it yourself, now, and puzzle your friends with your clairvoyant powers.

Another feat they claim as Spiritualistic is to place the performer in a large muslin bag, which is tied and sealed over his head. He is now placed in a "cabinet," and, in a few seconds walks out with the bag on his arm. The committee examine the fastenings and find they have not been tampered with. A pocket-knife and other articles that were put into the sack with him are found to still be inside. The bag is thoroughly examined and found to be entirely innocent of any break or rupture of any kind. How did he get out without breaking the seals put on by the committee?

The fact of the matter is that he has not been inside the sack at all, and the writer can prove it. Before the performer gets into the sack he is very careful to place a second one down his back and pants leg. His assistant takes from the committee the articles they desire to put in with you. These he lays on a table until he has placed the performer inside the sack. He now places the articles in the sack, and, pushing the performer's head down he gets the end of the sack that is concealed under his clothing, and drawing it up he gathers the outside sack around it and ties it with a large white handkerchief. The committee is now requested to further secure the mouth of the sack by tying, sewing and sealing with wax, and putting on private marks. They do all their work above the handkerchief, and, as the reader will readily see, they tie and seal the sack that is under the "medium's" clothing. The handkerchief conceals the top of the outside sack. The articles were placed in the inside sack that are supposed to be in with the performer. When the performer is placed in the "cabinet" he pulls the outside sack from under the handkerchief and gets out. This sack he conceals, and pulling out the other sack shakes it out and crumples it and steps to the stage.

It has not been necessary to tamper with the seals, hence the committee find them untouched. They may think that it is not the sack they tied until they examine the seals and take out the articles belonging to them, that they saw placed in with him. That is generally convincing and they go away talking of mesmerism and other occult forces.

Their "spirit cabinets" are quite wonderful in their way, and one, in particular is especially worthy of mention, so simple in its construction and yet so very wonderful the phenomena occurring with it. The committee is allowed to make a thorough examination of it, and find it to be constructed of inch lumber. After thumping and taking measurements to be sure there is no private compartment in it the "medium" takes his seat in front of the small square post that reaches from the floor to the ceiling in the center of the "cabinet." It stands on legs about two feet high and the audience can see under it at all times. After the "medium" is seated the doors are closed. After a few seconds they are opened again and the "medium" has vanished. The stool he sat on is still there but the "medium" has disappeared. The doors closed and opened again and the stool had disappeared. The doors are closed again, and one of the committeemen's coats is passed in through the aperture in the door. It is opened and the "cabinet" is perfectly empty.

"Where do all these things go? Where is the man?" asks one committeeman of another.

Well, where *do* they go?

After more opening and closing of the doors all the articles and the "medium" are produced. This is called the "spirit vanishing cabinet." It stands any amount of investigation at the hands of the committee.

The "cabinet" is supposed to be constructed

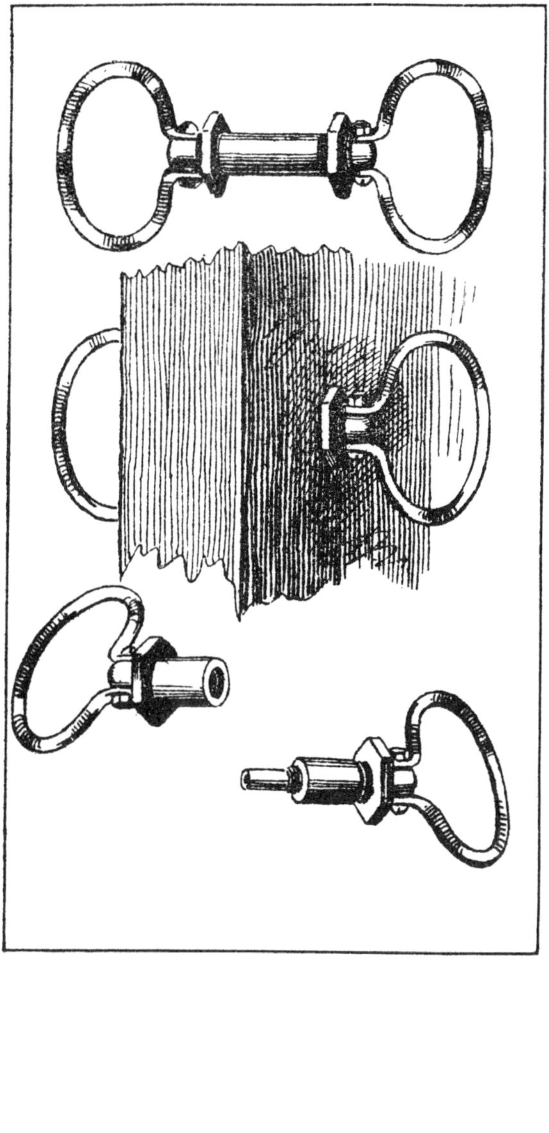

of inch lumber throughout, but the sides are not. The sides are double and are made of lumber a little less than a half-inch thick. The inside side wall is hinged at the back corner so that they can be swung from the front toward the opposite wall. These walls open out until their edge is just behind the square post in the center. This encloses the back quarter of the "cabinet." The "cabinet" is painted a dead black with the exception of the post, which is white, hence, when the doors are opened the "cabinet" appears perfectly empty, yet the "medium" is in the triangular shaped space behind the swinging walls. Care must be taken to so place the "cabinet" that no light falls directly in it. Many have undertaken to explain this deception on the mirror theory and others on the trap-door plan. None that the writer ever heard of ever offered the correct solution. It is generally the case that a man will explain these things in so wonderful and complicated a way that, when he reviews his explanation he is surprised at the wonderful amount of complicated machinery he has invented.

The "physical seance" of the magician is dependent on a great many pieces of apparatus for its success. If he is secured with ropes they are tied to "rings," "bolts" and "staples" that are not what they appear.

He does not become as expert as the "medium" in rope tying feats and makes use of apparatus that is a "sure thing" as to his becoming free or obtaining the use of his hands.

One of these pieces is a steel bolt with a ring in one end. The other end is put through the side of the "cabinet" up to a shoulder that has been turned on it and a tap is turned on until the bolt is immovably fixed to the side of the "cabinet." The bolt has been handed around for examination previous to having been put in place and nothing wrong discovered in its make-up. Something *is* wrong, however, and if it were not the magician would have no use for it. The shank has been decorated by turning two or three deep narrow grooves around it. After the bolt is fastened in place a sharp twist to the left will make two pieces of it, as it comes apart in one of the ornamental grooves. It need only be turned half way 'round to get it apart when there will be one piece of it fast to the "cabinet" and the other to the "medium's" wrist. He can do his work, replace the bolt, turn it to the right until it stops, and call for an examination. While the bolt is free of the "cabinet,"

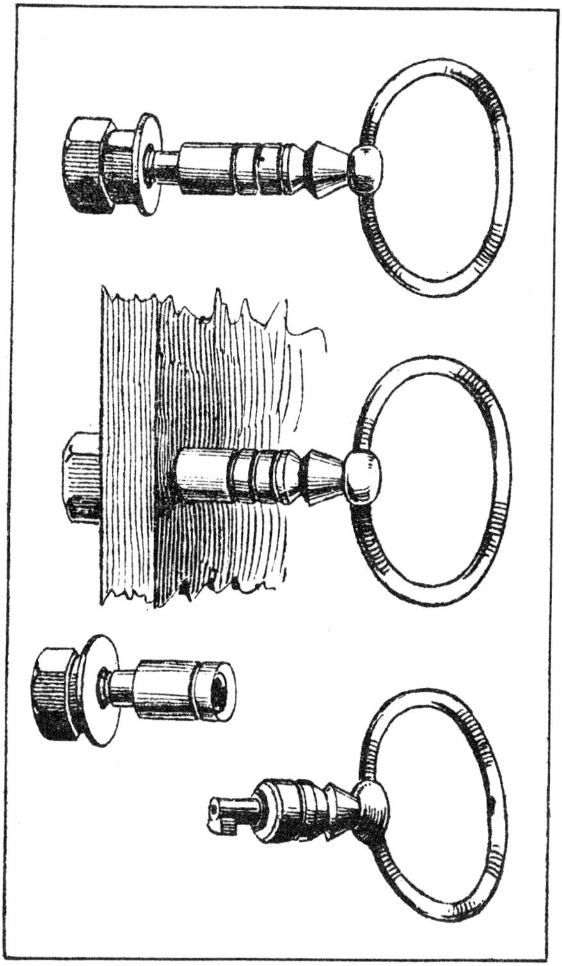

no man is strong enough to twist it apart for the reason that he can not get sufficient leverage. When it is fastened into the side of the "cabinet" so that it can not turn, the ring in the end furnishes the "medium" the leverage he requires.

There is another bolt in use that is quite clever and defies detection. This bolt is seven inches long and three-quarters of an inch in diameter, and is so constructed that an iron ring screws over each end. In using this bolt, a piece of timber five inches square and two and a half feet long is fastened by one end to the floor, between the "medium's" knees as he sits in a chair. Through the top of the post a hole is bored through which the bolt will slip easily. The bolt is taken apart and passed around for examination, different persons examining different parts at the same time. After examination one of the rings is turned on and the bolt pushed through the hole in the post, then the other ring is turned on. Sealing wax is now poured over the threads on the ends of the bolt so that the rings can not be turned off. They could not be turned off after the "medium" was tied without this precaution, except his arms were twisted off, but the wax is put on for an appearance of greater security. As in the case of the other bolt, this one has a joint in its middle that a half turn will open, and the "medium" will have one half of it pendant to each wrist. After doing his work he inserts the bolts into the holes, pushes them together, gives them a half-turn and he is ready for the committee. The bolt itself is perfectly smooth, but the joint is so nicely fitted that, after it has been rubbed around with a piece of coarse emery paper, the joint can not be detected with a glass. Where the bolts and staples are used the "medium" is tied either with wire or strips of muslin.

Another piece of apparatus much used is the "spirit collar." This is made of iron, and fits close to the "medium's" neck. It is hinged in its middle, and is secured by a padlock, the keyhole of which is then sealed. The collar is decorated by having mock bolts along its edge. One of these bolts really is a bolt, and can be turned out, when the collar comes apart at the hinge.

The stocks and pillory that is used are wrong at the hinge.

Now that a great many persons know the secret of their table lifting with ring and pin a

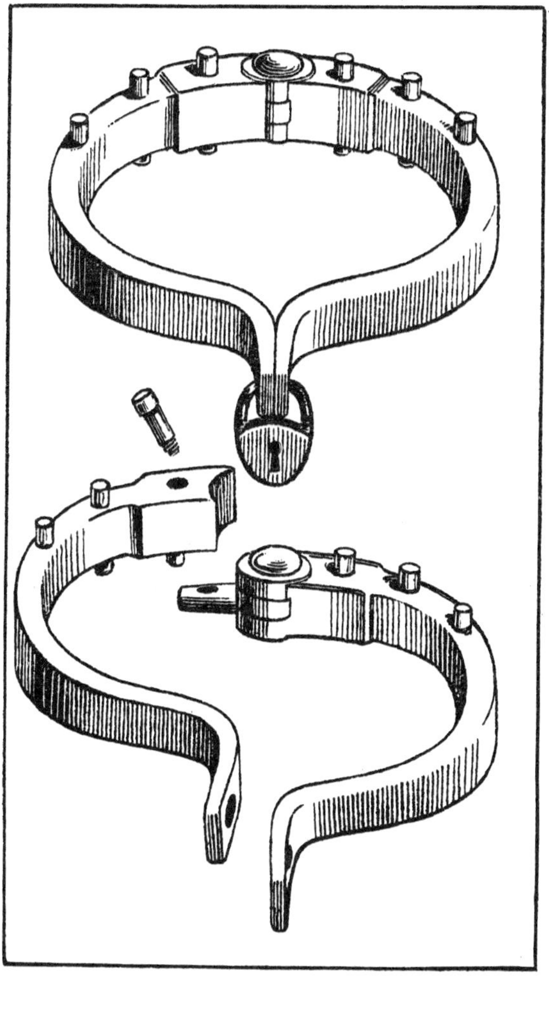

new illusion in that line is out. It is called the "spirit basin." The performer shows an ordinary tin wash basin to be empty, and pouring about a pint of water into it from a pitcher places his finger tips in the water and the basin clings to them. There is no chance for the pin racket in this trick for it could not be driven into the tin. Besides the basin is given for examination before and after the trick. It is accomplished by the use of the suction hat-hook which is in the pitcher of water and is poured in with it. The performer pushes it down hard on the bottom of the basin and it adheres. He hooks the wire under his ring, and the basin must cling to his fingers. When he has finished he pulls the hook loose and pours it back into the pitcher, giving the basin for examination.

These feats are given as the work of the "medium," but the "medium" can make no possible use of them. They are fit only for work on the stage and could not be used in a private house or at the "medium's" "seance."

Reader, have you ever attended a "seance" for "full-form materialization?" Have you ever thought you had met your dead relative's spirit at these "seances?"

If you have never had the pleasure of attending a "seance" of this "phase" you have missed a rare treat. The writer has assisted at many a one and will relate to you some of the wonderful phenomena occuring at them and the means used to produce it. He will mention no names but has no doubt that many will read these pages who will know who is referred to in the accounts of the "manifestations." Many, too, may read who have been duped and deceived at the identical "seances" mentioned.

There are hundreds of "materializing mediums" doing business in this country, who are swelling a good sized bank account. Their business sometimes runs into the hundreds of dollars in a single week. This phase of "mediumship" is considered by the Spiritualist as the highest possible attainable, and if you are a clever "full-form medium" your financial welfare is assured.

Many and various are the methods employed by the different "mediums" in producing this phase. It is in Boston, New York and San Francisco that it is worked the finest. The full-form "seances" most often met with are very simply worked, and easy of performance by the "medium." You are usually given a seat in a circle of chairs about the front of a "cabinet" made by hanging heavy curtains across the corner of the room. If you are a stranger or one who looks or acts as though he would "grab" the "spirits" you are seated at the furthest point from the "cabinet," or, if there are two rows of seats, you will be given a seat in the back row. There are usually three or four persons present who are regular attendants and who are placed in the front row and near the "cabinet." These persons may not be confederates, but simply ardent believers in that particular "medium," and, on account of their constant attendance are admitted at half-price. This is a very acceptable state of affairs for the "medium" or her manager, for they help to fill the front row with persons who can be depended upon to do no harm. After the spectators are seated and a song has been sung an Indian "control," or a "control" other than an Indian, usually has something to say before any manifestations occur, especially if the "medium" has not had time during the singing to get herself in shape to begin the manifestations. It is always a female "medium" who gives *this* description of "seance." You will notice that before the "seance" begins the manager takes a seat close up to one corner of the "cabinet." The room has been made so dark than you can scarcely distinguish your neighbor. After the Indian "control" has unburdened itself of a lot of nonsensical trash, it will announce:

"Me's maked up a pitty white squaw, and she's tummin out."

The curtains part and there is a strip of white visible to the "sitters."

"Who is this spirit for?" will ask the manager.

The "spirit" will probably raise a hand and point in some direction, but it is hard to tell to what particular person, and it is necessary that the "sitters" ask:

"Is it for me?"

"Is it Mary?"

"Is that Agnes?" etc.

One of them will be selected by the "medium."

"Can you speak to me?" is asked.

If the person is some Spiritualist on whom the "medium" has "tests" the spirit can usually say a few words and retires to the "cabinet." The next apparition, it is likely, will be a child or some "spirit" smaller in stature than the "medium." After it has been made known for whom it came it will disappear. If a stranger or one other than a Spiritualist has been claimed as a relative the spirit has been unable to talk except the "sitter" has inadvertently dropped some word from which a "test" can be worked up, as, is brother Willie with you; or, "have you met uncle Harry?" Now, one of the "medium's" "controls" puts in an appearance.

The "control" may be Queen Catharine or some less celebrated a personage. However, when they make their appearance they are attired in snowy white robes with a golden crown glittering with gems. They are gorgeously gotten up and the wonder is, where did the "medium" keep the yards of white material in which they were clothed? She has no guitar to help her out this time. No; but the folds of her skirt will conceal much that she uses. Her stockings are very good receptacles for various articles, and if her manager is worth his salt in the position he occupies, there is no reason why he should not pass in a great many things she requires. Many persons recognize their friends in some of the make-ups of the "medium." The writer has masqueraded as a spirit scores of times and been recognized by three or four different persons at the same "seance" as brother or father and even mother.

A very little apparatus is necessary to make

several changes in your appearance in the dim light that is furnished you to investigate by. The one robe answers for forty spirits, and, with two or three wigs and beards of different shapes, the color amounts to nothing, as it is so dark you cannot distinguish red from any color save white, a crown, a cap or two, a piece of chalk, and you can by changing your height by stooping, and getting on your knees to represent children produce quite an army of spirits, each differing in appearance from any other.

A large "spirit" leading a child can be produced by the "medium" stepping out and holding at arms' length a piece of the white robe-cloth. She has no white on the arm that is supporting the child. Her dress being dark and the curtain behind it dark, the arm is not seen and the child appears separate and apart from the large "spirit." Of course no handling is allowed, and, for all you can see, the shape is a child. The "medium" simulates child's talk and the child is supposed to have spoken.

When there are present a very particular lot of "sitters" the "medium" allows the ladies to search her and takes off all white skirts. The manager loads up with the apparatus and after the light has been turned down, he either passes it inside as he sits in his chair, or the "medium" puts her hand out from underneath and takes it from under his coat. If he sit in an upholstered chair, there is no end to the apparatus she can lay hands on. It is ready for her at any time after the chair is in its place whether her manager is in it or not. Where an upholstered chair is used the "medium" can have several different costumes. No one thinks of searching the manager or chair.

There are no such things as rubber spirits that are blown up, although many hundreds of persons think there is. You frequently hear of "spirits" "materializing" from the floor and again disappearing through the floor outside the "cabinet." In this deception, you will notice that the floor is covered with a very dark carpet. When the "medium" desires to make her appearance through the floor she first puts on a glove that reaches her shoulder, and one that is about the same color of the carpet or darker. She now takes in the hand a piece of the white netting that when shook out is about three yards long and one yard or forty-two inches wide. This is easily concealed by the hand when it is rolled into a ball. She now gets down on the floor inside the "cabinet" with her head gear on, and crawling as far to the front as the curtains will permit, thrusts out her arm as far as she can reach in front of the "cabinet" and on the floor. Her hand and arm cannot be seen. The white netting will show when she turns her hand over, appearing a white spot. She begins to shake it loose and the spot appears to grow. She continues to shake and release the netting raising her hand all the while until it is about four feet high, when, with one big flounce she darts from the cabinet and pulling the netting about her, there is your spirit. If she desires to depart through the floor she gets partially into the "cabinet," and getting hold of the netting so that she can dodge behind it, she suddenly raises it above her headgear and dodges behind the curtains. She now allows the netting to drop to the floor and slowly gathers it into her hand, when she so suddenly takes it into the "cabinet" that, in the dim light it seemed to fade into the air.

There are several methods of materializing a spirit from the floor and the different ways will be given. The manner just described is very effective and in the dimly lighted room is very well calculated to deceive. There are better methods that will be described later on when writing of the "medium's" "seance" who use the better method.

The "seance" just described is the work of

the ordinary "medium," one who is not at all clever, and who depends rather upon the gullibility of her "sitters" than the excellence of her work to pull her through all right. She will go along and make money though, even if her work is raw and bungling.

The writer has often been amazed that the "mediums" putting up this work should ever give a second "seance" in the same city. However, he was not looking with an unpracticed eye or in ignorance of the methods and movements of the "medium," and of course could see many things that the investigator would not observe. After all, it is not always the excellence of the work so much as the ignorance of the observer, that makes many things appear wonderful. Persons who give this description of "seance" sometimes catch some very nice "suckers."

What is meant is that some gentleman who is either wealthy or earning a large salary will become interested, and, finally convinced that "spirits" do return and materialize, and will be a constant attendant at the "seances" of this particular "medium." When such a man is caught by the "medium," plans are laid to relieve him of his wealth, of a goodly portion of it. The spirits give him to understand that they can work much better when he is present and that the Princess so-and-so, his soul-mate of affinity, is always at the "seances" to meet him. This affinity Princess is supplied with an elegant costume that will glitter with tinsel and gems. She will wear a white crown (signifying purity) on the front of which blazes a star, indicative of the advanced sphere in which she exists in spirit life. This Princess will conduct herself very much like an ordinary mortal, in the private "seances" she induces him to obtain from the "medium," at twenty-five or more dollars per "seance," at which time he is always welcomed with a royal kiss and embrace, and will sit on his lap a half-hour at a time, telling him of the beauties of spirit life, and the home they are to occupy together when he comes to her side of life. These loving actions are not always confined to the "private seances," but the writer has been present when a gentleman met his royal spirit lover, and kisses and embraces were indulged in in the presence of a public circle of as many as twenty persons. He would call her his "pet," "darling," "sweetheart" and other endearing names, until he made the writer most outrageously "tired." Others were "tired" too, judging from the smothered exclamations heard in various parts of the room.

When he has arrived at the kissing and embracing point, he is ready to pluck. There are various ways of doing this. He is given to understand by the spirit lover that her "medium" must have certain things that she will not herself purchase, in order that "conditions" be made more perfect, for their communing together. No sooner is this left-handed request made, than a check is written and the spirit sees to it that "her medium" gets it. There are a great many things, now, found necessary to secure better "conditions" and a great many checks written, ranging from ten to two or three hundred dollars. When he has been bled until he will stand it no longer, or has no more money, his Princess tells him she must return to her heavenly sphere again, not to return for a number of years; or he is sent to Europe on a fool's errand, to find something or to take his place in her family. If it is the latter, he is, no doubt, speedily shown the door, and possibly kicked through it. The reader may think such a thing as the foregoing never transpired, but it has. The man, in this case, appeared a thorough gentleman, and was certainly educated and intelligent enough to make considerable money. He is now "broke."

You may think he was crazy but he transacted business all the time that a crazy man could not handle. He was no more crazy than the women who become nuns or the men who will fortunes to the church, leaving their relatives out in the cold. He fell in love with the "spirit" and did no more than men will do who are madly in love with a *mortal* woman. Men are continually doing crazy acts when they are in love, up to their ears. These love affairs between mortal and spirit have even gone on to a termination in marriage, an account of which will be given later on. The writer knows all the details in this case, as he was an acquaintance of one of the "spirits" who brought it about, and also partook of the wedding supper that was given in honor of the occasion, at the bridegroom's expense.

When a victim is being "worked" he is always cautioned against ever speaking of the phenomena he is witnessing or telling any of his friends of the experiences he is having, as their minds being in conflict with any such ideas would utterly ruin the "conditions," thus stopping any further benefits he would secure from their communion together. By securing his silence their victim will not be likely to be "queered" by any of his friends or relatives, for they will know nothing of the matter.

Large sums of money have been secured by "mediums" from men who were wealthy, and men, too, who were highly educated, and had business qualifications sufficient to manage great mercantile and other institutions of business.

It sometimes happens that the victim discovers the game that is being worked on him after he has been swindled out of hundreds or perhaps thousands of dollars. Does he ever prosecute the "medium" or attempt to recover any of the money? Not one time in ten thousand. Why? Simply because he has a reputation to sustain. He is at the head of a large business and it would not do at all to have his escapade become public property. He has the reputation of being a brainy ihdividual by hundreds of persons, and would rather give up twice the amount he has been swindled out of than have his friends and business associates know what an ass he has made of himself.

The "medium" is sharp enough not to attempt his or her games on a man who is not either wealthy or the head of some large firm or business that brings him a large salary or income, so that the money he gives up will not be *very* hard to spare. Should they work a man who has only a moderate income or salary, without any great number of friends and he "tumbles,' to their game, he is liable to 'roar," and if the "medium" does not disgorge will probably see to it that they are placed where they will do no more "spooking" for some months or years.

The man of brains and fortune will say to himself: "Well! I have been taken in and nicely done for. Should my family or associates learn of this affair I should be the laughing-stock of several States, and my good name for business tact and intelligence suffer a terrible blow. I will just drop the matter, hoping it will never leak out. I have had some experience that I have paid dearly for, but the price is nothing if I can keep it dark."

The other man will probably think differently. He will say: "Of all the infernal swindles that I have ever heard of, this one is the most damnable. These people have preyed upon my most sacred affections in order to get money from me. Well! I will see to it that they pay dearly for it. But what will my friends say when they know what a fool I have made of myself. I don't like to have it get out. Let's see; how much have they got out of me?"

He will now figure up the different amounts

paid the "medium" and will probably ruminate as follows:

"Great Scott! I had no idea I was spending that amount of money on the infernal swindlers! Why in fourteen months it amounts to over two thousand dollars. That is enough to make quite an addition to my stock of goods or would go a long way on my years rent and expenses. or would make a comfortable addition to my bank account. They are making money faster than I, and they have nothing invested. I can not afford to lose that amount of money for nothing, friends or no friends. I will first go to them and if they will settle, it need not get out.

If they do not, I will send a lawyer and see it through, no matter how much publicity my foolish actions receive.

You will see, that it does not pay the "medium" to pluck the small fry, for ninety-nine times in a hundred they would be compelled to disgorge, and all their hard work would be wasted. The only thing necessary to accomplish in order to get such a "sucker" is to convince the man of the truth of your claims and the genuiness of your phenomena. After that is made sure of the remainder will be easy. When he is converted he can be led to believe almost anything that comes from the lips of a "spirit."

There are many plans that will bring money, or perhaps the "sucker" (they are called "suckers" by the "mediums") will have some particular "hobby" regarding Spiritualism that will suggest a scheme. Those plans based on some idea held by your victim are always the best and easiest, for you know that it is no no trouble at all to "make a thirsty horse drink." If he be not thirsty your success in making him drink will end when you have led him to the water trough. Just so with your "sucker." You may present your bait, and while he may look it over and not run away from it he will not take it. It is possible you could keep him in contemplation of it until he became interested enough to work, but that would be a tedious operation, and it is likely the money would come too slowly to be a *good* thing, and the chances are he would the sooner get on to your "fake."

Nothing is so good to give a man as something he *wants*. He will take more of it, take it faster and pay more for it than anything you attempt to substitute for it.

Some men want a "spirit Princess" for a bride, and this man can be "nailed to the cross" (that is the way the "mediums" express it) for a good round sum: others want tips on stocks and pay a twenty-five per cent commission to the "medium" on all their earnings besides a five dollar bill for the "sitting" to get the "pointers." When his deal is a failure the "medium" does not return a twenty-five per cent commission on what he has lost. It sometimes happens that the "medium" is given three or four hundred dollars to invest for the "sucker." He does not go near the stock board, but obtaining some of the stock blanks fixes them to show that he has won four hundred dollars and hands it to his "sucker" at his next visit. He now gets his twenty-five per cent. commission.

In the course of a few days the "spirits" tell the "sucker" they have the points by which they can cause the "medium" to win from three to five thousand dollars from an investment of two thousand. The "sucker" had four hundred won from three hundred, and will furnish the two thousand required. The "medium" now has his four hundred dollars back besides one hundred dollars commission and sixteen hundred dollars that he is to invest. One way to invest it is to "slope," another way is to return four or five hundred dollars saying the balance was lost. This actually occurred in one case the writer knows of.

The "medium" took the money and by giving a large commission induced the book-keeper of the bucket shop to fix the books and blanks to show that every dollar of two thousand furnished had been lost. This netted the "medium" a clear gain for his day's work of twelve hundred dollars, he having three hundred dollars in the money furnished and gave the book-keeper five hundred for his part of the transaction. When the "medium" wins the "sucker" will make no investigation, but when he loses such an amount things must be fixed to account for it.

Some are working on inventions and want "spirit" assistance; some want to secure a certain phase of "mediumship;" some want to find certain valuable papers; some want gold or diamond mines or buried treasures; others seek the aid of the spirit-world in securing the heart and hand of some lady or gentleman, etc. They are all "worked" to the limit by the "medium" who delays on one pretext or another, through the "spirits" the completion of the task undertaken as long as the "sucker" will continue to "produce." However, we will return to our "materializing."

The reader is aware that the only difficulty the "materializing medium" encounters is the getting into the "cabinet" of the apparatus and costumes used. The "manager" and chair method have been described, but there are others. One of them is to make a trap in the base or mop-board and stowing the apparatus behind it. It is a very easy matter to cut out a small section of the mop-board and so arrange it that it can be replaced or removed at pleasure without danger of the investigator discovering it. A small trap can be made in the floor, and your carpet so laid that you can turn back enough of it to get at the trap. These traps will be described in detail later on.

Another way is to have a small snare drum in your "cabinet" for the use of your "drummer-boy control." In it can be kept all the laces and netting used by the "medium."

A small table is sometimes placed at one corner of the "cabinet" on which is kept slates and pencils, lead pencils, writing tablets, and a pitcher of water. This table contains a drawer that is locked, apparently, but the "medium" needs no key for he or she enters it from below. This drawer, it is needless to say, contains all the apparatus needed. This table could also be very much in the way if any one attempted to "grab."

When the "cabinet" used is a closet, the most convenient place for a trap is the door framing. You can take off the piece that makes the facing and hinge it so that it swings open from the floor to the top of the door, thus getting rid of a joint that may result in your detection.

Now, you will be treated to a description of a "seance" given by a male "medium" and where you will get your money's worth. The manifestations, in this case, are the work of an artist, in his line, and who is in the business for the money he can get, and is doing his best to give satisfaction. The "medium" is a member of the Brotherhood, and is sure to have the freshest of everything. The writer will describe the "seance" as though he were an investigator, and will assume the personality of one who received just what he will describe as occurring to himself. Afterward it will be explained to you so that it will not puzzle you at all to account for many things you have yourself witnessed or heard of others experiencing.

The location of this particular "medium" will be the city of San Francisco, perhaps on Mission street. Previous to the narrator's having visited the San Francisco "medium's" place, he had been investigating the philosophy and phenomena of Spiritualism for some months. He had attended their lectures and "test-meetings" in New York City, where he resides. At one of these test-meetings the "medium" had given him a good description of a little boy child he had lost, and told him that a visit to a certain independent slate-writing "medium" would result in his having some word from others of his friends and relatives. The "test medium" gave the first name of the child, which was Eddie. I now repaired to the slate-writer and received some astonishing "tests." He requested that I write a couple of questions on a card and seal them in an envelope, writing on the card the name of the "spirit" I desired to have answer them. After sealing them in the envelope there was no way in which the "medium" could know what I had written. My questions were to my father, J. A. Smith, and were as follows:

"Father, are you present? If so, is there any one of my loved ones with you?" The "medium" laid the envelope on a slate and placed it under a table that was draped with a curtain that hung nearly to the floor. He held the slate with one hand and in a few moments withdrew it and on it was written in a hand-writing that strongly resembled my father's, the following:

"My dear son George: I am not only present but am much pleased to meet you here investigating the glorious phenomena and philosophy of Spiritualism. There is one here whom you have heard from before, and who is a bright little spirit. I refer to my beautiful little grandson, Eddie. He sends his love to you and says that he goes every Sunday to the hall."

I was more than astonished at the result of this trial, and acting on the suggestion of the "medium" prepared other questions addressed to other friends. What I wrote this time read like this:

"If my sister, Harriet Mansfield, is present, I would ask her how she fares in her present state, and if she holds the same religious opinions as while on earth? Your brother, George." The answer was in the following language:

"Dear brother: My religious opinions have undergone an entire change since I have passed to the higher life. Spiritualism is the grandest of all truths. Continue to investigate and you will find a solace in its teachings afforded by no other religion. Abner is here. Harriet Mansfield."

Here was a surprise, indeed. My uncle Abner Smith was present, a relative I had not thought of in a number of years. I had not thought or written of my uncle, yet he came to me, making quite a good "test." I now addressed a question to him, and as he died in San Francisco, I wrote:

"I am contemplating a journey to 'Frisco where you died and will visit your grave. Do you think my trip will prove successful? Your nephew, George Smith." The answer came as follows in a handwriting differing from the others:

"My dear nephew. I am pleased that you are investigating Spiritualism. It will bring only contentment and will rob death of its sting. When you visit my grave away out on the western shore of the continent my spirit will be with you. I knew of your intended trip and will accompany you. I can see no reason why you should not have an entirely successful trip. We spirits can sometimes advise in business matters, and if you will visit Mr. ———— ————, clairvoyant and business medium at No. — M—— street, we may be able to be of service to you. Abner Smith."

This was certainly satisfactory coming under such strictly "test conditions" as it did. I now wrote the following:

"If my wife, Alice Smith, is present I should be pleased to hear from her or my brother Alex."

This was placed under the table and elicited the following reply from John King, the "medium's" "control."

"Dear sir: Your wife is not present. Your Bro. Alex. is present, but the forces are exhausted and he can not write at this time. Jno. King, control."

I asked the "medium" concerning the business "medium" in San Francisco, referred to by my uncle Abner, and he said he did not know him, in fact had never heard of him before, and requested that if I found such a a "medium" there that I drop him a card, as it would be something of a "test" to him.

The author should write Mr. Smith's Spiritualistic experiences under the caption "The Fakes that made him a Spiritualist." On the next Sunday I was in attendance at the meeting held by the "test medium," and was surprised and pleased to hear from my son Eddie, my sister Harriet Mansfield and my uncle Abner Smith, each one giving their full name and evidencing a knowledge of the business trip that was under consideration. I was surprised that I did not see the slate-writer there and on asking the "test medium" why he was absent was told that he was unacquainted with the gentleman and did not believe he ever visited the Sunday meetings.

There were several Sunday meetings held in the city, and happening into one farther down town the next Sunday I met the slate-writer. He was not taking an active part in the exercises but sat in one of the rear seats. I sat down beside him, and when the "medium" who was to lecture came in he introduced us. After the lecture "tests" were given and my son Eddie was among the first to announce himself, and expressed great pleasure at the opportunity of demonstrating to me that he followed me about. He said his grandpa J. A. Smith was with him. Toward the close of the meeting my brother Alex. made his presence known by saying he was sorry he had been unable to communicate with me on a late occasion, but would do so at the next opportunity offered, and said his name was Alexander Smith, which was correct. He also said others were present, but would not occupy the time from other spirits who desired to have a word with their friends. This was the first time this "medium" had ever met me, and I felt sure my friends were in the hall, else through what means did the "medium" give their full names.

I left New York the following evening for San Francisco and had a very pleasant trip. On arriving at my destination, and registering at the Russ House, I repaired at once to the office of the "medium" I had been referred to by my uncle. On arriving at his office, I was told that I would have to register and leave an appointment, that Mr. —— was so busy that one could not tell when they might see him except they appointed a time beforehand. Accordingly I registered my name, and left one-half the fee. I found that I would not be able to get a "sitting" until the afternoon of the second day. At the appointed time, I was at the "medium's" door and was admitted to his reception room. After sitting a few moments the "medium" made his appearance and conducted me to his "seance-room." He now instructed me that I observe great caution in my movements and conversation that I give him no knowledge of the purpose of my visit or the names of any of my spirit friends. I was instructed to write a list of questions on a sheet of paper that he furnished me, and to address it to only the *initials* of the spirit I desired to have answer it. This I did, and was given two slates, a gimlet and six screws and screw driver. I was instructed to place the written page between the slates and to fasten them together. When I had done this the "medium" covered the screw heads with heated letter-wax which he stamped with a seal ring that he wore. He now lifted the drapery from a square table and asked that I make an examination of it. This I did and found nothing suspicious about it. The "medium" seated me at one side of the table and himself sat at the side opposite me. He now took the slates from my hand and held them beneath the table with his right hand. On the sheet I had written the following:

"If the spirit of A. S. is present will he reply to the following questions and write any further communication he may desire: 1. Have you communicated with me previous to this time? 2. If so, where? 3. Where did you die? 4. Can you give me any business advice that will be of use to me? 5. Will my trip prove successful? 6. Are there others of my friends present? 7. If so, will you give their names?"

If those questions were correctly answered

there could be no doubt as to the source from whence the answers came.

The "medium" kept up a continual knocking of the slates against the top of the table, and at one time took them out and handed them to me thinking the writing finished; but a loud rap on the table caused him to again place them under with the request that I assist in holding them. This I did by putting my hand through a slit in the drapery over and around the table. I now held one end of the slates and the "medium" the other. While we were thus engaged the "medium" said he felt as though he would see something clairvoyantly for me. He said he saw a child—a little boy, apparently six years of age, with light hair and light blue eyes. His complexion he said was very clear and white, and he thought he could see a strawberry birth-mark on the back of his head. He further said the child called me father and gave his name as Eddie Smith. "Now," said the "medium," "I see an old gentleman, also light of complexion, of medium height with a sandy beard, and gray or light blue eyes. He says he is glad to meet you here, and to know that Spiritualism had enlisted your attention. He says that he is your father and that his name is J. A. Smith."

He described a young man that I did not recognize, and was told he would come again and identify himself.

By this time the "medium" received knowledge that the writing was finished, and took the slates out on his side of the curtain as the slit on my side was just barely wide enough to admit my hand. We repaired to another room and, after examining the fastenings on the slate I opened them and to my surprise and delight one of them was written full. The writing was on straight lines, even and regular. The writing was as follows.

"My dear nephew, the spirit of A. S. or Abner Smith *is* present, and it will please him to answer any questions in his power. 1. Most assuredly I have communicated with you previous to this time. 2. It was in New York City, and the last time quite recently. I will do all in my power to keep my promise, made at one sitting to give you business advice. 3. I died here in San Francisco, and you will keep your promise to visit my grave. 4. I am not prepared, at this sitting, to give you any *advice* but will say that I can see you will be successful in your business. If you will come here again I will probably have some advice to offer. 5. Your trip *will* prove a success, and a material financial benefit result. 6. Yes. 7. Your father, J. A. Smith; your son, Eddie; your sister, Harriet Mansfield, and your brother, Alexander. If you will visit the materializing "seances" of Mr. ———, on ——— street, next Thursday evening, you will meet some of us face to face. It would please me very much to demonstrate to you our ability to make ourselves visible to the eye of mortals. We will expect to meet you there. Abner Smith."

By what process of reasoning could I arrive at the conclusion that I had not been in communication with my uncle? I had received the full names and the relationship of five spirits, through the organism of a "medium," I had never before met, and who said he had never been outside the boundaries of the State of California. I had also received an exact personal description of my son Eddie, even to the strawberry birth-mark under his hair, with a good description of my father, two persons the "medium" had never seen.

On the following Sunday evening I was in attendance at one of the meetings of the "mediums" for "test-giving" and my son Eddie was described, as was my father, and their names given. A young man was described as coming to me who was one of my regiment comrades, and whose name was Rich rds. I could recognize the description but the name was Rickard. I presume the "medium" gave the name wrong and he said it was possible he had misunderstood it. This "medium" told me of a scar on the inside of my left hand, made by a severe cut. There was no doubt but my spirit friends were present, for the evidence was ample.

On the next Thursday evening I made my way to the "materializing seance" at which my friends hoped to materialize." I was admitted to the "seance room" and found about twenty persons already assembled. I was seated in the front row of chairs. The "cabinet" used was a closet about six feet long and four feet wide. The ceiling of both the room and "cabinet" was of wood. After a thorough examination had been made of the "cabinet" by all those who cared to do so, the "sitters" were rearranged to suit the "medium." There were present, now, thirty-five persons. The "seance room" was very large. The door had been taken off the closet that served as a "cabinet," and in its stead was hung heavy curtains. The floor of the room was carpeted with a dark carpet as was the "cabinet." The light was furnished by a lamp placed in a box that was fastened to the wall some eight feet from the floor. This box had a sliding lid in front, controlled by a cord passing into the "cabinet." By this means the spirits could regulate the light to suit themselves, without any movement on the part of any of those in the "seance room" being necessary. When everything was in readiness the "medium" entered the "cabinet," seated himself and was tied, and so secured to his chair that it was impossible that he could have any use of himself. He was most thoroughly secured to his chair and his chair nailed fast to the floor by passing leather straps over the rounds in the side and nailing the ends to the floor. After it was shown to the "sitters" that he was utterly helpless, the curtain was drawn. The manager now placed an ordinary kitchen table in front of the door of the "cabinet," so that it stood away from it about two feet. The table contained no drawer. On the table was laid writing material, a guitar and small bell. The manager seated himself close to one side of the "cabinet" entrance, and started a large Swiss music box. Before it had finished the first air the lamp was shut entirely off, making the room inky dark.

An illuminated hand and arm was now seen to come from between the curtain and played an accompaniment to the music box on the guitar. We could see plainly the movements of the hand, arm and fingers as it manipulated the strings of the instrument. It did not appear necessary to finger the strings on the key-board, although the air was in a key that made it impossible to tune the guitar so that an accompaniment could be performed *without* fingering. However, but one hand was visible, and it was picking the strings. After the tune was finished the hand left the instrument, and moved out into the room to the front of the table, and from the sound we knew it was writing on the tablet that had been placed there. The arm was of bluish light and appeared to end just above the elbow, and to have no connection with a body. It finished writing and seemed to float into the "cabinet," near the top.

The light was opened and the manager requested those who had tied the "medium" to examine his condition and see if the ropes had been tampered with. The examination was made and it was evident that the fastenings were undisturbed. The communication was read aloud to those present and contained the following.

"We are pleased to meet so many seekers after light and truth here this evening and from the conditions, as we sense them, we will have a satisfactory and pleasant "seance." The way to obtain the best results is for each person to maintain a passive condition and take what we are able to give. You may rest assured that our best efforts will be put forth to give you entire satisfaction. The Control.

The writing was exactly on the ruled lines although written in absolute darkness. The hand and arm, although luminous did not give out a particle of light. The arm had been at least five feet from the "cabinet" opening and seven feet from the "medium." Surely, it was not he. The message read, the light was again shut down and the music again started.

Once more a hand appeared and, floating out to the table again began writing. Of a sudden the hand disappeared, and, after a few seconds I was astonished to feel a hand thrusting a paper into my top coat pocket. Now appeared two hands and they played an air on the guitar. Now came three, then four hands were visible, bright as the day. Two of them began writing again and when they had finished, two more "sitters" were the recipients of sheets of paper. Soon the light was opened for an inspection of the "cabinet," which was made, with the conclusion that the "medium" had not moved. Those of us receiving communications were afforded an opportunity to read them. We found them nicely written as before and all contained "tests," of which I will give my own. On my sheet was written:

"My dear brother, I can not express the pleasure I experience on this occasion. We will, before the "seance" closes, endeavor to so "materialize" that you can see and recognize us. Spiritualism is a most glorious truth. Continue to investigate until you are so positive of your knowledge that nothing can shake you. Spiritualism will answer both to live and die by. Your sister, Mrs. Harriet Mansfield."

One of the other gentlemen receiving communications had been investigating Spiritualism for a few months and this was his first visit to this "medium," while the other was a Spiritualist and had visited this "medium" once before, although he had not received any communication on his previous visit, nor seen any spirit he recognized. This time his communication contained very fine "tests."

After the light went out again, more hands were seen, the table was floated about, over the heads of the circle, as was the music box, which weighed at least fifty pounds, two more satisfactory communications written. Another examination of the "cabinet" was made and everything found satisfactory. This time the light was not put entirely out, but a very dim light was allowed.

The music-box was again set playing, and while yet it was playing the first time a tall figure, robed in creamy white with gleaming sparks in her hair and on a sort of crown she wore. She was recognized by a gentleman present, a Spiritualist, whose spirit guide she was, and who addressed her as "my queen." She stood a few seconds behind the table and then stepped out in the open space between the "sitters" and the table. The gentleman now arose from his seat and standing beside her, holding her hand, conversed in a whisper with her for some seconds,

This was most assuredly a lady, if appearances go for anything. Her hands were quite small, and were warm and life-like, as several, including myself, can testify, having been permitted to shake hands with her. At last she started to the "cabinet," and as she went appeared to grow shorter, until, as she disappeared between the curtains she was not much taller than the table. The manager now explained that the spirit had remained out rather too long and came near dematerializing before she reached the "cabinet." Now came the spirit of a young man, dressed in a light suit of clothes, who gave his name and said his mother was present. She was, and had a few words of conversation with him when he disappeared into the "cabinet." The lady said that it was unmistakably her son; but there was *something* that was not as he had been, but what it was she was unable to describe.

The next spirit to present itself was my son Eddie. He came from out the "cabinet," calling papa, papa. The manager asked, "who is your papa?" and he replied, "Mr. Smith." All this time he stood between the table and "cabinet," and only his head and shoulders could be seen. The manager told him to step out where he could be seen, when he came around to the front of the table.

It was rather dark but I would swear it was my son. He was just the right size, with long flaxen hair, with a very pale face. He wore a light-colored waist and darker knee-breeches and stockings, with a large black bow at his throat, just as I remembered seeing him last in health.

While Eddie was still standing in front of the table a large man came out and took him by the hand. Eddie spoke, saying:

"Must I go back, grand pa?" The form turned toward me, saying:

"My son, this is a great pleasure to us, but we must not long remain, as it is our first attempt at "materializing." He turned to go when the manager said to him:

"If the gentleman is your son you ought to give him your name."

"The name of the child is Eddie, and my own is J. A. Smith." replied the form as they vanished into the "cabinet."

The manager suggested that it would be well to examine and see whether the "medium" had been out or not. The "cabinet" was examined and everything found satisfactory.

Spirit after spirit came from the "cabinet," one and two at a time for an hour, some of them came to friends and others were "controls" of the "medium." Many of them were recognized by different ones of the "sitters" in the room. I, for one, could swear to the identity of my own son Eddie, while my father was plainly recognizable.

The "control" announced from the "cabinet" that a very distinguished spirit would now present itself, if the music-box was started. Accordingly the manager allowed the box to start, and but a few bars had been played when there appeared from the "cabinet" and to the front of the table a tall spare man. The light was made a trifle brighter and each one present recognized the form and features of Abraham Lincoln. He spoke a few words relating to the progress of the country since the troublous times at his death. He was dressed in a black suit with a white shirt to which a rolling collar was attached and around his neck was tied the old-fashioned black choker. It was certainly Abraham Lincoln. After speaking he retired to the "cabinet," and was seen no more that evening.

When he had disappeared into the "cabinet" the room was again made dark. Suddenly there appeared on the floor in front of the table a light about as large as a base-ball. It moved about in a circle of perhaps a foot in diameter and grew larger. It soon lost the shape of a ball and appeared to be a luminous cloud. Seemingly we could see into and through it. In the course of thirty seconds it had become as large as a six-year-old child, still there was no definite shape, only a fleecy cloud-like mass, turning, twisting and rolling. At the end of perhaps a minute it was the size and shape of an adult person. The face could not be seen, but bright, luminous spots were visible as though the hair and ears were decorated with gems. The shape spoke and requested light. As the light was turned on the luminousness disappeared, and we beheld a beautiful young lady clothed in a dazzling white costume. Her arms and shoulders were bare, and about her neck there was a necklace of what appeared to be very brilliant diamonds. Her feet were encased in white slippers, with straps across the instep. In her ears and hair glistened and shimmered beautiful diamonds. Her face and arms were as alabaster, and altogether she was one of the most beautiful women I had ever beheld. She was recognized by a lady and gentleman present as their daughter. They had met her here before. They were from the East and were wealthy. The spirit requested that they come to her, which they did, and were each kissed and embraced by it. They held a moment's conversation with her and resumed their seats, when the lamp was slowly turned down. As the light became dim the spirit became luminous. The face and arms disappeared and the body became as a cloud again, turning and twisting and growing smaller until it was nothing but a small light spot on the carpet, which of a sudden disappeared entirely.

Immediately after this "manifestation" an examination of the "medium" and "cabinet" was made, and it was certain the "medium" had not been away from his chair. The light was again turned out and the music-box started, when *two* bright spots appeared on the carpet, one at either end of the table. These went through the same process of development until, when the light was turned on there was another beautiful female spirit at one end of the table, and a child of perhaps eight years of age at the other. The child was recognized by a lady present as her daughter, while the adult spirit was recognized and rapturously greeted by a gentleman who sat near me on my left, as his "darling angel guardian." They had quite a long conversation in which they made use of very endearing language, each to the other. I supposed it was the gentleman's wife. The spirit's name was said o be Isis, and he was said to be a denizen of the planet Jupiter. [More about them later.] These spirits did not disappear as the first one had, but when the light had been turned off, the luminous shape revolved a few times, and on two occasions assumed the garb and shape of men, and when the light was turned on again there stood the men with beards and men's forms.

After some eight or ten of these "materializations" and "dematerializations" before our eyes, the last couple completely disappeared.

The light again turned down and a luminous shape came from the "cabinet" followed by others, until seven of them stood on the floor. The light was turned up until we could see the seven spirits. Five were females and two males. They were of different sizes. The curtain at the door of the "cabinet" was pulled aside and we could see the "medium" sitting in the chair in which he was bound. The forms now filed into the "cabinet" again, while the music-box played. After they had disappeared, the light was turned up, an investigation made of the "cabinet" and the "seance" was over.

There, reader, is a truthful description of what can be witnessed at the "seances" of "mediums" who are artists. None of your bungling, amateur work here. The work of such a "medium" is always satisfactory for the reason that if a man feels *sure* that the "medium" is a fraud, he has been so well entertained that he does not regret the money paid for the opportunity to witness it. This is the class of "medium," also, who frequently succeed in getting large sums of money from wealthy persons they have converted to Spiritualism.

Did the writer not give you the true explanation of the manner in which these things were produced, you would probably say it was a "fish story," conceived by a very fertile imagination. If you believed that he saw these things you would perhaps offer the preacher's explanation, by saying, "it is the work of the devil;" or of the scientist, by asserting that "it is the mesmerist's power over your mind; or the operator has discovered an odd force in nature;" or go off on a long dissertation on hypnotism and fourth dimension of space problems. However, it is not the work of the devil, neither is there any but *natural* laws necessary to its production.

The "seance" described actually occurred and was described in writing by Mr. Smith in the language used, although it was not printed, and the writer was one of those who assisted in its production. He will now proceed to explain this particular "seance," and, in order to do so will find it necessary to begin back in New York City at the public meeting where Mr. Smith was told through a "test medium" to visit a certain "slate writer."

You will remember that he was requested

by the slate writer" to address the spirit by name on the question cards. The "medium" read the cards by the alcohol method and copied them on his cuff or a card. The communication which mentioned in the information that "Abner is here" was a *feeler* for more names. If Abner had not been recognized, the spirits would have written that he was a distant relative and one of Mr. Smith's "controls" or "guides. It happened that Mr. Smith had an uncle by that name and admitted it, besides inadvertently supplying the "medium" with the information that he died in San Francisco and was buried there. You can see how the names and information was obtained, and, although the answers were satisfactory to Mr. Smith it will be plain to you that *anybody* could have written all they contained. The "medium" discovered that Mr. Smith intended visiting Frisco, in fact, he gained all the information from Mr. Smith that Mr. Smith has since gained from the different "mediums." Our slate-writer now hastens to the "test medium" who had sent Mr. S. to him and gave him all the details of the "sitting." The "test medium" is now prepared for him and gives him a couple of the names. It would not do to give them all, else Mr. Smith might suspect a connivance with the "slate-writer." When Mr. Smith remarks the "slate writer's" absence, he is told by the "medium" that he is unacquainted with, and has never met the gentleman thus "nipping in the bud" any thought of collusion.

When Mr. Smith visited the down-town meeting the following Sunday and met the "slate writer" the names of his spirit friends were written on a card and slipped into the hand of the "test medium" by our "slate-writer." Of course Mr. Smith gets a "test." He intends visiting San Francisco and his uncle has named a "medium" there through whom he and others will communicate if Mr. Smith will visit him. All the information possible to be obtained regarding his friends and business, along with a personal description of Mr. Smith is mailed this "medium," with the information that he will visit Frisco in the near future and has been instructed to visit him by his spirit uncle Abner. On his first visit to the San Francisco "slate-writer" and business "medium," he is made to leave his name and come three or four days later. This was done that the "medium" might have time to look him up. Again, he may have been sent from another city, and information may be coming in the mails concerning him. By delaying three or four days the

the mail, if there is any, will come to hand, and the "medium" have time to "fix" it. When he gets his "sitting" with the "medium" he is instructed to be careful to conceal from the "medium" any knowledge of himself or spirit friends. Oh! the honesty of that "medium." He instructs his "sitter" to be careful. He already knows enough to "paralyze" him, and will perhaps know more before his "sitter" gets away. You have read the questions he asked and the answer he received. The slates were screwed together and stamped with the "medium's" ring. The "sitter" held the slates a great portion of the time, and it does not appear possible that the writing could be accomplished by other than spirit power. Another and more convincing proof of its genuineness is the information contained in the communication. By what means could the "medium" know the full names of his spirit friends and that his uncle Abner died in Frisco. How was it possible that he knew of the promise given that uncle to visit his grave.

The writing was obtained by the trap door system that has been described. The assistant in the cellar had the New York "medium's" letter of information and finds it an easy matter to answer the questions propounded. While the writing was being done, the "medium" has clairivoyant visions for the "sitter," thus attracting his attention from the time consumed in getting the slates prepared for him, besides, it was possible he would stumble on some *new* "test." That was the idea in mind when he described the young man Mr. Smith could not recognize.

After Mr. Smith has gone, and it is sure that he will visit the "materializing seance" as requested by his spirit friends, the "medium" makes out a list of names of his spirit friends with the descriptions of those he had described and takes it to the "materializing medium" and the "test mediums" who do public work. Mr. Smith can now visit but few "mediums" in San Francisco who can not give him "tests" that are "clinchers." We will now see how the "materializing medium" produced the wonderful phenomena Mr. Smith witnessed at his "seance."

It will be remembered that the room and "cabinet" was carpeted with a dark carpet, and that the ceilings were of wood. The ceilings were decorated by being put on in panels. The ceiling of the "cabinet" would not have been like that of the room, had the closet been a part of the architect plans for the house. It was not, but was made by the "medium." He simply built a lath and plaster partition from the corner of a wide chimney to the wall, thus inclosing a space six by four feet. The panel in the ceiling of the closet was twenty inches square. This panel was "doctored" and could be displaced leaving an aperture large enough for the "spooks" to get through with perfect ease. A light ladder that reached within three feet of the floor of the "cabinet" was hooked fast above and furnished the means of getting down and up again. There were eight persons connected with the "seance" described by Mr. Smith seven up stairs and the "medium" in the "cabinet." Of course it was not necessary that the "medium" get out of his fastenings, and the facts are that he did *not*. The table was placed across the "cabinet" door; not to lay the instruments on, but to be very much in the way should any one make a rush and "grab" for the "materialized forms." In case this occurred, the "spooks" above would close the light, making the room perfectly dark and the manager would do his utmost to turn the table on end, or side, with the legs out in the room. Before the "grabber" could get the lay of things and get past it, the "spooks" would have gone through the trap, pulled up the ladder and have closed it. The "grabber" would have found the "medium" writhing and groaning and bleeding from the mouth. The bleeding was for effect and would be caused by sucking very hard on his teeth or gums.

The table also served a convenient purpose in the "materialization" and "dematerialization" through the floor. You now know where the "spooks" came from, in this particular house, and how they got in and out. Now let us see how they managed the "manifestations," and the properties used to produce them. The trap and ladder were practically noiseless in their operations, but the music-box made assurance doubly sure that the least sound from the "cabinet" should not be heard in the "seance-room."

When the box began its first air the trap door opened and down the ladder came a young man clad in a suit of black tights. He was entirely covered with black with the exception of his right arm, which was bare to a point a little more than half way from the elbow to his shoulder. The bare arm glowed with a luminous bluish light.

This condition of things was brought about by powdering his arm with pulverized luminous paint. If you are not told the method of transforming the sticky paint to powder, you will not be able to do it and conclude the writer was romancing in this case. The most essential thing to you, will be to know where you can procure this paint. The writer has been unable to procure it anywhere except of Devoe & Co., of New York City. It is put up in a package resembling six-ounce jelly glasses, and you will get six of them for five dollars. In order to reduce it to powder, thin the contents of one of the glasses with one pint of turpentine. When it is thoroughly cut and incorporated into the turpentine, soak strips of muslin in it and hang them up to dry. When thoroughly dry you can shake the powder from the cloth. In order to powder one of your arms, gather one of the cloths in your hand, and use it as a powder puff on your arm. You will not be able to get *all* the paint out, but the pieces will make luminous crowns, slippers, stars and luminous decorations for your robes. You will be under the necessity of perfuming your robes each time they are used, for the odor of the turpentine will always remain to a greater or less degree. To illuminate a robe or costume (the "mediums" always say robe) you proceed the same as in the powdering process, except that to the pint of paint you will add a wine glassful of Demar varnish which will prevent its falling or being shaken off in powder. You are not to make the robe of muslin, but of white netting. Every lady will know what the netting is. It is the lightest, thinnest material the writer ever saw sold in a dry goods store. Ten yards of it can be put into the vest pocket. Do not scrimp the material, but get as much of it into your "robe" as possible.

When he of the luminous arm steps from the "cabinet" into the dark room no part of him is visible save the arm. He picked the strings of the instrument with the illuminated hand and fingered the key-board with the other. He makes a sound of writing on the tablet and tears off a leaf which he conceals, and, drawing a long black stocking over the luminous arm places in the pocket of the "sitter" a communication that had been written upstairs in a good light. This accounts for the even beautiful writing, supposed to have been done in the dark. He covers the luminous arm so that any one so inclined could not locate it in order to "grab" when he is near enough. By mounting the table, that luminous hand and arm can be made to show as though it was floating about near the ceiling.

When four hands were visible there were

two "spooks" at work with both arms illuminated. You already know where the spirit got its information regarding Mr. Smith. You can readily understand the forces that floated the music-box and table above the heads of the "sitters," and an explanation is useless.

When the first female spirit appeared, it was, in reality a young woman, dressed in a gorgeous white costume without paint, hence the light was turned up instead of down, in order that she be visible. Rhinestones and Sumatra gems being cheap she was plentifully supplied with "diamonds," although many of those who are the "queens" or "spirit guides" or "controls" of wealthy Spiritualistic fanatics wear real diamonds, the gift of their wealthy charge or "king" as they usually call them.

When she started for the "cabinet" she used her hands to keep her "robe" from under her feet and as she went stooped lower and lower, until as she disappeared in the "cabinet" she was on her hands and knees. This is what caused the appearance of "dematerialization."

When Mr. Smith's son, Eddy, came from the "cabinet" he was represented by a boy about eight years of age, the son of one of the female "spooks" up stairs. He receives two dollars a night for his services, the same as the larger spooks. He was powdered until he was very white, a blonde wig put over his own hair and dressed as most boys are at the age Mr. Smith's son died. Mr. Smith recognized him by his size, his light complexion and flaxen hair, and the fact that he called him papa and gave the correct name. His father was "made up" from the description given by the "medium" and acknowledged by Mr. Smith as correct. Of course he knew his own name, for it was given him by the slate-writer.

Mr. Lincoln was represented by one of the "spooks" who could easily "make up" for him. These "materializations" of illustrious persons are only fancy pieces and used to fill in with.

Now we come to a part of the phenomena that all Spiritualists who have witnessed it will swear by. What is referred to is the "materializing" and "dematerializing" of the spirit from the floor and before your eyes. In this, you see first a small light, which grows larger and larger, until there stands before you a fully formed lady or male spirit, as was described in Mr. Smith's experience.

In order to accomplish what he witnessed, the same "spook" who had before been recognized by a gentleman as his "queen," prepared herself in the following way. Divesting herself of all clothing she donned simply a long chemise that reached her shoe-tops. She drew on a pair of white stockings and over them a pair of white slippers. Into her hair and ears she put rhinestone diamonds, and around her neck a necklace of the same beautiful but valueless stones. On each ear lobe and around her neck were put small spots of the luminous powder to represent the diamonds while it was dark. Her face was powdered and her eyebrows and lashes darkened, while a dark line was drawn under each eye. She now took a black mask that covered her head, and her "robe" in her hands and went down to the "cabinet." Arriving there she put the black mask over her head to prevent the luminous diamonds being seen until the proper time. She carried her robe in a black bag. Crawling from between the curtains and under the table, she exposed on the floor a small part of her "robe." This she shook and moved about, allowing it to escape from the bag until it was all out. She was now from under the table and on her knees, and it was time the head show on the form, so, getting close to the robe she threw off and under the table the black mask. The shape was now the size of an adult, she adjusted the robe to her person, and rapped for light. As a matter of course, when any light was made the luminousness of the robe was drowned, and she appeared in simply a white costume. The necklace and eardrops could now be seen, but when the light was such as to reveal them the luminous spots had disappeared, leaving the spectator to think the ones he now saw were the ones he had seen in the dark. The process of "dematerialization" will now he apparent and a description will only tire the reader. One small "spook" was all that was required as he could be made to represent boy or girl as was desired by clothing him in the garments of either sex.

At the close of the "seance," the full force of "spooks" came into the room. After disappearing they shinned up the ladder, drew it after them, closed the panel and the trap in the floor above it, replaced the carpet and pushed over the place a heavy bed stead from which they took the castors. They now carried the ladder down stairs and concealed it in the coal house as they went through it on their way home. They will get their pay next day.

Should ever so close an examination of the "cabinet" be made you would not find anything wrong. This particular "medium" has taken investigators into the cellar beneath the "cabinet" and the room above it scores of times, yet nothing was discovered.

You are not always to search for the trap in the ceiling, nor yet in the floor. A trap is not possible in the ceiling except a closet is used as "cabinet" and the ceiling is of wood. Where this condition of things does not exist you must search elsewhere. The floor is a very likely place when it can not be made in the ceiling. If you do not find it there examine the base or mop-board. If it is in the mop-board, you will find upon examination that there is a joint in it near the corner of the "cabinet," but you will find it solidly nailed with about four nails each side of the joint. This appearance of extraordinary solidity will be absolute proof that it is *not* solid.

The nails are not what they appear, but are only pieces about one-half inch in length and do not even go through the board. The piece is fastened on the other side with a couple of bolts that hold it very firmly in place. There is a corresponding opening in the mop-board in the next room, although no attempt is made to so carefully conceal it as no one is ever admitted to it. Through this trap the "spooks" enter the "cabinet" by crawling and wriggling. It is not a very desirable trap for the mop-board is scarcely ever wide enough to permit of a trap that the "spook" could get through in a hurry, besides they must assume their costumes after they get into the "cabinet" or tear them to pieces. You can see how this would make it very inconvenient.

If the room is wainscoted the "spook" will have all the sea room necessary in his trap, for it will extend from just below the molding on the top of the wainscoting to the floor behind the strip of quarter-round. Four of the five-inch boards will be arranged to double together from the middle and open by swinging inward.

This would give a space three feet high and twenty inches wide, through which the "spook" could make good time and not disarrange or tear his or her costume.

It is next to an impossibility to detect these traps by examining in the "cabinet." They were constructed to avoid discovery and no pains spared to make them so absolutely perfect that not one chance in a million is taken.

The proper place to seek for traps is in the adjoining room. upstairs or in the cellar. One is foolish to undertake to find a trap by thumping the walls or floor; for if you happen to thump one the "medium" who is smart enough to make use of a trap is also sharp enough to make provision for its being thumped, and your sounding method goes for naught. Bear in mind that when you are examining the "cabinet," you are seeking at the very place that is prepared most effectually to withstand your investigations.

In the "cabinet" of the "medium" who does not use "spooks" but do the personating themselves and through the use of "dummies" it is well to expect to find the traps *in the "cabinet"* for if they could not be opened from the "cabinet" they would be of no use to the "medium." If *they* open it from the "cabinet" you will be able to do so, providing you find the means. The trap will be either in the mopboard, the floor, the door-jam, or a chair or table on the outside. If you find it in neither place, and have searched thoroughly, take the "manager" into a room and go through his pockets and clothing. You are sure to find an assortment of robes, wigs and various articles of spiritual apparel in one or the other of the places mentioned. Do *not forget* the "manager" in your search. He or she is never searched, or never has been, up to date, which has been the cause of many a failure to find the "properties" of the "medium" when the "seance" was given in a room and "cabinet" furnished by a stranger and skeptic. Do not be deceived into a belief that each one of the "sitters" are strangers to the "medium." There may be from one to five persons present who pay their money the same as yourself, and who may appear to be the most skeptical of any one in the room. They will generally be the recipients of some very elegant "tests" and weep copiously great grief-laden tears when they recognize the beloved features of some relative.

They are the most careful of investigators, and when the "medium's" trap is located in the door-jamb, will pound the walls, and insist on the carpet being taken up, when they will get upon hands and knees and make a most searching examination of the floor. They are the closest and most critical of investigators, but they are very careful to examine everywhere *except where the defect is located.* Because one or two men *seem* to be making such a critical investigation, do not allow that fact to prevent you making one on your own responsibility. Wait until they have finished and then examine not only where they did, but most particularly where they did *not*. Their examinations are only for the purpose of misleading others. Their "tests" are received in a way to cause those about them to think they admit them very unwillingly or because they were so undeniable that they could do nothing else.

A great many will probably deny that confederates are ever employed. They are not by "mediums" who are not smooth enough to produce that which appears so wonderful as to make a good business for them. The writer would advise those "mediums" who give such rank "seances" to employ a few floor-workers, they are easily obtained, and see what a difference it would make in the amount of business they will do. Get good ones—those who know human nature, and know when they have said all that is necessary. Most of them are inclined to say too much, thus causing the ordinary man to suspect that he is a confederate.

It is only in a few cities of the United States where the expert and artistic "mediums" are to be met with, men who invest considerable money in the business, and do business with the intention of puzzling every class of man who attend their "seance." It is true, though, that hundreds of "mediums" are to be met with all over the country who carry several "test" or note-books, and who furnish much information to the located "medium." Once let a man get into the hands of the Brotherhood and he will have no trouble at all in receiving "tests" all over the country.

The writer agreed to give the details of the courtship and marriage of a mortal and spirit, and this is a fitting place to give it. The real name of the gentleman will not be given, but the name of the spirit was supposed to be Isis, and she an inhabitant of the planet Jupiter. Mr. Smith, on his visit to the "materializing seance" witnessed a meeting of the gentleman and his spirit bride. The conditions that led to this marriage were as follows:

The bridegroom, whom we will call Mr. Brown, began an investigation of Spiritualism in one of the Eastern cities. He was a man of wealth and traveled much as a means of pleasantly passing away the time. He was educated a bachelor, and held that all the planets were inhabited by races of human beings similar to ourselves, though much in advance of us in everything. He believed that the inhabitants of Jupiter were once the people of this earth, but that since death they may have lived on several of the different planets, and as they progressed were placed on planets that contained everything and every condition that their state of development entitled them to.

How much of this strange belief was obtained through the "medium" the writer cannot say. However, when the 'Frisco "medium" learned these views he at once set to work to make them pay him. He, Mr. Brown, was first convinced that the "medium" was genuine. His own views were then made to appear as correct, thus he was certain to continue his investigations with this "medium."

At one of the "materializing seances," one of the female "spooks" was made as handsome as a new robe trimmed with satin and other things, a Rhinestone necklace, ear-drops hail-pins, bracelets and brooch, along with plenty of powder and pencil-work would make her, and she "came" for Mr. Brown.

It was no one Mr. Brown remembered, and he was told that it was a spirit from Jupiter and was his spirit guide or guard, and his "affinity." He was also told that he had just begun to attain a Spiritual "condition" that would permit her to communicate with him.

In her "make-up" the "spook" was certainly very beautiful. Especially was this true when she was looked upon in the very dim light of the "seance-room."

Mr. Brown fell in love with Isis, very much in love. So much so that he was present at every public "seance," and had one and two private "seances" each week. It may not have been so much the physical beauty of the spirit as the supposed exalted sphere of progression she existed in, and the thought that she was his guardian angel.

Besides this, her conversation with him was always of spiritual sciences and matters that were of interest to him. She also gave him to understand that they always had been "affinities," and that some time in the future they would be mated. He was informed that the reason he had never married was because of her "influence," that had she remained on earth they would as certainly have met and married as it was that the sun rose and set that day, also that it would have been infinitely easier for both to have reached the perfect state if it had transpired that way. He was told that these communions together would materially aid him in his progression when he came to that side of life. This was kept before him so constantly that he finally asked if it would not be possible to consummate the marriage between them.

This was rather unexpected and the "medium" and "spook" consulted on the matter and concluded they could get a little extra, perhaps, by getting up a mock marriage ceremony. The "medium" set his wits to work, and when Mr. Brown had his next private "seance" he was told that the marriage could be consummated if it could be arranged so as to not kill or injure the "medium." It was satisfactorily explained to him why there was danger of anything of the kind occurring, and that the "medium" ought to be handsomely rewarded if he could be persuaded to sit for him for that purpose. It was left to her to name the amount and she made it five hundred dollars. She bade him make the arrangements with the "medium" and confer with her again next day. This he did, and the "medium" after *much persuasion* was induced to accept a check for five hundred dollars, the "seance" to occur at any time named by the spirit Isis.

At the private "seance" the next day Isis informed Mr. Brown that a large amount of fine silks and jewelry would have to be purchased and placed in the "cabinet" so that she and the company would have abundance of material from which to "materialize" their clothing. He was told that the occasion should be honored with a grand supper after the ceremony, and would he see to it that it was arranged for. She said there would be six "materialized" spirits present and twenty who would be invisible. The date for the wedding was named and the number of private "seances" to be had previous to it. He was instructed to give the money to the "medium" to purchase the silks and other material they were to "draw from."

These things were to be touched by no hand save the "medium's" else they would receive a "magnetism" that would prevent the purpose for which they were furnished. The "astral magnetism" would control all the proceedings, and none other must be allowed to contaminate it.

The wedding night came around and the "seance" room was decorated with flowers and shrubs, besides a long table being laid for twenty-one persons. It will suffice to say that the wines and viands on the table cost close to three hundred dollars. No one was present save the "medium" and Mr. Brown. The "medium" entered the "cabinet" and went into a trance.

Soon there stepped into the dimly-lighted room a tall and magnificiently gowned and crowned person who appeared to be a priest or a high functionary of some sort. He was followed by the "bride" and she by four other beautifully costumed "spirits," two ladies and two gentleman. The writer will only add that the tall spirit performed the marriage ceremony, after which all sat down at table although nothing was eaten, as Mr. Brown had not yet been brought to a point where he could believe a spirit could eat and digest solids. They were supposed to feast on the aroma or essence or spiritual part of the feast spread for them.

The "medium" had fine wines and high living for several weeks after the wedding. He did not purchase silks and laces with the money furnished but placed in the "cabinet" some bundles of paper.

All the properties furnished for the wedding went to the "medium." He made in the entire transaction, including "private sittings," more than four thousand dollars in six months. This from *one* man, alone. He may have had three or four "suckers" beside Mr. Brown. To be sure, the "sucker" is cautioned to secrecy regarding all these occurrences, for were it to become known by any of his friends it might result disastrously to the "medium."

The recital of Mr. Brown's experience will not be believed by a great many who read this book; but it is a *fact*.

The writer knows of another case of mortal falling in love with a spirit, in which the spirit, too, became smitten. It resulted in the "spook" going to the gentleman and confessing that she was the spirit. They are married, now, and as the gentleman is wealthy, the "medium" has levied blackmail on the poor "spook" wife until life is a burden to her. The "medium" threatens to tell the public how she obtained her husband.

Perhaps the render witnessed or read of the wonderful spirit parafine moulds that created so much astonishment some years ago in London. It was supposed that the spirits "materialized" and in the presence of the "sitters" made parafine moulds of their faces, feet and hands.

They would prepare for this "phase" by placing in a basin of hot water a large piece of paraffine wax. This would melt and float on the surface of the water. This would be placed on a table in front of the "cabinet" with a basin of cold water. The spirit would come from the "cabinet" and bending over, apparently dip their faces in first the paraffine and then the cold water. It would require three dips to have the sheet of paraffine sufficiently thick to retain its form. After dipping, the spirit would stand erect and apparently pull the mould.

from the face and hand it to one of the "sitters." This was all performed in a *very dim* light.

The explanation is simple enough and lies in the "medium's" having prepared in advance by making paraffine masks from plaster of paris moulds. When the spirit came from the "cabinet" it had fitted over its face the prepared mould, and, in reality, did not dip into the paraffine but *did* dip into the water, so that when the "sitter" got them they were wet and dripping.

Many persons have these moulds mounted and framed hanging in their apartments thinking them the work of the spirit-world and prize them highly. Usually they cost enough to obtain so that they *should* be prized.

Many were the attempts to solve the mystery of their production, but all resulted in failure, for the reason that they were supposed to have been made before the eyes of the "sitter" and pulled from the faces they were moulded over. As the "mediums" were men with beards it was impossible that they be moulded over *their* faces.

The reader can perform some wonderful work with the guitar when *both* his hands ARE held if he will experiment a few times and follow up the following instructions.

Place in your room an oval dining-table and

on it place a guitar, tea-bell and a tambourine from which the head has been cut. In your top vest pocket place a long lead pencil. Now seat your "sitters" around the table and have them clasp each the other's hands, including your own. Seat yourself so that the end of the neck of the guitar is lying toward you and quite close to the edge of the table. Have the tambourine lying close to your edge of the table, while the bell can be placed anywhere. Make the room perfectly dark and begin operations by catching the edge of the tambourine frame in your teeth and by leaning well back put it over your head. It will settle down around your neck. Now draw the neck of the guitar out over the edge of the table and by leaning forward the tambourine about your neck will hang down to as to allow you to get the neck of the guitar through it a few inches. On straightening up you will find that the guitar will bind against the ring and your chest so that it will rise from the table. It lay on its back on the table and the strings must be on the side toward you. Now take the pencil between your teeth and proceed to thrum the guitar. By moving it about your "sitters" will think it is travelling about the room. In order to disguise your movements in causing the "manifestations" you will find the jumping and jerking tactics of all "mediums" to quite effectually fill the bill.

Now we come to the "sack-test" that has caused so much astonishment among the uninitiated. This "test" is in use to-day by a great number of "mediums," and is the one the magicians were attempting to expose when they invented the sack trick already described. You will readily perceive the difference between the two feats.

In this "test" the "medium" is placed into a sack of heavy material, usually dark canton-flannel, that is just long enough to admit of its being tied around the neck. Before he gets into the sack, each of his wrists have tied and sealed about them pieces of colored braid. These have ends long enough to be put through holes in the sack and tied to the back of the chair in which he is sitting. When he is secured, he is inside a flannel sack that has a draw-string in its top which is pulled up until it brings the mouth of the sack snugly about his neck and the ends tied and sealed with wax. The knots and seals are at the back of his neck. The tapes on the hands are pulled through small holes in the sack behind and tied to the chair back, thus his hands are firmly tied behind him.

SPIRITUALISTIC MYSTERIES EXPOSED. 315

In this condition the poor, helpless "mecium" is placed in the "cabinet" and expected to aid the spirits to produce "physical manifestations." Of course the investigator has a sure thing on the "medium" not being able to perform any tricks except he break the tapes and seals. It is impossible that he have the use of any of his members or get away from the chair.

Notwithstanding all these "test conditions" the "manifestations" occur just as though the "medium" was entirely free; hands and faces are seen, the instruments are played upon, and "full-form materializations" walk from the "cabinet."

After the "seance" is finished an examination will show you that the "medium's" condition is the same as before the "manifestations." Not a tape or seal has been touched. Fullforms have come from the "cabinet," yet here is the "medium" tightly tied up in the sack and it is not possible that it was he.

Of course you know what it was that walked out of the "cabinet" and spoke. It was a rubber form that the "medium" blew full of wind, and, being a ventriloquist he threw his voice into the form's mouth, thus causing it to appear to speak. Was that it, or did the "medium" have a confederate come up through the floor? If you can not solve the mystery satisfactorily to yourself as being either of the above explanations nor the result of mesmerism, or that the "medium" sprayed the room with a liquid that robbed you of your senses for the time being and caused you to *imagine* you saw the form, go to a preacher and ask him for the explanation. You will get it, for they *ought* to know *everything*, and if you believe all they say, they *do*. The preacher will look wise (just like the doctors do) and after turning your question over in his mind a few seconds will turn upon you a face expressive of pity for you and horror of your late experiments and say to you in a voice solemn as death and calculated to carry conviction of truth with it, "My dear man, it is the work of the evil one. It is the Devil's work in leading mankind astray from the truth."

I suppose he would be right if he did not happen to be wrong. The devil is a very convenient person for them. What they cannot explain they lay to him.

In this case they would be wrong, as usual, for it was none other than the "medium" who came from between the curtains all robed in white. It was not the devil nor a rubber form nor a confederate, neither were you mesmerized or drugged. I might add that it is not necessary to the "medium's" success that his "sitters" be crazy, either.

Here is an explanation that entirely wrecks the "devil theory." We have said it was the "medium," now let us *prove* it. As we *know* how he accomplisbed it, it will not be a difficult matter to demonstrate the truth of *our* explanation.

The sack had withstood the closest inspection and had been pronounced perfectly straight and sound. In fact the "mediums" will sell these sacks to the investigator, and they can take them home and make a most thorough examination of them and yet discover nothing wrong in their construction. However, because the investigator discovers nothing is no proof that the sack is faultless.

The sack is perfectly sound with the exception of a small hole in the hem around the top of the sack. This hole is made by ripping open the seam made in sewing up the side of the sack, inside the hem around the top, through which passes the tape that serves as a draw-string. When the "medium" is placed in the sack this seam is in front of him and he gets hold of the tape, drawing in and fastening to a vest-button enough of it so that when he releases it, it will permit of the sack being opened wide. It is now easy enough to get out and in again if his hands were not tied. The hands are *not* tied.

The tapes were tied and sealed around each wrist, separately, leaving ends sufficiently long to put through the holes in the back of the sack and tie to the chair. When the "medium" gets into the sack he gets out of his pocket two pieces of tape of the same color as that on his wrists. He doubles one piece and puts the ends through one of the holes, keeping tight hold of the other end. He does the same with the other piece, and the investigator ties them to the chair thinking them the ends of the tapes that are around the "medium's" wrists.

You can see, now, reader, how easy a matter it is for the "medium" to get out and in again without any aid from the devil or anybody else.

When the "seance" is at an end, the "medium's" assistant cuts the tapes that are supposed to bind the hands, and the "medium" puts the pieces he holds into his pockets. The asssistant now cuts the tapes around the neck, and, pulling out the slack that the "medium" used, cuts it off and puts it in his pocket, leaving the tape just the length it should be.

In conclusion the writer does not wish to be understood as maintaining that there is nothing in the Spiritual philosophy. Far from it. Although he has cursed the teachings of the *Religio-Philosophical Journal*, while traveling about the country giving his "seances," he is free, now, to admit that the journal in question is pretty generally sound in its doctrines and opinions, and is the paper *par excellence* of the entire number published. While it may appear severe or too general and far reaching in its accusations of fraud among the "mediums," the trouble is the editor does not lay hands on but a very small per centage of the fraud and dishonesty practiced. Were there more papers published on the same principles Spiritualism would soon reach a more elevated plane, and the hundreds of rascals who are coining money at the Spiritualist's expense would be compelled to stop their miserable work. It is not the writer's desire to deprive any Spiritualist of the comfort they must certainly derive from their belief in Spiritualism. There is nothing so calculated to give the believer such solace in their hours of trial and tribulation. No church deals out to its congregation anything so satisfactory, so comforting and so much in accord with our ideas of Almighty and indiscriminating justice. The author's entire family are Spiritualists, made so from "mediums" who were frauds, but the writer would no more take their Spiritualism from them, even though he *knew* it was a farce *from beginning to end,* than he would deliberately set to work and take their lives. What he has undertaken has been to convince the reader that there are thousands of persons earning a dishonest living through the practice of various deceptions in the name of Spiritualism. He feels satisfied that what he has written is done so in such a manner as to be convincing that he is not writing "fairy tales," but of things that, perhaps you have spent many a dollar on, under the impression that it was very different. He has attempted to show that the "professional medium" is to be watched, and that few, if any, are what they claim. He hopes that he has so fully explained their tricks, that the fraudulent rascal will find it a hard matter, indeed, to capture your silver, and that if you are ever "nailed to the cross" it will be through means other than those used by the gentry treated of. The author sincerely hopes, and firmly believes that wherever this book is read, it will result in a general purging of the ranks of the Spiritualist of all unclean "mediums" and hangers on. The writer is, perhaps, more Spiritualist than anything else. He believes that he will live again although that belief was not the result of listening to the sermons of the preacher, nor through anything read in the Bible. If the writer live again he is sure others will, and it is probable that he will meet the friends that have preceded him, and it is more than likely he will be able to see and visit his friends on earth. If it does transpire that he can return to earth and visit those he loved, he is positive he will not do so through performing feats with heated lamp chimneys, or controlling a lecturer and attempting to deliver an impressive oration in the language of a coal heaver. He would not attempt to return through a "medium" through whom an Indian "control," who is at least sixty-eight years of age, converses to an audience in the language of a prattling child, through fear that his relatives and friends would not believe the "medium" even though she *were* genuine. He does not believe that he or any other spirit can or would return through the organism of any man who is an habitual drunkard and depraved in other ways, nor through a woman who is worse than a common prostitute. Many such persons are to be found among the "mediums."

It is not at all probable, either, that he would go into the business of materializing lace for the entertainment of a number of sitters at fifty cents or a dollar a head, although he is familiar with the methods employed in that manifestation. No religion is so satisfactory nor so reasonable and just in its teachings, to the writer's best understanding; but his own career and the fact that he has met no other *professional* "medium," male or female, in his long experience and extensive travels, who were not "crooked" leads him to the conclusion that from the professional you are to expect nothing genuine. Reader, investigate Spiritualism. It will do you no harm, but may do you much good. Do not investigate through the professional "medium," but form a circle of your own family and admit none other. If there is anything for you, you will get it in that way as easily, or more so, than any other. Do not set out with the intention of getting rich in worldly goods through their aid nor attempt to find buried treasures, pots of gold, mines of silver or in fact anything you can better attend to yourself, but to receive anything that it may be their pleasure or license to give you. Do not attempt to develope the phase of "materialization" or any physical manifestations, for the chances are you will sit in vain. Subscribe for the *Religio-Philosophical Journal*, edited and owned by Jno. C. Bundy of Chicago, and you will get as clean, honest literary work and opinions along with articles from the pens of clearheaded able writers and correspondents, as it is possible to obtain. You will gain much that is not misleading and that will materially aid you in your investigations.

Bear in mind that men and women may be mistaken in regard to a great many things and still be of sound mind. You will find also that Spiritualism numbers among its believers hundreds of persons against whom no breath of scandal has ever been breathed, and who are learned, and many who occupy positions of honor, trust and responsibility. Read the history of the various denominations of orthodox Christians, and you will find that all that is said against the Spiritualist has been said of them. Remember, that no matter what manner of man or woman the "medium" may be, that it does not follow that the Spiritualist has the same taste and desires. If you must have it that there is nothing in the Spiritualist's belief, do not set him down as a fool or a knave, or as one who is insane; but say, simply, that he holds mistaken ideas. You would not accuse a man who was color-blind of all these things because he mistakes red for yellow

This work will receive unlimited amounts of abuse at the hands of the "medium" and some of the Spiritualistic journals; but in the case of the "medium" it will be found that they will no longer attempt to produce certain phases or manifestations which have before been a feature of their seances. Yet do not despair You will find in the chaff that is so plentiful some good grains. Because one does not find it does not signify that none will.

The writer could tell a strange story regarding the origin of the desire to write this book and circumstances surrounding its production but, as not one reader in a hundred would believe or understand it, it will be left unwritten No one should allow this book to stop their investigation of Spiritualism, but should continue their investigations with the book in a convenient pocket.

INDEX

Abbot, Mr., husband of "electrical woman," 163, 164.
Abbott, Mrs., the "electrical woman," xxiii., 157 ff
Acid, for independent slate-writing, xxii., 120
Affinities, 307
Albums, family, as a source of information, 199
Alcohol, baths, xxiv., 167; to render paper temporarily transparent, xxv., 179, 288
Animal Magnetism, as agent for healing the sick, 165
Apparatus, mediums and, xxii., 11, 17, 22, 237, 238
Arm, blood-red writing on, 181; in varnish, 182
Baldwin, 11
Banner of Light, 63
Bard, Mr., 59
Bearded "spirits," 285
Belts, magnetic, 169
Bibles, family, as a source of information, 199
Billet reading, *see* Pellet reading
Billiard cue trick, 163
Bishop, Washington Irving, xxvi., 225
Bleeding from the mouth, for effect, 293
Blood-writing test, 181
Bolts, faked, 238-242; illustrations of, 234, 239
Book, faked, and slate trick, 225-8
Box, musical, floating, 279-80
Bride, spirit, 256, 305, 310
Brimstone, smell of, 82
Bundy, Jno. C., 323
Bundyite Spiritualist, 176
Business, mediumship, as a, 304
Cabinet, description of spirit, 67, 233-4
Cagliostro, 23
Cameras, twenty-five cent., 112

Carpet trick, 140 ff.
Catharine, Queen, as spirit control, 249
Ceilings, faked, 291, 301
Cellar, use of, 153
Cemeteries, information found at, 196
Chair, faked, for slate writing, 123
Charges, a medium's sliding scale of, 213
Chase, C. M., xviii., 22
Cheeks, clapping of, as substitute for hands, 190
Cincinnati, note-book for, 110
Circles, private, 42 ff.
Clairvoyant sittings, 45 ff, 180, 211
Collar, spirit, 242; illustration of, 243
Committees, learned, 13, 23 ff.
Confederates, xxii., 140, 202-11, 225, 304
"Controls," spirit, Indian, xix., 53-54, 247, 248; Queen Catharine, 249; Katie King, xxvii., 254
"Cough Medicine," 83
Cuff, shirt, use of, 138
Development of mediumship, 68, 214-217
Devil, mediumship and the, 61 ff.
Devoe and Co., 294
Dictionary trick, xxvi., 226
Doors, use of partition, 156
Drum, as a means for concealing articles, 263
Drummer-boy control, 263
Ears, searching the, xviii., 26
Electro medical "cures," xxiii., 178
Erastus, 50
Escape, from muslin bag, 232-233; from sack, 314-318
Fakirs, Indian, 27
Finger-writing, 147 ff.
Fire test, prescription for, 98
Flap, silicate, 122

325

Floor-traps in séance rooms, 263 ; how to find, 301-304
Flour in hands as a test, xxvi., 195
Fox Sisters, xxiv., 170-171
Funeral notices, information derived from, 196
Gaiters, congress, 119
" Generals," 108
Georgia Wonder, the 157
Gloves, stuffed, 34
Grabbing the " spirits," xxvii., 247, 264 ; how to prevent, 292
Guitars at dark séances, 32, 185, 276, 312-313 ; self playing, xxii., 33, 115
Hands, dummy, 103 ; pasteboard, 104, 189 ; opening and closing, 105 ; luminous, 187 ; changing at séances, 187 ; method of changing, 188 ; clapping of, 190 ; shot, placed in as test, 190 ; flour placed in, 195
Heel, fake boot, xxii., 117, 119
Heller, 11, 16
Hermann, 11, 16
Hypnotism, xxiii., 28
Illusions, description of spiritualistic, 228
Information, sources of, xx., 196-199
Insanity, spiritualism and, 18, 20
Inspirational speakers, 95
Instruments, musical, at dark circles, 185
Investments entrusted to the medium, 261 ; how they are " fixed," 262
Isis, 284, 305, 307-308
Judd, J. W. 22
Jupiter, the planet, as the home of Isis 284, 305-306
Kellar, xviii., 16
King, John, xxvii., 81, 85, 268
Kisses, spiritual, 254
Languages. messages in different, 14. 39
Lead, sheet, xx., 103
Letters, reading sealed, 173-181

Lights, match heads used for, xix., 73, 83, 90 ; floating, 185 ; regulation of, 276
Lincoln, Abraham, 283, 297
Lovers, spirit, 254-255 ; 308-310
Luck and the Medium, 212
Luminous paint and powder, 187, 293-295 ; how made, 294, mask, 92
Maggie, xviii., 45
Magnetised paper, 168-169
Magnetism, curing by, 167-169
Martin and Co., 22
Masks, gauze, 92, 117
Massage, 167
Mat, fur, use of, 153
Match-heads, xix., 73, 82 ff.
Materialism, mediums and, 8
Mediums, female, 95 ff., 106-107 ; test, 199 ; charges of, 213 artistic, 304 ; materializing, 107, 200, 202, 246, 263-311
Midget, the pony, 79
Mock-marriage, 307-310
Mop-board, 263, 300
Morality of spiritualists, 19
Mouth, searching the, 26
Muslin bag, escape from, 232-233
Mustard, essential oil of, xxiv., 167
Names, guessing, 45, 89
Note-books, xx., 108-109, 136, 305
Pads, writing, for sealed letter reading, 180 ; waxed, xxv., 181
Paint, luminous, 187, 293-295
Paper, burnt, use of, 182
Parafine mould test, 311 ; how made, 312
Pellet reading, 124 ff. 147
Pencils, fake, how to prepare, 149
Phosphorus, smell of, 82
Photographers, spirit, 112 ff.
Photographs, copying, 112
Pictures on slates, how to get, 145-146
Pillory, 242
Plumbago, powdered, xxv., 181
Pockets, secret, 123
" Pony " books, xx., 108

Index

Powder, luminous, how made, 294
Prairie Flower, the control, 53
"Pumping" information, 197-199
Questions, difficult, for the "spirits," 177
Raps, produced by Fox Sisters, 170; by hands and knees, 171-172; at dark séances, 70, 186
Religio-Philosophical Journal, 319, 323
Rhinestones, 296, 298, 306
Ripley, Frank T., 63
Robes, how to illuminate, 294-295
Rod, tapering steel, 104
Rope, neck-tie trick, 22; binding with, 31, 74 ff.; escaping from, xix., 81, 86 ff.; soft cotton, 88
Rubber "spirits," 251, 315
Sack trick, 232-233; 314-318
San Francisco, 100; Mission St., 118, 264
Sealed-letter reading, 172-176; by means of slates, 178-179; by writing pads, 180; by confederacy, 230-231
Search, methods of, 26
Shot, small, as test, 195
Slack, stealing, xix., 86 ff.
Slate-writing, through acids, 120; with silicate flap, 122; by exchange, 122-123, with pellet reading, 124 ff; in locked slates, 126 ff, 139; by confederates, 140; by the carpet trick, 140 ff; in screwed slates, 154 ff; with sealed letter reading, xxiv., 178-179; sitting for, 214; and book trick, 225
Slates, faked, xxii., 127 ff; illustration of, 129

Snare-drum, 263
Soul-mate, spiritual, 254
Spirit basin, 245
Spirit collar, 242; illustration of, 243
Spiritual Journals, 199
State Library, 196
Steen, Mr. and Mrs., 217; their methods exposed, 218-20
Stick, pointed, for writing on arm, 181
Stocks, 242
Styrax, liquid, xx., 98
Substitution of slates, 122-123; of hands, 188-189; illustrations of 192-193
Table, fake, for concealing articles, 263
Table lifting, fake for, xxiv., 228-229
Tea-bell, use of, 120
Tests, fire, 97 ff.; *sure*, 201; some remarkable, 202-211; slate-writing, 271-272
Torn corner test, 132
Traps, in floors, 153, 263, 292-302; in wainscot, 157
Trumpet, séances with, xxv., 186
Tumbler trick, 163-164
Varnish, writing on arm with, 182
Victims, why they do not prosecute, 257-258; why they do, 259
Wall trick, Mrs. Abbott's, 163
Watch, as apparatus carrier, 119
Wax, for pads in sealed letter reading, xxv., 181
Wedding of a "spirit," 256, 308-10
White, Erasmus, 51
Wine and horn test, 119.

PRINTED IN GREAT BRITAIN BY THE DEVONSHIRE PRESS,
TORQUAY.

PERSPECTIVES IN PSYCHICAL RESEARCH

An Arno Press Collection

Carrington, Hereward. Laboratory Investigations Into Psychic Phenomena. [1939]

Colquhoun, J. C. Report of the Experiments on Animal Magnetism. 1833

Coover, John Edgar. Experiments in Psychical Research at Leland Stanford Junior University. 1917

Cumberland, Stuart. A Thought-Reader's Thoughts. 1888

Doyle, Arthur Conan. The History of Spiritualism. 1926. 2 vols. in one

Driesch, Hans. Psychical Research: The Science of the Super-Normal. 1933

Ehrenwald, Jan. New Dimensions of Deep Analysis. [1952]

Esdaile, James. Natural and Mesmeric Clairvoyance. 1852

Fukurai, T. Clairvoyance and Thoughtography. 1931

Garrett, Eileen J. My Life as a Search for the Meaning of Mediumship. 1939

Geley, Gustave. Clairvoyance and Materialisation. 1927

Gregory, William. Animal Magnetism. 1909

Gudas, Fabian, [editor]. Extrasensory Perception. 1961

Haddock, Joseph W. Somnolism and Psycheism. 1851

Hibbert, S. Sketches on the Philosophy of Apparitions. 1824

Mulholland, John. Beware Familiar Spirits. 1938

Murchison, Carl, editor. The Case For and Against Psychical Belief. 1927

Myers, Frederic W[illiam] H[enry]. Human Personality and Its Survival of Bodily Death. 2 vols. 1954

Podmore, Frank. **The Newer Spiritualism.** 1910

Podmore, Frank. **Studies in Psychical Research.** 1897

Price, Harry. **Fifty Years of Psychical Research.** 1939

Price, Harry and Eric Dingwall. **Revelations of a Spirit Medium.** 1922

Prince, Walter Franklin. **The Enchanted Boundary.** 1930

Richet, Charles. **Thirty Years of Psychical Research.** 1923

Roll, William G. **Theory and Experiment in Psychical Research.** 1975

Salter, W. H. **Zoar:** Or the Evidence of Psychical Research Concerning Survival. 1961

Saltmarsh, H. F. **Evidence of Personal Survival From Cross Correspondences.** 1938

Saltmarsh, H. F. **Foreknowledge.** 1938

Sidgwick, Eleanor Mildred. **Phantasms of the Living: Cases of Telepathy Printed in the Journal of the Society for Psychical Research During Thirty-Five Years** and Gurney, Edmund, Frederic W. H. Myers and Frank Podmore, **Phantasms of the Living.** 1962

Thomas, John F. **Beyond Normal Cognition.** 1937

Tyrrell, G. N. M. **Science and Psychical Phenomena.** [1938]

Von Schrenck Notzing, [A.] **Phenomena of Materialisation.** 1920

Wallace, Alfred Russel. **Miracles and Modern Spiritualism.** 1896

Warcollier, René. **Experimental Telepathy.** 1938